THE EVOLUTION OF THE FISHING VILLAGE

LEICESTER EXPLORATIONS IN LOCAL HISTORY 1
Series Editor: Harold Fox

THE EVOLUTION OF THE FISHING VILLAGE

Landscape and Society along the South Devon Coast, 1086–1550

by

Harold Fox

*Senior Lecturer in English Topography
Department of English Local History, University of Leicester*

with the maps of
Kenneth Smith

Leopard's Head Press
Oxford

ISBN 0 904920 43 7

This book is sold subject to the condition that it shall not, by way of trade or otherwise, be lent, re-sold, hired out, or otherwise circulated without the publisher's prior consent in any form of binding or cover other than that in which it is published and without a similar condition being imposed on the subsequent purchaser.

No part of this publication may be reproduced, stored in a retrieval system, or transmitted in any form or by any means, electronic, mechanical, photocopying, recording or otherwise without prior permission of the author and the Leopard's Head Press.

© H. S. A. Fox, 2001

Reprinted 2004

Typeset by John Chandler
Printed and bound by Short Run Press, Ltd, Exeter, Devon

First Published in 2001 by LEOPARD'S HEAD PRESS LIMITED
1-5 Broad Street, Oxford OX1 3AW
Trade enquiries to
Explorations: Marc Fitch Historical Institute
5 Salisbury Road, Leicester LE1 7QR

For Margaret Meeres,
to record expeditions by Dart, Teign and Exe

CONTENTS

List of illustrations	ix
List of figures	x
List of tables	x
Series editor's foreword	xi
Preface and acknowledgements	xiii
Abbreviations	xvii

1	Introduction		1
2	The coast		7
	2.1	A classification of coastal settlement	8
		2.1.i Port towns	8
		2.1.ii Cellar settlements	12
		2.1.iii Fishing villages	12
		2.1.iv Quays	14
	2.2	A tour of the coast	17
		2.2.i The Exe Estuary	18
		2.2.ii From Dawlish to Dartmouth	24
		2.2.iii From Dartmouth to the Tamar	29
	2.3	Conclusion	35
3	The fisheries and the foreshore		47
	3.1	Early evidence for fisheries	47
	3.2	'Thirty shillings from the fishery this year'	51
	3.3	Seigneurial fisheries	57
	3.4	The technology of the fisheries	59
	3.5	The foreshore; hunting and gathering	64

4	Consumption and distribution	85
	4.1 Consumption	85
	4.2 Marketing	88
	4.3 Distribution and redistribution	95
	4.4 The westwards reach	99
5	Fishing farmers and cellar settlements	107
	5.1 Fishing farmers	107
	5.1.i The Woodbury tithe payments	107
	5.1.ii The Kenton cellar rents	115
	5.1.iii The Stokenham custumals	122
	5.2 The cellar settlements	129
6	Transition: from cellar settlement to fishing village	145
	6.1 Dating	145
	6.2 Climatic change and coastal security	150
	6.3 Social and economic contexts	154
7	Conclusion: fisheries and settlement history	177

Indexes   195
List of Occasional Papers, Department of English Local History, University of Leicester   207

LIST OF ILLUSTRATIONS

(between pages 106 and 107)

1. Coombe Cellars and the River Teign, watercolour by John Swete, 1795 (Devon Record Office, 564M/F8/87, reproduced by kind permission of the Office and the Devon Gardens Trust)
2. Sidmouth beach, watercolour by John Swete, 1795 (Devon Record Office, 564M/F8/3, reproduced by kind permission of the Office and the Devon Gardens Trust)
3. Beer, East Devon, a fishing place with no protection, drawing of 1807, unsigned (West-Country Studies Library, P & D 8726, reproduced by kind permission of the Library)
4. Warfleet, Dartmouth, watercolour by John Swete, 1800 (Devon Record Office, 564M/F2/161, reproduced by kind permission of the Office and the Devon Gardens Trust)
5. The Exe Estuary, map of 1743, possibly by William Chapple (Devon Record Office, 96Madd./E11, reproduced by kind permission of the Office and Clinton Devon Estates)
6. Barrepta, Carbis Bay, Cornwall, drawing by E. W. Cooke, 1848 (Royal Institution of Cornwall, reproduced by kind permission of the Institution)
7. Part of a tithe account for the parish of Woodbury, Easter 1432 to Easter 1433 (Exeter Cathedral Archives, Vicars Choral, 3363, reproduced by kind permission of the Dean and Chapter of Exeter Cathedral)
8. Coombe Cellars and the River Teign, photograph of around 1900
9. Lympstone and the Exe Estuary, watercolour by John Swete, around 1799 (Devon Record Office, 564M/F16/102, reproduced by kind permission of the Office and the Devon Gardens Trust)
10. Minehead, Somerset, watercolour of around 1800, unsigned (Somerset Archaeological and Natural History Society, Braikenridge Collection, reproduced by kind permission of the Society)
11. Pilchard fishing in St Austell Bay, map of the late sixteenth century by John Norden (Trinity College, Cambridge, reproduced by kind permission of the Master and Fellows)
12. Torcross, watercolour by John Swete, 1793 (Devon Record Office, 564M/F4/160, reproduced by kind permission of the Office and the Devon Gardens Trust)

13. The Exe Estuary, from a map of landing places and defences of around 1540 (D. and S. Lysons, *Magna Britannia: Devonshire*, 1822, vol. 2, opposite p. 320, redrawn from the original in the British Library)
14. Hooe manor house and fishing village, drawing by Edmund Spoure, 1694 (facsimile in Cornwall Record Office, FS3/93/3/130B, reproduced by kind permission of the owner, *via* Cornwall Record Office)
15. Shaldon, map by William Doidge, 1741 (Devon Record Office, 563Z/P1, reproduced by kind permission of the Office)

LIST OF FIGURES

2.1	The coastline from Exmouth to the Tamar	17
2.2	Fisheries and coastal settlement in the sixteenth and seventeenth centuries: the Exe Estuary	19
2.3	Fisheries and coastal settlement in the sixteenth and seventeenth centuries: from Dawlish to Dartmouth	26
2.4	Fisheries and coastal settlement in the sixteenth and seventeenth centuries: from Dartmouth to the Tamar	30-1
3.1	Detached parts of the parishes of Haccombe with Combe and Kenton	49
3.2	Detached part of the parish of Stokenham	50
4.1	Carriage of fish by land and sea from South Devon to Exeter, late fourteenth century	97
4.2	Transport of fish to aristocratic households and religious houses	101
5.1	Kenton manor: cellars and settlements	119
5.2	Stokenham manor: settlements and fishing according to the custumal of 1360	125
6.1	Population growth and village origins: some links	164

LIST OF TABLES

3.1	Littleham and other small manors (E. Budleigh Hundred) in 1086	48
3.2	The species which were caught	60
4.1	Mileage of coasts and poll tax payers, 1377, by county	102
5.1	Value of payments of tithes on fishing at Woodbury, 1423-35	112
5.2	Kenton manor: size of farm holdings and occupation of cellars at Starcross, 1578	120
6.1	Demand for land at Sidbury and Stoke Fleming as indicated by numbers of holdings remaining vacant at the end of the year, 1420s-1490s	157

SERIES EDITOR'S FOREWORD

'Leicester Explorations in Local History' will be a series which continues the old 'Occasional Papers' of the Department of English Local History at the University of Leicester, full bibliographical details of which are given at the end of this book. Works published in the new series will all have three distinctive characteristics.

First, they will be on novel themes and will open up new areas of research, either by dint of highly intensive local study, perhaps on newly discovered sources or types of sources, or by pioneering examination of local themes across regions or provinces or nations, of which England will be but one. This characteristic the new series will share with the old, described as Finberg's 'brilliant series' and, recently, as 'the glory of Leicester University Press'.[1] The small claims which the present book may have in these respects are set out in the Introduction and have been approved by the readers who scrutinized the text and notes on behalf of the Leopard's Head Press.

Second, I want each title in the new series to be attractive and accessible not only to the very many historians in universities who have an interest in local research but also, and perhaps especially, to the greatly more numerous army of dedicated, knowledgeable and learned men and women who have an interest in their own localities or in the subject in general. The 'Occasional Papers' were innovative, elegant and exciting in their themes, and were written by a glittering array of scholars, but there is good evidence to show that they did not always reach a wide audience in the counties to which they related.

Third – and following on from the above – this new series will be accessible in style, will be illustrated and will have an attractive exterior format, including the wide spine which many booksellers reasonably require if they are to agree to display a book. Accordingly, in word-length these new 'Explorations' will be longer than the old 'Papers' (a description not now appropriate), usually of between 40 and 60 thousand words – long enough to give the appropriate bulk to the physical object and for adequate exploration of a novel theme, yet of a length which will not deter either reader or author. I do not wish to bore the reader with details of the conversations which I have had over the last ten years, with more publishers than I care to remember, about format and pricing and spines and booksellers and publicity . . . . All I can hope for is that the present book, a result of those discussions, lives up to the aspirations set out in this Foreword.

Harold Fox

[1] *Times* obituary of Professor H. P. R. Finberg; M. W. Beresford in a review in *Agricultural History Review* 41 (1993), p. 197.

PREFACE AND ACKNOWLEDGEMENTS

> Then thought I, Virgil, how from Mantua reft,
> Shy as a peasant in the courts of Rome,
> You took the waxen tablets in your hand,
> And out of anger cut calm tales of home.
> (V. Sackville West, *The Land*)

A tentative outline for this book came to me on the waterfront at Starcross in July 1984. I was in Devon to finish preparing a course of lectures for the following year, on the topography of the county. I already had material for some of them, but for two – on fishing villages and ports – I needed to undertake much more work. 'When are you off to Devon?' asked Alan Everitt, as he always did towards the end of June. I replied that it would be as soon as I possibly could and so, that July, I was on the shore at Starcross with a good deal of time ahead in which to explore ports and fishing villages in the field and in the archives. Nothing could have been more delightful and exciting.

Already in 1984 I had some material on fishing villages stored away in three files. My Ph.D. thesis had been on aspects of Devon's agrarian history and, scouring the archives as a research student, I could not fail to come across references to fishing settlements and fishing people. Already in 1984 I had gathered a good deal of material for my chapters for the Cambridge *Agrarian History of England and Wales, 1348-1500* (part of a pioneering series initiated in the Department of English Local History by Herbert Finberg and later overseen by Joan Thirsk). This time I made sure that I transcribed and filed away any references to fishing in the largely agrarian documents which I examined. Then there was a third file containing some earlier thoughts on fishing settlements, a few paragraphs only from the previous decade, written for a popular publication which never saw the light of day. These had been compiled quickly, and with the undue confidence of youth, in my first years at Leicester. Coming as an outsider to the Department of English Local History, it truly seemed to me to be an intellectual court of Rome, so glittering was it with new ideas, approaches and possibilities. In my first years, Alan Everitt and Charles Phythian-Adams (finding me to a degree wanting) infected me with their thinking on and enthusiasm for a whole range of new topics – not least by-employments and linked settlement structures (themes which surface in the pages which follow) – and these affected what I said in that first, tentative, unpublished piece on fisheries, written late in the 70s. It was a period of great excitement and discovery, which I look back upon now with unclouded affection.

And so to return to the beach at Starcross in the summer of 1984. I planned my lecture and, at the same time, saw that it could be expanded into a short paper, a mode of origin for certain work published from the Department, not least my own. I gave the course, including the lecture on fishing settlements, the following autumn and repeated it, with much change of detail, in subsequent years. However, the published paper which was to have been based upon it became delayed by other writing and editing commitments, not least for the *Agrarian History* and for the Department's Occasional Papers, as well as by the growing number of silly things which we now accept – with resignation rather than anger – as having to be done for university and government administrators. A window of opportunity opened up a few years ago but by then the projected paper had turned into a book, so many were the new ideas given to me by my student audiences. I spent some time in making a systematic attack on more source materials, both in the Public Record Office and in Devon and in revisiting documents which I had already examined some time before, as described above. At last all the materials were assembled and this book could be started.

Over a long period many people have helped me along the way. Foremost debts – beyond that expressed in the dedication – are to our students who have explored the Devon coastline with me over the years, pointing out new observables and making new points; and to Alan and

Charles, two sympathetic heads of department who have already been named in this Preface. I am most grateful to the two official readers who examined my text and notes on behalf of the Leopard's Head Press. Then there are the friends who read early drafts of the text and provided me with so many corrections and additions, some of them Honorary Research Fellows in the Department of English Local History, others drawn from the circle of well-wishers and unpaid helpers which a unique department has always attracted. Kenneth and Joan Smith together read the text and the former drew the lively maps; as in many other aspects of my work, it is difficult to think how I could have done without them. Dr Mike Thompson, who bore the brunt of my criticism when he was my research student, got his own back, so to speak, by providing trenchant evaluation of style and logic. Eleanor Vollans did the same and also shared with me her extensive knowledge of maritime topics; the Department will always have reason to be glad that, after a fruitful career at Bedford College (University of London), she retired to Oakham, close enough to us to be of assistance both in ways which can be publicly acknowledged with much gratitude, as here, and also in ways which cannot. As for those who helped me by inputting and by tidying up the references, I have been extraordinarily lucky to have had the services of Dr Lucy Faire, Sylvia Pinches, Rosie Keep and Paul Wilcox because each of them is an expert historian, Leicester trained, with an eagle eye for the conventions of historical writing. Some of the text was input by Pauline Whitmore to whom I owe thanks for so much help in all ways over the past ten terms. Dr John Chandler is the typesetter and also a distinguished west-country professional historian, a combination which was a great comfort to me in the final stages. The Short Run Press, Exeter, is the printer, providing its usual very high standards and rapid service. Roy Stephens is the publisher; he has courteously helped me with this book, and in many other ways, over several years.

I cannot mention by name all of the archivists and librarians who have kindly provided help and services and must limit myself to thanking Margery Rowe and John Draisey of the Devon Record Office, Audrey Erskine and Angela Doughty of Exeter Cathedral Archives and Ian Maxted of the West-Country Studies Library. Five scholars and friends have helped me on countless occasions with discussion, facts and references to source materials. Foremost is Maryanne Kowaleski, of Fordham University, with whom I have had many friendly conversations in Exeter and London; her very great contributions to medieval Devon history are mentioned many times in the text below and readers will also notice the constant repetition of her name in the notes, an indication of how indispensable her work is. Todd Gray's published and unpublished work has also been indispensable to me, dealing as it does with fisheries and fisherfolk in a period which follows directly on from my own, and I recall many pleasant conversations with him too. Tony Collings has always shared with me his extensive knowledge of the South Devon coast and, far beyond the call of duty, has consulted local source material when I, at a distance, needed a reference urgently. Oliver Padel patiently helped with Cornish sources and place-names, and in other ways. Linda Pinkham provided much information which I had myself missed, on Kenton and Starcross. To the following people, collectively, the book also owes much: Derek Aldcroft, Mark Bailey, John Blair, Nick Corcos, Paul Cullen, Chris Dyer, Ian Friel, Frank Galbraith, Mark Gardiner, Terry Hartley, Peter Herring, Richard Hoyle, Jeanne James, Evan Jones, Ian Maxsted, Michael Nix, Dave Postles, Bob Roberts, Richard Smith, Robin Stanes, Robert Swanson, Bob Sylvester, Chris Thornton, Bob Tulley, Penny Upton, Victor Watts, Chris West, David Williams and Angus Winchester. I am most grateful to them all. I also acknowledge small grants given from time to time by the University of Leicester's Arts Faculty Budget Centre committee, and its predecessors, and generous contributions to the cost of production by the Friends of the Department of English Local History and the Marc Fitch Fund.

Harold Fox
Department of English Local History
University of Leicester
November 2000

ABBREVIATIONS

BL	British Library
CRO	Cornwall Record Office
DCNQ	*Devon & Cornwall Notes & Queries*
DCRS	Devon and Cornwall Record Society
Domesday	C. and F. Thorn, eds, *Domesday Book, Devon* (2 vols, 1985)
DRO	Devon Record Office
ECA	Exeter Cathedral Archives
Gray, *E-SMS*	T. Gray, ed., *Early-Stuart Mariners and Shipping* (DCRS, new ser., 33, 1990)
Kowaleski, *LCAPE*	M. Kowaleski, ed., *Local Customs Accounts of the Port of Exeter, 1266-1321* (DCRS, new ser., 36, 1993)
Kowaleski, *LMRTE*	M. Kowaleski, *Local Markets and Regional Trade in Medieval Exeter* (1995)
Kowaleski, 'Markets'	'Markets and fairs in Medieval Devon', pp. 353-70 of her *Local Markets and Regional Trade in Medieval Exeter*
Leland, *Itinerary*	L. Toulmin Smith, ed., *The Itinerary of John Leland* (5 vols, 1906-10)
NMHD	M. Duffy, S. Fisher, B. Greenhill, D. J. Starkey and J. Youings, eds, *The New Maritime History of Devon* (2 vols, 1992-4)
PDAS	*Proceedings of the Devon Archaeological Society* (formerly Devon Archaeological Exploration Society)
PND	J. E. B. Gover, A. Mawer and F. M. Stenton, *The Place-Names of Devon* (2 vols, English Place-Name Society, 1931-2)
PRO	Public Record Office
TDA	*Report and Transactions of the Devonshire Association*
VCH	*Victoria County History*
WDRO	West Devon Record Office

In addition to the above, some words in the titles of periodicals, of calendars to collections in the Public Record Office and of record societies have been lightly abbreviated. The version of Domesday Book published by Phillimore has been used, despite some misleading translations, because it is generally available and because of its expert critical material, the work of Caroline and Frank Thorn.

Note on place-names. An italicised place-name indicates a place not generally named on Ordnance Survey maps of the nineteenth or twentieth century; or an old form of a current name.

Chapter One

INTRODUCTION

Mark Bailey writes of 'an alarming gap in our knowledge' of fishing in the Middle Ages and adds that 'historians might justifiably despair of discovering anything about fishermen in small coastal villages'; even for some of the larger port towns evidence on fishing can be scanty. In similar vein, Peter Heath claims that the subject of medieval fisheries 'should entice the student by its manifold problems no less than by its obvious importance'. He concludes, moreover, that 'a major impediment to the study is the very frugal and random nature of the sources', so that 'the scholar who embarks on the early history of the fishing industry . . . will need good fortune as well as pertinacity'.[1] I am eternally grateful that I read these comments only when this book was nearing completion, for had I seen them earlier, I might, faint-hearted, have been deterred forever.

    Both Heath and Bailey are absolutely right, of course. There is a great deal that we shall never know or understand properly about fishing in the Middle Ages. Medieval documents are rarely systematic in their references to fisheries. Many of the sources are indeed 'random in their nature' although, having trawled several times over the medieval and post-medieval collections relating to coastal manors in Devon (as described in the Preface), I did find that even from random sources a coherent, if sometimes faint, picture was emerging. Lords made profits from the fishing of their tenants and they drew rents from buildings used by fishing families, so that seigneurial surveys and financial account rolls contain relevant references. Ecclesiastical authorities gained from tithes of fisheries, so that fishing is obliquely mentioned in documents concerning tithe, including early grants. Tenants who fished were as likely to transgress against one another and against their lord as were ploughmen who ploughed or herdsmen and shepherds who tried to keep their charges in order, so one finds references in court rolls to disputes over fishing gear and about use of the lord's shore. And then, in the course of this research, there were the occasional lucky finds of rare types of documentary source (Peter Heath's 'good fortune'): the fine tithe accounts of Woodbury parish, with detail about people who fished, where we meet the fishermen face to face at last; the custumals of Stokenham with their detailed accounts of the operation of a fishery; surveys of the manor of Kenton with their rich detail concerning structures on the shore from which fishing was practised; documents relating to the share which the abbess of Syon took of the porpoises captured by her tenants in Sidmouth Bay.

    It would be immodest of me to make too great a claim for this monograph. To say that it is the first to deal in depth with medieval fishing on a relatively long stretch of coast is perhaps true; but in saying so I do not wish to belittle important, but more geographically limited, earlier studies such as Peter Heath's on the Scarborough fishing fleet or Mark Bailey's on the south-east Suffolk fisheries – studies which are both quoted above – or A. J. F. Dulley's on the fishing industry of the town of Rye; nor to belittle work on medieval inland fisheries, like McDonnell's study of Yorkshire or the many papers brought together by Mick Aston.[2] Alison Littler's thesis on medieval fishing in England at large and Simon Pawley's on Lincolnshire unfortunately remain unpublished but a major contribution to the history of the craft is now in print: this is Maryanne Kowaleski's brilliant reconstruction of the medieval trade in fish centred on the city of Exeter, a work much exploited in this monograph.[3] Very little else has been written on medieval sea fishing along Devon's coasts, so that when, in 1987, Mike Dickinson produced his excellent edited collection on fishing in Devon called *A Living from the Sea*, none of the contributions went back before the sixteenth century. My research claims to be primarily a study of fisheries, fishers and fishing settlements – all examined in depth – but it includes also some treatment of other activities, of the marketing and disposal of fish and of medieval economic development more generally insofar as those topics are relevant to the development of fishing. As explained above, I have been fortunate enough to discover new sources and these have naturally brought with them new slants and interpretations.

I shall end this introduction with a few words about what I do not intend to omit and about what is intentionally omitted. I occasionally use the word 'fishermen' in my text by no means as an affront to fisherwomen nor as a signal to indicate that women will be omitted, but simply to translate *piscator* (masculine) in the Latin and to avoid the monotonous repetition of 'fisher', 'fishing family' and so on. We encounter many women in the following pages: the famous cockle-rakers of Starcross; Joan the widow of Gervase who sat near the shore of Stokenham manor (around 1346) from the Purification until Hockday, watching for the arrival of the mullet; 'the wife of Thomas Wyse' who controlled the Dawlish fish market; the anonymous women of the port towns who repelled invaders while their men were at sea. Nor must we forget that when men fished as a more or less full-time occupation, or when they were away from home as mariners, then tasks which were normally expected to be performed by males fell to women: hence the surprised descriptions of women at the plough, given to us by travellers along the shores of the Exe Estuary in the eighteenth and nineteenth centuries.[4] If fishing itself is often hidden from us in the Middle Ages, we would expect that all of the ancillary activities associated with the craft, and probably in the hands of women to some large degree, would be hidden more deeply still (e.g. mending nets, caring for hemp gardens, gutting and curing).[5]

Now for deliberate omissions. First, in order to curtail the time taken in making the final documentary searches on which this monograph is based, I have limited it to the coastline of South Devon, between Exmouth in the east and the Tamar – the border with Cornwall – in the west. Naturally, though, where I have discovered some important and telling piece of evidence from the coastline east of Exmouth, or from North Devon, or from Cornwall or Somerset, I have not hesitated to include it, though without implying that settlement on those coasts was similar; the Cornish 'porths', for example, may have a history all of their own, one which certainly needs to be written. The final chapter takes us further afield with a few comparisons from some other parts of

England. Second, I have omitted much detail of technical matters (insofar as they are known) because the focus here, as I have said, is on fishers and fishing settlements; a short section is devoted to this topic but an examination in great depth must be left to the historian of technology. Third, I deal exclusively with the inshore and estuarine fisheries and largely with fishing as practised by the people of rural manors. The great majority of the fisheries along the coast of South Devon were of this kind and, one suspects, a majority of those who fished were employed in them, at least before the middle of the sixteenth century, and perhaps after that. The fisheries of the port towns are mentioned in Chapter 2 but are not studied in detail; in Chapter 6 mention is made of what we are beginning to learn, thanks to the researches of Maryanne Kowaleski and Todd Gray, about the fishing craft of South Devon which set out (from the fifteenth century onwards) to distant, longshore fisheries along the coastline of England and then, eventually, on fishing expeditions overseas.[6] These were precursors of the great ventures to the Newfoundland cod banks, pioneered by Devon men around the middle of the sixteenth century, but I do not see my study as setting the scene for those international developments. It is not necessary to do so, for the local South Devon fisheries studied here made their own significant and independent contribution to fish supply, to the lives and incomes of those who fished and to the diet of consumers in both England and also (through exports) abroad. I have mentioned the sixteenth century so, finally, I should say that this is largely a medieval study, beginning in the eleventh century and extending until around the middle of the sixteenth. It cannot exclude later periods entirely; for example, some of the detail in Chapter 2, which describes shoreline settlement, is drawn from the end of the sixteenth century and from the seventeenth when the sources become fuller. Other evidence is occasionally taken from later periods and this makes the point that, in studies in medieval local history, we cannot ignore subsequent centuries from which pieces of evidence can sometimes throw a sharp ray of light on the Middle Ages, if we are patient enough and loving enough in our treatment of them. But the stress is on medieval sources and fisheries and the story told here ends with the late fifteenth century and the early sixteenth, when fishing villages proper began to be established along the coast of South Devon.

In this monograph I try to show how a *genre* of place came into being, leaving the later history of fishing villages to other historians. An important concept in local history is that the nature of the origins of a place colour and guide its subsequent character, including its landscape and the character of its people, for many subsequent centuries. As we move into the second half of the sixteenth century and into the seventeenth a whole array of types of historical sources, not available to the medievalist, may be used in order to bring these distinctive communities more fully to life. Records now relate to poverty, order and disorder, to birth and marriage, to vagrancy, apprenticeship, occupations, public health, literacy, religious beliefs, dissent, authority – all of these topics are available for the student of later periods to study in depth, whereas the medievalist normally gets only occasional glimpses of them, or none at all. Study of any of these topics in relation to fishing villages – or, preferably, study of them all in a rounded picture of those communities from the sixteenth century onwards – is now possible. When it has been carried out, we shall know at last if some of the stereotypes associated with fishing villages were really the common experience of the people who lived within them in the past. Were fishing villages really separate from agricultural communities, 'standing back to back and not face to face, one … [looking] outward to the far horizon over the glistening sea, the other inward over the fruitful plain'?[7] Were they and their people marginal and vulnerable? What of the supposed solidarity of fishing communities? What of their superstitions? What of their nonconformity and resistance to authority? I touch upon some of these traits in a final chapter but, as I have said, their detailed exploration I commend to others who, I hope, will trace, link by link along the chains of the evidence, some of the continuities which begin in this monograph.

The continuities may be extended ones which, in terms of landscape, certainly, come down to the present day and, in terms of *mentalité*, certainly into the nineteenth century. When Sydney Smith wished to illustrate independence and resistance to authority – in the context of opposition to parliamentary reform – he used the example of

Mrs Partington who attempted to sweep the waves of a high storm away from her shoreline fishing cottage.

> In the winter of 1824, there set in a great flood upon that town – the tide rose to an incredible height – the waves rushed in upon the houses, and everything was threatened with destruction. In the midst of this sublime and terrible storm, Dame Partington, who lived upon the beach, was seen at the door of her house with mop and pattens, trundling her mop, squeezing out the sea-water, and vigorously pushing away the Atlantic Ocean. The Atlantic was roused. Mrs Partington's spirit was up; but I need not tell you that the contest was unequal. The Atlantic Ocean beat Mrs Partington. She was excellent at a slop, or a puddle, but she should not have meddled with a tempest. Gentlemen, be at your ease – be quiet and steady. You will beat Mrs Partington.

Mrs Partington, made famous solely by the comparison, was an inhabitant of the Devon coastal village of Sidmouth.[8]

---

[1] M. Bailey, 'Coastal fishing off south east Suffolk in the century after the Black Death', *Procs Suffolk Inst. of Archaeology and History* 37 (1990), p. 102; P. Heath, 'North Sea fishing in the fifteenth century: the Scarborough fleet', *Northern History* 3 (1968), pp. 53-4.

[2] A. J. F. Dulley, 'The early history of the Rye fishing industry', *Sussex Archaeological Collections* 107 (1969), pp. 36-64; J. McDonnell, *Inland Fisheries in Medieval Yorkshire* (Borthwick Papers, 60, 1981); M. Aston, ed., *Medieval Fish, Fisheries and Fishponds in England* (2 vols, British Archaeological Reports, British Series, 182, i and ii, 1988).

[3] A. S. Littler, 'Fish in English economy and society down to the Reformation' (unpublished Ph.D. thesis, Swansea, 1979); S. Pawley, 'Lincolnshire coastal villages and the sea c.1300-c.1600: economy and society' (unpublished Ph.D. thesis, University of Leicester, 1984); Kowaleski, *LMRTE*, especially pp. 307-21.

[4] 'We here [near Starcross] saw women employed at the plough': R. P. Chope, *Early Tours in Devon and Cornwall* (1918), p. 237, citing W. G. Maton, *Observations on the Western Counties of England* (1794-6).

[5] P. Thompson, T. Wailey and T. Lummis, *Living the Fishing* (1983), especially Chapter 10, 'Women in the fishing'.

[6] T. Gray, 'Devon's fisheries and early-Stuart northern New England', *NMHD*, vol. 1, pp. 137-46; M. Kowaleski, 'The expansion of the south-western fisheries in late medieval England', *Ec. Hist. Rev.*, 2nd ser., 53 (2000), pp. 429-54.

[7] T. C. Lethbridge, *Boats and Boatmen* (1952), p. 27.

[8] W. H. Auden, ed., *Selected Writings of Sydney Smith* (1950).

Chapter Two

THE COAST

This chapter sets the scene. It includes a discussion of types of shoreline settlement and a tour of the stretch of South Devon coast explored in this monograph, from Exmouth in the east to Plymouth in the west. (Readers who do not need the level of detail contained in the tour may wish to pass over that section.) For the Middle Ages we are not fortunate in having detailed and comprehensive sources describing the shoreline, its settlements and the occupations of its people: here and there the evidence is good, but in general it is patchy and partial. It is not until we come to the sixteenth and seventeenth centuries that there is anything like a reasonable picture of the coastline, though even then it is far from perfect. From near the beginning of that period (around 1540) there survives the huge map, nearly 10 feet long, of the coast from Land's End to Exeter, drawn up to record the state of coastal defences at a time when Henry VIII feared imminent invasion by several continental countries; from near the end of it there are the maps in the atlas called the *Coasting Pilot* (1693), commissioned by Charles II and executed by Captain Greenvile Collins.[1] Neither of these have the mapping of coastal settlement as their principal objective. The former is a picture-map of the make-up of the shoreline (cliffs on which fortifications could be placed and sands which might make 'good landing' for the enemy) and of public and private defensive works both existing and projected, while the latter is concerned primarily with bearings and landmarks, with depths of water and with shoals, rocks and channels. Nevertheless, they do not fail to show useful, though partial, information for the historian of coastal settlement, and the same can be said of other charts produced for the purposes of navigation and defence.[2] The maritime survey of 1619, listing the human resources and shipping of South Devon, and recently edited by Todd Gray, is another official source which adds much to our knowledge of the coast in the seventeenth century.[3]

Every stretch of the coastline was part of some manor (or borough) and when written manorial surveys become especially detailed, towards the end of the sixteenth century, these can give good pictures of coastal settlement, albeit pictures which have to be constructed in the mind's eye. Their coverage is not, of course, complete: probably less than half the coastline surveyed here belonged to a manor for which a survey (or rental) survives from the sixteenth century or the seventeenth. Other manorial documents, such as court rolls (with, in some cases, by-laws concerning fishing) are also useful in reconstructions of the activities of the coastline, as are many miscellaneous sources such as the seventeenth-century record of Blackawton's parish boundary which, almost incidentally, refers to a fishing village, and the probate inventories for Cockington (a rare survival for Devon) which mention fishing gear and boats.[4]

When brought together all of these sources provide the earliest picture we can reconstruct (albeit incomplete) of shoreline settlement and shoreline occupations. Later on in this chapter we take a tour of the South Devon coastline, beginning with settlements as they were in the sixteenth and seventeenth centuries, with some earlier references where that is possible. In order to make this tour more manageable we begin with a simple classification of coastal settlements, always bearing in mind that there are some places which do not fall easily into any one of the suggested categories.

2.1 A classification of coastal settlement

2.1.i Port towns
The expected attributes of a port town are as follows: an adequate anchorage for ships, safe from the battering of wind and wave; facilities for the loading and unloading of merchandise, a quay especially; ships which were thought of as 'belonging to' the port, which means, before the days of official systems of registration, their return to the place when

a craft needed repair or was to be laid up between voyages; residence by ship-owners and merchants; residence by masters and mariners; facilities for the repair, fitting-out and victualling of ships; and certain demographic and sociological characteristics stemming in part from the fact that large ports were in a sense 'frontier towns'.[5] Because they were places to and from which merchandise was brought by land and sea, and because of their role in victualling, most ports had markets. If a few of these attributes were absent from a place, it can sometimes still be called a port, especially if strength in some of the others compensates. (This bundle of characteristics is relevant for the High Middle Ages and later. Earlier on, places at which merchandise was imported and exported would not have boasted all of these features by any means: for example, the sixth-century trading station on the River Avon at Bantham may simply have been a beach site to which foreign ships came, perhaps at certain seasons only, to discharge and pick up merchandise.)[6]

As an example we may take the town of Dartmouth, a port whose medieval trade was dominated by imports of wine from Gascony, although many other commodities of lesser value passed through it, and privateering and piracy (or one disguised as the other) were important sources of income.[7] In the seventeenth century the port was dominated by the Newfoundland trade which involved a voyage to distant cod fisheries, the catching and salting of cod, its transport to the Catholic countries of southern Europe for sale and, to complete the triangle, return to England with Mediterranean imports. It is notable that none of these activities, medieval and early modern, relied on the produce of the port's surroundings: the same geomorphological history which rendered the port's anchorage so deep and spacious had also shaped the steep hills all around, making access to the immediate hinterland very difficult while, further to the north, the wider hinterland was restricted by the uplands of Dartmoor. A port can function without a good hinterland, although only through sustained resourcefulness among its inhabitants which, in Dartmouth's case, meant the capture of distant and dangerous trades exemplified by Gascon wine imports, the profits of privateering and the Newfoundland venture. The mayor of Dartmouth, writing to the Privy Council in 1609, made this point very well: the town's merchants 'trade not with any [of] the staple commodities of this kingdom'; neither, he continued, 'do these parts yield . . . merchandise . . . where with the shipping of this port may or can be . . . employed'.[8]

Of other port attributes, what was probably a public quay is mentioned in 1344 at Dartmouth, at a time when there were also private quays here. In the late sixteenth century and the early seventeenth the corporation of Dartmouth arranged for the financing of a new, long, straight quay which is shown, with crane and with ships drawn up alongside, on a seventeenth-century map and which can still be seen, incongruously stranded, today. W. G. Hoskins perceptively noticed that one of the earliest Dartmouth streets of which we have the name was *Smithenestrete*, 'the street of the smiths' (note the plural); these men were no doubt engaged in ship repair. According to the official survey of coastal occupations made in 1619, no fewer than 55 shipwrights worked in Dartmouth, almost one-third of all the wrights recorded along the South Devon coast; there were also 14 coopers. Earlier on, the port ranked high among places required to send men to work on Henry VIII's *Henri Grâce à Dieu*.[9] Other occupations connected with the activity of a port (mainly taken from medieval Dartmouth surnames) were those of merchant, captain, hooper, porter (a quayside activity), and cog's master, as well as the cooks, taverners, bakers and millers who were associated with the victualling of ships.[10]

A market at Dartmouth is recorded in 1205, burgesses are mentioned in 1270 and burgages a little later; the place may have been regarded as a borough by the middle of the thirteenth century. In 1341, Edward III granted a charter of liberties (including the right to elect a mayor) to the burgesses of Dartmouth who, in return, were to find and maintain two ships of war of 120 tons each.[11]

Many ports naturally housed people engaged wholly or partly in fishing. A sheltered harbour, a familiarity with maritime ways, the presence of crafts associated with ships and boats, a demand for dried fish to be used in victualling, easy access (in most cases) to a hinterland in which there would be further demand – all of these features meant that many port towns were settlements in which it was relatively easy to make a livelihood from fishing full-time or part-time. The maritime survey of 1619 gives the names of no fewer than 371 'sailors and mariners' at Dartmouth, and Todd Gray's analysis of this document has shown that some of these would have been full-time or part-time fishermen, although the proportion cannot be calculated.[12] John Leland, viewing the port in the early sixteenth century, noted that one part of it was 'inhabited mostly by fishermen', seeming to contrast them with the 'good merchant men' elsewhere in the town. Earlier references to fishing at Dartmouth are an ordinance in the mayor's court concerned with the freshness of the fish sold there; a probable seller of fish named in the poll tax of 1377; a Scottish maker of nets recorded in the alien subsidy of 1328; and local custom dues, first mentioned in 1275, on conger and other fish. The town had a *Fishmongers' Lane* although how old the name is we do not know.[13]

Other ports of the South Devon coast contained their contingents of full-time fishers. For example, a royal inquisition of 1383 was concerned to find that certain fishermen of Sutton (i.e. the port of Plymouth) were selling fish at unaccustomed places; a complaint to Chancery in the 1440s records that four boats from Dartmouth and Teignmouth were fishing together off the coast near the mouth of the Dart when they were captured by Bretons; at the port of Topsham the earls of Devon ran a seigneurial fishery in the thirteenth century.[14] At all of the South Devon ports seine nets, probably for local use, were recorded in a survey made by the Vice Admiral in 1566, and by this time many of them were sending fishing vessels to overseas fisheries and were exporting cured fish to foreign countries, enterprises which in general began in the fifteenth century.[15] In South Devon the contribution of the medieval fishers of ports to the total catch of the coast cannot have been small. But it is equally true to say that it must have been dwarfed by the catches not made by the ports, at least until the sixteenth century, because medieval references to fisheries on rural manors, on which this monograph concentrates, are very great in number. So now we must turn to types of settlement associated with fisheries in rural places.

2.1.ii Cellar settlements

Most of the rural settlements of Devon's coastal manors – typically small hamlets and isolated farms – were situated away from the shore and often out of sight of the sea. The reasons for this were probably fairly simple and basic: a desire to avoid the fiercest of winds and a need for security, which was still strong enough in the seventeenth century to encourage the owners of relatively small properties to construct crenellations from which intruders from the sea, especially pirates, could be deterred (Blegberry in Hartland parish, north coast of Devon, and Roscarrock in St Endellion parish, north coast of Cornwall).[16] Such considerations, and, in South Devon, rich farmland inland, drew rural settlements away from the coast. On the other hand, when and where fishing was a by-employment among farmers, fisheries in estuary or sea drew people towards the waters. The Devon solution to this tussle (with parallels in other parts of Britain, as shown in Chapter 7) was for farmers living inland to use cellar settlements, collections of storage huts on the beach which served as bases for their fishing operations. The *Oxford English Dictionary* defines a cellar as a 'store-house . . . whether above or below ground'; the name Coombe Cellars (on the shore of the River Teign) and other similar names show that this was the word used in Devon for a fishing place – Coombe Cellars was the fishing station of the inland rural population of Combeinteignhead. Cellar settlements were uninhabited insofar as they were places for working and not for night-time use (except, one might guess, when moon and the movement of shoals combined to make night-time fishing highly lucrative). They were not seasonal *habitations* as, say, the hill shielings of northern England and Scotland were, but, in many cases, they were used seasonally or at least not continuously. They were an integral part of the occupation of fishing when that was a by-employment among the farming population, and such a fascinating and characteristic feature of the South Devon coast, yet hitherto unknown and undescribed, that a separate section of this monograph is devoted to them.

2.1.iii Fishing villages

At Hallsands, according to the census of 1851, there were 26 heads of households of whom 18 were described as fishermen or (in the case of some widowed female heads) as paupers who had once assisted their husbands at fishing; there were also coastguards, victuallers and a thatcher.[17] There can be no doubt that nineteenth-century Hallsands should be classified as a fishing village. For earlier centuries historical sources which give such precise details about occupational structure are generally lacking; manorial surveys from the sixteenth and seventeenth centuries – one of the principal sources for the tour of the coast which follows – give the names of tenants but are usually silent as far as occupations are concerned. Written surveys and rentals do, however, contain other clues which indicate that the people of a particular settlement lived from shoreline activities among which fishing was probably dominant: location of dwellings on the shore, dwellings mostly described as 'cottages', absence of land attached to cottages, the presence of buildings called cellars, 'fish-houses' or the like, and lack of any (or many) of the attributes of ports as described in the previous section. Cross-checking between written manorial surveys and maps will indicate shoreline location, although sometimes the survey tells us as much, describing a dwelling or storehouse as 'on the beach' or 'next to the sea' or *apud litus maris*.[18] A rental of Kenton manor, from around the end of the seventeenth century, may be used as an example to bring out the humble nature of the dwellings of the fishing village of Starcross, and their landlessness: it lists 28 dwellings, all described as cottages, without gardens or any kind of land attached, and only 6 with gardens; the rental distinguishes 'cottages', the smaller dwellings, from 'tenements', the term used for the larger farmhouses of inland Kenton. Starcross, then, had a very basic, simple and undifferentiated social structure: all dwellings were small cottages, rents were standard, almost all had no gardens. At this time there were also about five cellars at Starcross.[19] The landless character of fishing villages is a result of their location on very restricted sites, for the cultivated fields of a typical manor stretched as far as was feasible towards the shore and the highest tides combined with high winds brought the waters close to the limit of cultivation: they were divorced from the land rather than being linked to farms as the cellar settlements were. 'Fishing village' is used as a convenient shorthand term for a coastal settlement where fishing was a dominant occupation although, as will be seen in the following chapter, the waters, mudbanks, beaches and cliffs close to such a village yielded a variety of other valuable products, apart from fish and shellfish, and gave occupations and livelihoods to local people.

2.1.iv Quays

Because of its tourist industry, the best known settlement on the South Devon coast is probably Torquay, the quay belonging to inland Torre, and the same could be said for Newquay on the north Cornish coast. These names raise questions about quays and their relationship to medieval coastal settlement. The whole topic is an exceedingly difficult one with, apparently, very little existing literature to guide the historian along.[20] Four basic questions need to be asked. Were quays of different types? What was their chronology of development? Who built them? What relationship did they have with settlement? At this stage we must be content with skirting around these questions, for firm answers will only come with further research.

It is clear that there were two types of quay, which, for convenience, may be called riverine and maritime quays. A riverine quay was essentially a wide wall parallel to a river bank, converting a shelving surface to a flat one. By reclamation it extended the bank out into the river channel, thereby providing a greater depth of water at high tide and a flat surface on which cargoes could be placed and from which cranes could be operated. In one document such a quay is called a 'sea wall' (*murus maris*, 'sea' in this context meaning 'estuary').[21] The maritime quays of the South-West, of which we have such good pictures on the coastal map of Henry VIII, were stone jetties in the true sense, walls thrown out (Old French *getee*) into the open sea, often with a gentle curve, which gave deeper water for ships loading and unloading and also acted as breakwaters, protecting craft lying in the lee.

As for chronology, this is not the place to discuss the wider European, or even British, contexts although it should perhaps be said that maritime trade routes must have been highly effective means of diffusing knowledge about the benefits of quays and their method of construction. In the South-West, riverine quays are known from the thirteenth and fourteenth centuries. Some were located at the larger ports, for example at Dartmouth where there was one by 1344 and at Topsham, by 1316; these are the earliest known references and may post-date quay construction by some time.[22] Some smaller riverine places also had quays by the fourteenth century and earlier, for example at Warfleet (Dart, possibly thirteenth-century), Morwellham Quay (Tamar, early thirteenth century, and therefore the first quay known from Devon) and Halton Quay (Tamar, Cornish side, possibly late fourteenth century). At the last mentioned place, in the fifteenth century, an enterprising lord gathered in as much as 30*s*. yearly from the keyage (landing fees) on wine, sand and iron.[23]

In the South-West, maritime quays built to facilitate loading and unloading, and to give craft shelter or succour (to use John Leland's term), may be a little later. From Devon and Cornwall the earliest references seem to be from 1392 and 1412: the bailiffs of Mousehole had a grant of quayage for five years to enable them to finish a quay, and a petition to Chancery complains that a French wine ship, seized as a prize of war by the men of the *George* of Paignton, was subsequently stolen by Dartmouth men while moored at *le Getee de Torrebaie*.[24] If the name Tor Bay applied, in the fifteenth century, to the great bight which later bore its name, rather than to the small indentation on the manor of Torre, the jetty or quay referred to could have been the one at Paignton: this would have been the logical place to which the *George* would have taken its prize.[25] Alternatively, as has usually been assumed, a quay at the site of the present Torquay harbour, in Torre manor, could be implied. All we can tell for certain from this reference is that at least one of the quays of Tor Bay was in existence in 1412; by the sixteenth century, the bay had become a veritable nest of quays, probably four in all, perhaps because of ease of construction (gently shelving shore), perhaps as a result of competition between settlements.[26] If we move forward in time, we find a flurry in the building of maritime quays in the 1420s and 1430s along the coasts of western Cornwall, with what seem to have been new structures in at least four places, Marazion, St Mawes, Newlyn and Newquay,[27] and it could well be that others, at Padstow, Lelant and St Ives, date from this time.[28] The storm-battered coast of North Devon had to wait until later: until the late sixteenth century at Hartland ('bill for the finishing of the port of Hartland' passed by an Elizabethan parliament) and at Clovelly ('late erected . . . pier or key' in the will of George Cary, 1601) and until the seventeenth century at Buck's Mills ('harbour . . . to shelter ships and boats').[29] Some stretches of coastline never received quays, on account, one might guess, of exposure, lack of access from the land, or shores which shelved too steeply. The famous Cobb at Lyme Regis, mentioned in the 1290s, stands out against the generalization that most maritime quays in the South-West date from around the beginning of the fifteenth century or later.[30]

Some quays were built as an investment by lords of manors. The riverine quay at Halton was referred to as 'the lord's quay' (*keia domini*) in a financial account (for 1434) of the Hylle family and may be seen as a minor landlord's attempt at increasing income: the family had interests in tin-making and lime-burning (near the quay, to which the limestone was imported) as well as in quay profits. Hartland's quay, likewise, was a landlord's investment: in this case the lord was William Abbot, inheritor of the manor of Stoke St Nectan which had passed to his family at the Dissolution, and the construction of the quay (for commodities in a minor coastal trade) may be seen as part of a programme of estate development.[31] Other quays were built by local communities, like 'the men . . . of *Marghasyowe*' who were building the structure at Marazion in 1425, or the community of burgesses at Lyme Regis which built the Cobb there.[32] Such quays were local 'public works' and – as with bridges, chapels of ease, and church naves and towers – local people could be encouraged to provide work or cash for their construction through indulgences, grants made (usually) by bishops to excuse members of the laity from penance so long as they made a contribution to a scheme for the public good.[33]

Most of the classes of settlement discussed earlier in this chapter might have quays. The large riverine ports such as Dartmouth and Topsham had them. A community of fishermen might build a quay, such as the riverine one at Dittisham probably constructed towards the end of the fifteenth century.[34] In some cases quays attracted settlement

The Coast

to them. Thus a cottage 'at the quay' (*apud* . . . *kay*) is recorded at Halton in 1473 and, after the making of Hartland quay at the end of the sixteenth century, a house for a quay-master, warehouses and other buildings were eventually constructed.[35] In other cases coastal settlement preceded quay: this was almost certainly so at all of the ports, where the building of a quay may be seen as a significant step forward in their commercial development; and also at some fishing villages, such as Mousehole in Cornwall.[36]

2.2 A tour of the coast

This tour of the coast, with its accompanying maps, concentrates on settlements as they were in the sixteenth and seventeenth centuries when the evidence first becomes reasonably abundant, though by no means comprehensive, but some earlier references are given, especially for larger

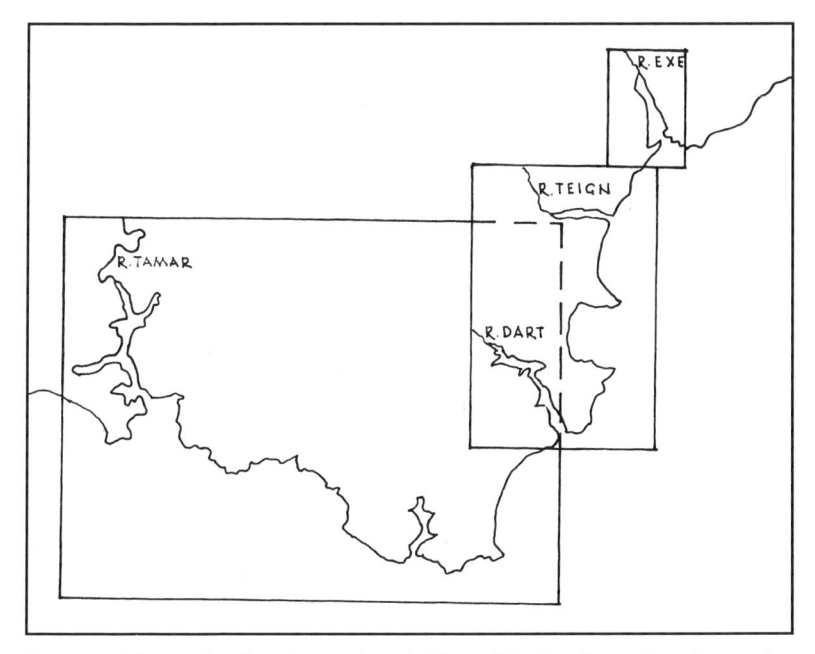

Figure 2.1 The coastline from Exmouth to the Tamar. The three boxes show the stretches of coast covered, from right to left, by sections 2.2.i, 2.2.ii and 2.2.iii of the text.

places. The maps attempt to show fisheries, ports, fishing villages, cellar settlements and quays known, from documentary evidence and cartographic sources, to have been present in the landscape of the seventeenth century. Use of sixteenth-century and even earlier evidence has been permitted, where necessary, on the grounds that most fisheries, where it can be proven, have been exploited with a good deal of continuity. It will be seen from the maps that the type of settlement, if any, associated with many fisheries is unknown or uncertain. It must be repeated that the maps are bound to be incomplete, both through lack of record of a fishery and through my own failure to locate records. For the sake of convenience the tour is divided into three parts (Fig. 2.1).

2.2.i The Exe Estuary (Fig. 2.2)
On a good day and at high tide the Exe Estuary has the appearance of a broad, placid lake. The sea seems very far away because it is at many points blocked from view by the curving sand spit of Dawlish Warren which closes the entrance to the estuary except for a narrow channel. At the head of the estuary is the city of Exeter which had its own medieval quay, just beyond the Roman walls, but which could be reached only by relatively small craft. Topsham, 4 miles downstream from Exeter, was the city's outport in the Middle Ages and perhaps as early as Roman times. In 1178 there is a record which indicates that ships laden with wine were discharging at Topsham, so it cannot have been the fish weirs set up there by the earls of Devon in the 1240s and 1280s which prevented large ships from reaching Exeter itself: the channel upstream from Topsham had become shallow well before the weirs were built. The weirs were, however, a great frustration to the city of Exeter whose citizens used force in the 1260s first to vandalize them, then to lead an attack on Topsham quay.[37]

Topsham was the only port town and borough on the Exe Estuary. In the sixteenth and seventeenth centuries it was at the height of its prosperity, for through it went the output of the expanding East Devon cloth industry, a trade which, by 1700, almost equalled London's. Prosperity was further increased by large-scale participation in the Newfoundland trade and by import, export and coastal trades in a great

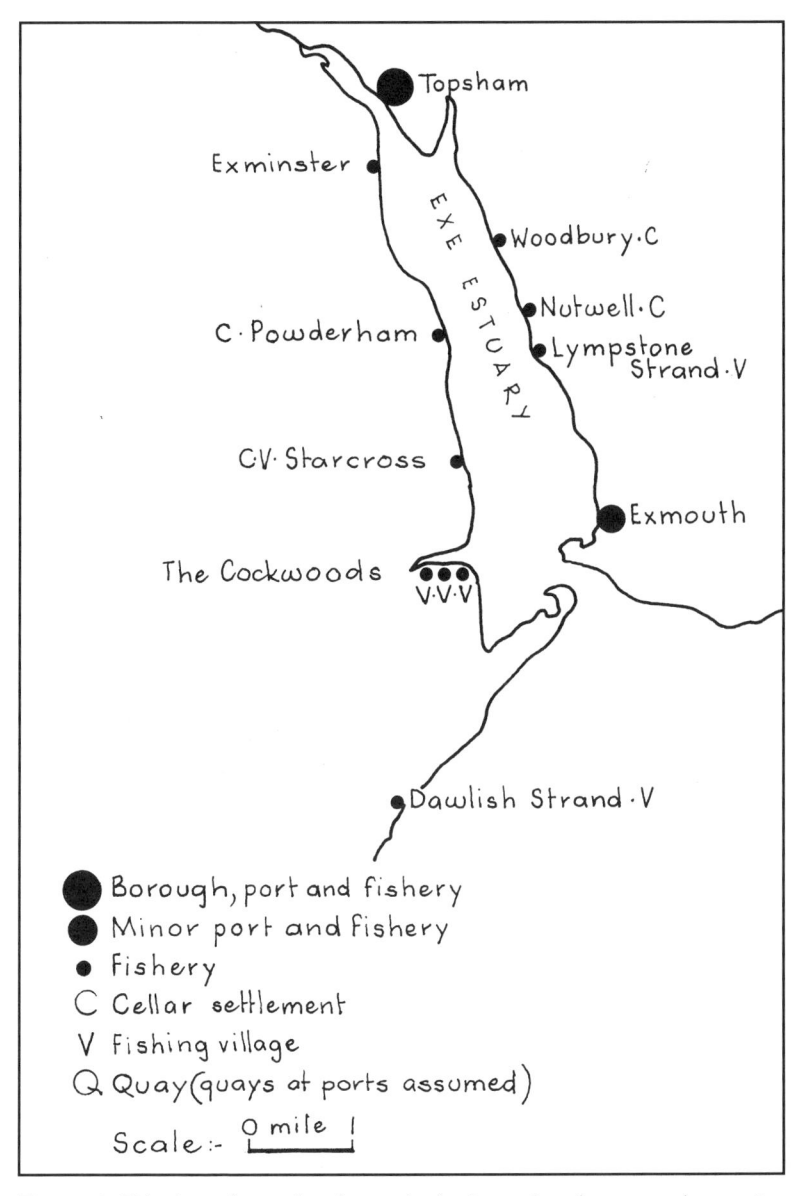

Figure 2.2 Fisheries and coastal settlement in the sixteenth and seventeenth centuries: the Exe Estuary. In cases where a fishing place has no known name, it is given the name of the manor to which it belonged, as in the documents.

variety of merchandise both exotic and humdrum.[38] Lightermen, customs officials, wharfingers, porters, shipwrights, carpenters, ropemakers, sailmakers, anchorsmiths, shipsmiths, brandy distillers, pipe-makers, millers – all of these occupations which have to do with the loading and unloading and transport of merchandise, and with the making, fitting-out and victualling of ships, are on record at the port in the early modern period.[39] Ports contained concentrations of sailors to be ready and available when crews were formed, and about 40 are recorded under Topsham in the maritime survey of 1619.[40] Some men so classified are likely to have been fishermen, for there are many references to Topsham's river fishery, from the beginning of the twelfth century when its tithes were granted to the Priory of St James in Exeter, extending through into the nineteenth century when White's *Directory* records 'eleven fishing boats employing about 100 men and boys in catching herrings, whiting, sprats, etc.', and later.[41]

Topsham's importance as a port extends back into the Middle Ages. A quay is referred to in 1316, stretching towards the river channel, and it was associated with a crane and sheds for storage. There are many subsequent references to these, for example from 1452 when expenses are recorded for 'the wall next to the crane', for *le slenges* (slings to do with the crane) and for lubrication of a mysterious 'machine' (*machina*) of unknown purpose, perhaps a giant pair of scales.[42] The medieval trade of the port was dominated by wine (mostly from Gascony) as the most valuable import and has been thoroughly documented, as has the coastal trade, by Maryanne Kowaleski.[43] Some ships were based in medieval Topsham but attributions are difficult because craft which documents call 'of Exmouth' could have belonged to any parish bordering on the Exe Estuary, though a good number of them would probably turn out to be Topsham ships if the documentary references were more revealing. Topsham also had some merchant importers, for example Robert Irlond who imported wine in 1298, 1299, and 1301 and frequently thereafter.[44] A man such as Irlond may not have been a substantial wine merchant for the bulk of that trade was in the hands of importers resident in Exeter. John Leland made this same point in relation to Topsham's trade in general, noting 'the great trade and road for ships' at Topsham 'and *especially* [my italics] for ships and merchant men's goods of Exeter'.[45] A market and a fair were established at Topsham during the thirteenth century, but references to stalls pre-date the institutional grants and suggest that trading was of some antiquity there. At the same point during the Middle Ages Topsham came to be regarded as a borough.[46]

Along the shores of the Exe the only other place with many of the attributes of a port town was Exmouth, on the eastern side near the estuary mouth. There is some doubt about the status of the place in the medieval and early modern periods, most recent opinions tending (wrongly) to play down its size and importance.[47] In the sixteenth and seventeenth centuries many of the ships belonging to Exmouth were involved in the Newfoundland trade. The survey of ships made in 1619 lists seven vessels here, none of them over 40 tons, their relatively small size being a result of the fact that the deep-water channel of the river makes for the western bank directly opposite Exmouth, so that even at high tide the port could accommodate only rather modest craft. Besides mariners and ship-owners (one of whom was Sir Richard Whitbourne, author of *A Discourse and Discovery of Newfoundland*, 1620), Exmouth was home to pilots who guided shipping through the difficult mouth of the Exe, and to customs officials who boarded incoming vessels as soon as they approached the estuary in order to check their cargoes. A survey from the early eighteenth century suggests a population of about four or five hundred, quite a sizeable nucleation by the Devon standards of the time.[48]

Medieval sources also indicate that the place called Exmouth today had some of the attributes of a port. In the Middle Ages it was called *Pratteshide*, the word Exmouth being then usually used to describe the whole estuary. The majority of ships tagged as being 'of Exmouth' in Exeter's customs accounts were probably not based at *Pratteshide*, but a few could have been, because an order of 1310 commanded that ships 'of *Pratteshide*' should join with others from the Exe Estuary to help in the war against Scotland, while Littleham (the mother parish) is listed among places at which ships were to be made ready for war in 1324 and 1326.[49] There was some kind of facility for loading and unloading ships, because the second element in the name *Pratteshide* is *hyth*, 'a landing place on a river bank',[50] usually with some implication of a built structure, however rudimentary (perhaps of wood rather than stone?). Here were unloaded, illicitly or with licence, cargoes from ships which, for some reason, were unwilling to sail up-river to the official quay at Topsham.[51] The ferry to Starcross, on the opposite shore of the Exe, also used the landing place at *Pratteshide*. Near to it was a mill, referred to as early as around 1240. This, almost certainly, was not the main manorial mill of Littleham (the manor in which *Pratteshide* lay), for that would have been inland; the presence of a mill near the landing place is suggestive of a port, albeit a minor one, because coastal mills are often associated with the victualling of ships.[52] There is a possibility of maritime activity of some kind here already by 1086.[53]

By the end of the Middle Ages, according to Peter Weddell's expert researches, the built-up area of *Pratteshide* was quite extensive. It is difficult to estimate the size of its population, because the settlement straddled a boundary, lying mostly in Littleham manor and parish but partly in the sub-manor of Hill in the adjacent parish of Withycombe Raleigh. A rental of Littleham, made in 1388, includes an abnormally large number (45) of small tenements and cottage holdings without land, many of which were probably at *Pratteshide* and which were almost certainly inhabited by people with maritime occupations, for this was a small manor (as its name implies) and would not have needed a sizeable complement of agricultural labourers. On the small adjacent sub-manor of *Hill* there were ten dwellings, almost certainly landless, in 1500.[54] Medieval occupations of smith, chapman and seaman are recorded; ferrymen and ships' masters are implied; excavations have yielded clench bolts, mainly used in ship building to join overlapping planks, so we may also infer shipwrights here.[55] Fishing was an important occupation – the local fishery is referred to as early as the middle of the thirteenth century and, by the fifteenth, fishing voyages to distant parts were being undertaken[56] – but it may by no means have been the dominant one. A market is mentioned as early as 1261 and was remarkably persistent despite being completely unlicensed.[57] At least two chapels of ease were built to serve the growing community, one known as early as 1329. The need for these chapels is well expressed in a petition of 1415: the 'vill' of Exmouth was 'situated on and hard by the sea', and when its inhabitants travelled inland to the mother church at Littleham they were likely to be cut off by the tide and their houses burned by pirates.[58]

Medieval *Pratteshide* (later Exmouth) was close to being a town if 'town' is defined by occupational diversity, non-agrarian base and the presence of marketing, yet it never acquired the status of a borough nor was its market licensed. Indeed, Christopher Dyer has recently included the place in his discussion of sites which had thoroughly commercial characteristics in the Middle Ages yet which flourished despite the efforts of 'lords and the state . . . to channel trade through the institutions which they created'.[59] *Pratteshide* takes its place alongside some other settlements on the South Devon coast (notably Brixham, Kingswear and Salcombe) which were ports, albeit relatively minor ones, without any of the institutional trappings of a town. To describe *Pratteshide* as a 'fisher townlet' – as John Leland did in the early sixteenth century – does not do justice to its size nor to the varied character of the occupations of the people there.[60] The internal evidence of his *Itinerary* suggests that he never visited the place but merely glimpsed it from the opposite shore or was told about it by an informant, so that his description of Exmouth may cast doubt upon the accuracy of his use of the terms 'fishing hamlet' or 'fisher townlet' at some other places in his notes.

Exmouth (*Pratteshide*) has been discussed in some detail here in order to introduce this type of settlement. Remote, mostly distant from seats of manorial authority inland, lacking their own courts or officers, lacking parish churches, sometimes straddling manorial boundaries, these places must have had a special and distinct character and quality of life in the Middle Ages; they are a fascinating sub-set within the category of port towns yet, by their very nature, relatively poorly documented, so that fascination is not rewarded by much historical and human detail.

The other shoreline settlements of the Exe Estuary (Fig. 2.2) present fewer problems of classification than Exmouth does: in the sixteenth and seventeenth centuries the estuary boasted at least five fishing villages – Westwood, Middlewood, Cockwood, Starcross and Lympstone

Strand – and at least three surviving cellar settlements. The three Cockwoods – still there for all to see today, though two are high and dry as a result of reclamation – are particularly well documented because their dwellings are recorded in a rental of 1515 and, when they changed hands, in the account rolls of their parent manor of Dawlish. The rental lists ten, thirteen and seven cottages, most of them landless, in the Cockwoods (from west to east) and a few decades later the great coastal map, drawn up on instructions from Henry VIII, gives a diagrammatic picture of these settlements. Starcross at the end of the seventeenth century contained 34 cottages, most without gardens, and five cellars; the earlier history of this settlement and some account of its diverse occupations, including fishing, are given in Chapter 5. The fishing village of Lympstone Strand was physically distinct from the inland settlement of Lympstone, near the parish church, as is clear from maps made in 1743 and 1765. A seventeenth-century survey of Lympstone manor lists no fewer than about 32 cottages with no land or only small acreages of land, as well as 13 cellars. All of the cellars would have been on the strand (one, indeed, was *apud les Chesills*, 'on the pebble beach') as would some of the cottages, though the precise number is unknown because the survey is topographically rather bland.[61]

Finally, extant records reveal cellar settlements which survived until the end of the sixteenth century or beginning of the seventeenth on sites which never developed into fishing villages: four cellars 'lying next the sea-shore' in Nutwell manor recorded in a survey of 1566, three in Powderham manor ('built upon the high strand, the lord's soil') recorded in a survey of about 1640, and probably others on the shore of Woodbury manor.[62]

2.2.ii From Dawlish to Dartmouth (Fig. 2.3)
From Dawlish to Dartmouth the coastline is dominated by imposing cliffs with many little coves below, some of them accessible from land only with the greatest difficulty or along steep, narrow paths perhaps commemorated in the name Anstey's Cove (perhaps O.E. *anstiga*, 'path for one person', 'single-file path'). In the major bight of Tor Bay the cliffs are lower and some larger 'sands' replace coves. One minor creek –

at Dawlish, now reclaimed and called The Lawn – and the long estuaries of the Teign and Dart complete this stretch of shoreline.

The settlements of this coast comprise two port towns which were also boroughs, Dartmouth and Teignmouth, two other minor towns and ports like Exmouth (described in the previous section) and numerous fishing places on rural manors. Dartmouth has been considered in detail earlier in this chapter, for it was used there as an exemplar for port towns in general. Dartmouth always outshone Teignmouth in terms of numbers of ships, having 45% of all Devon's ships in royal service during the fourteenth century, compared to the latter's 5%; 57 ships in the survey of 1619, compared to the latter's 7. Whereas the fjord-like mouth of the Dart could provide safe anchorage for huge fleets of ships of high tonnage – such as the 164 assembled there in advance of the second crusade of 1147, an event said in conventional histories to have caused the rise of the port – the far shallower mouth of the Teign was barred by a sandbank which made the channel entrance difficult to navigate. It may be that this impediment was not so severe in the early fourteenth century as it was to become later, for customs accounts from that period show quite large craft 'of Teignmouth' engaged in the Gascon wine trade.[63] Teignmouth suffered several vicissitudes: in 1340 it was fired and partly destroyed by the French and later it suffered partial silting of its harbour by detritus from tin works upstream – perhaps during the second half of the fifteenth century when tin output on Dartmoor grew very rapidly, although the first we hear of this damage is in the early sixteenth century. There was another French raid in 1690 when a reputed 116 dwellings were burned.[64] Even so, Teignmouth ships made a significant contribution to the Newfoundland trade in the seventeenth century, though one which was dwarfed by Dartmouth's.

Along this stretch of coast two other places qualify as ports, though of a relatively minor kind. One was Kingswear, Dartmouth's twin on the opposite side of the Dart. In the sixteenth and seventeenth centuries Kingswear was home to numerous sailors and mariners, some of whom were fishermen, and also to ship-owners and shipwrights. To judge from the number of seines recorded here in 1566, there was a greater emphasis on fishing than at Dartmouth on the opposite shore.[65] Medieval

The Evolution of the Fishing Village

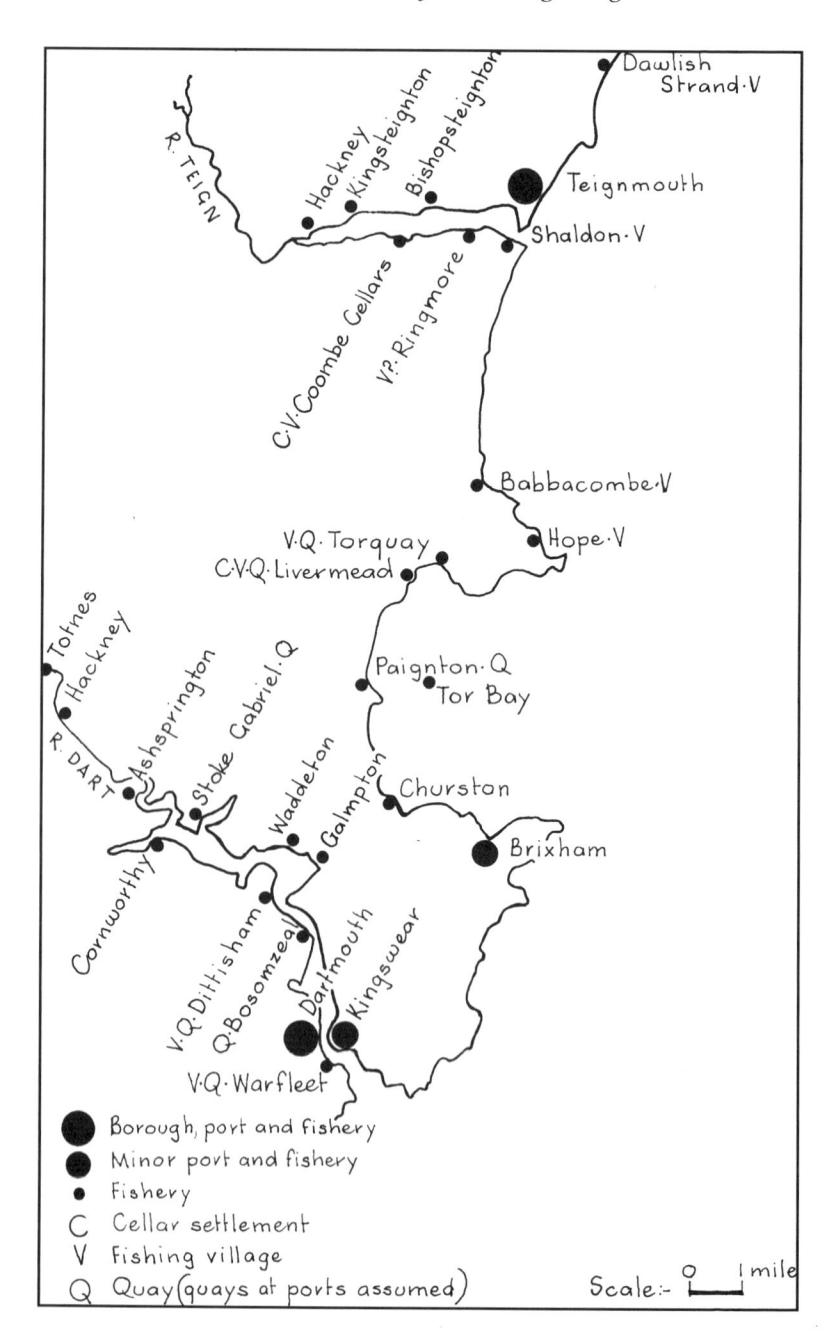

Kingswear also shows some signs of being a small port. There were warehouses and a ferry and several private quays.[66] Ships 'of Kingswear' were recorded in the local customs accounts of the port of Exeter and a few royal levies on shipping name the place separately from Dartmouth.[67] As early as the beginning of the thirteenth century some kind of maritime settlement had grown up here, for Kingswear is well documented at this time and all of the early charters relate to buildings with little agricultural land attached to them, that is to commercial premises of some kind.[68] Brixham was another place with some attributes of a port town although it is highly unfortunate that such an important place, with a valuable fishery – its fish tithes were worth £17 according to the *Valor Ecclesiasticus* (1535) – is so poorly represented in the medieval documentary record, as the expert researches of Percy Russell and John Pike make clear. Brixham quay, of the curved type protecting a fine natural inlet, is clearly shown on Henry VIII's coastal map of about 1540, but any attempt to trace it back further than that disappears into obscurity.[69] There are no good early modern surveys to help us. In 1295/6 we hear of a small craft (*batel*) of Brixham which docked at Topsham with a cargo of wheat and barley, typical South Devon crops bound probably for the food market of Exeter; in 1404 a barge of Brixham was reported as lying in the Thames, requisitioned for crown service, its master desperately trying to retain its crew despite lack of pay; in 1442 a ship in the harbour of Brixham, laden with imports of canvas, cloth and iron was wrongfully seized; in the 1460s the customs accounts of Exeter regularly record ships of Brixham, especially the *George*, the *Mary* and the *Rose*, which brought cargoes of fish, products perhaps of catches in Tor Bay, to Topsham and the fish markets of the city; a final example in this miscellaneous sample of references to Brixham's trade is of a ship of the port which was repaired at Bordeaux in 1502.[70] A single medieval manorial survey from the 1440s is brief and rather colourless, but it gives one tell-tale clue about the manor of Brixham, for there were three

---

Figure 2.3 Fisheries and coastal settlement in the sixteenth and seventeenth centuries: from Dawlish to Dartmouth. In cases where a fishing place has no known name, it is given the name of the manor to which it belonged, as in the documents.

times as many cottage holdings without land as there were farm holdings; a total of perhaps 90 cottages is a very large figure for a rural manor and there is little reason to doubt that some of their occupants would have had maritime occupations.[71] In short, here was another minor port with a varied trade (both coastal and overseas), which developed on the shore of a rural manor and which prospered virtually unnoticed by the Crown and with none of the fuss of borough status or burgage tenure.

The stretch of shoreline described in the previous section – the Exe Estuary – is particularly well documented, with good early modern sources, especially rentals and surveys, for all but one or two of those manors with a waterfront. The same cannot be said of the stretch from Dawlish to Dartmouth, so the map of this coast (Fig. 2.3) cannot claim anything like completeness. Despite gaps in the evidence, the number of fisheries shown on Fig. 2.3 is prodigious and, as usual, those on rural manors dwarfed, numerically, those of the port towns. In the previous section, the stretch of shoreline was shorter and the fishing places correspondingly fewer; it was possible to describe them all, however briefly. Here, by contrast, and in the next section, the reader must largely make do with the maps and with a few examples chosen out of many.

Livermead is one of the most illuminating of the settlements along this stretch of coast, because it shows how difficult classification is and demonstrates a slow transition from one type to another. There are good and clear medieval sources referring to fishing from Livermead Sands which were part of the manor of Cockington, the manor house and church lying a little less than a mile inland; but despite excellent manorial documentation there are no early references to dwellings on the shore.[72] Then, in financial accounts of 1528 and 1529, we read of a 'newly built small messuage [dwelling house]' at Livermead taken by John Martyn, and from that point onwards there is a growing number of references to built structures at the place, a snapshot of the stage of development reached by the middle of the seventeenth century being provided by a quite detailed survey of 1655. The surveyor clearly had a good eye for buildings and property generally, noting how one cottage property inland had been converted from 'half a barn', that another had once been a stable while a third was 'a pretty dwelling house and a little backside'.

These references, and others to cottages inland built on small plots of waste, show that the years running up to the making of the survey had seen an expansion in the manor's stock of landless cottagers. This trend also affected shoreline settlement, for just as agricultural buildings inland were being converted to dwellings, so too, at Livermead, were cellars being converted to cottages: the survey has two clear references to a 'cellar now a dwelling house' and to a 'dwelling house sometimes a cellar' and another entry where 'little dwelling house' has been added as an amendment to the word 'cellar'. At the same time, some cellars – or 'fishing houses' or 'poor cellars', to use the terminology of the observant surveyor – were still uninhabited buildings, such as one leased by a farmer with a dwelling house and an agricultural holding inland.

It is clear that the snapshot provided by the surveyor in 1655 catches the settlement of Livermead in transition; in terms of our classification it is a hybrid. Some buildings were dwellings on the shore constructed *de novo*, others were conversions of cellars into cottages (occupied by landless individuals who, almost by definition, must have had maritime occupations), while yet others remained as storage huts used by fishing farmers living inland. Wills, leases and probate inventories confirm that, for some, dual occupations persisted on Cockington manor well into the seventeenth century.[73]

2.2.iii From Dartmouth to the Tamar (Fig. 2.4)
Along the South Devon coast, land meets the waters in many delightful ways and this is as true for the third stretch to be discussed here as it is for the previous two. For the most part this is a cliff coastline with few long sands: the longest are in Start Bay, viewed with great trepidation in the early sixteenth century, as the annotations to Henry VIII's coastal map show, because of their suitability for enemy landings. Here and there the cliffs give way to little coves. In addition, the shoreline is much extended by the estuaries of six rivers which wind many miles northwards so that the inland walker, feeling himself far from the sea, suddenly comes across bright glinting water among the farmland or, at low tide, senses the '. . . thrilling-sweet and rotten | Unforgettable, unforgotten | River smell . . .'.

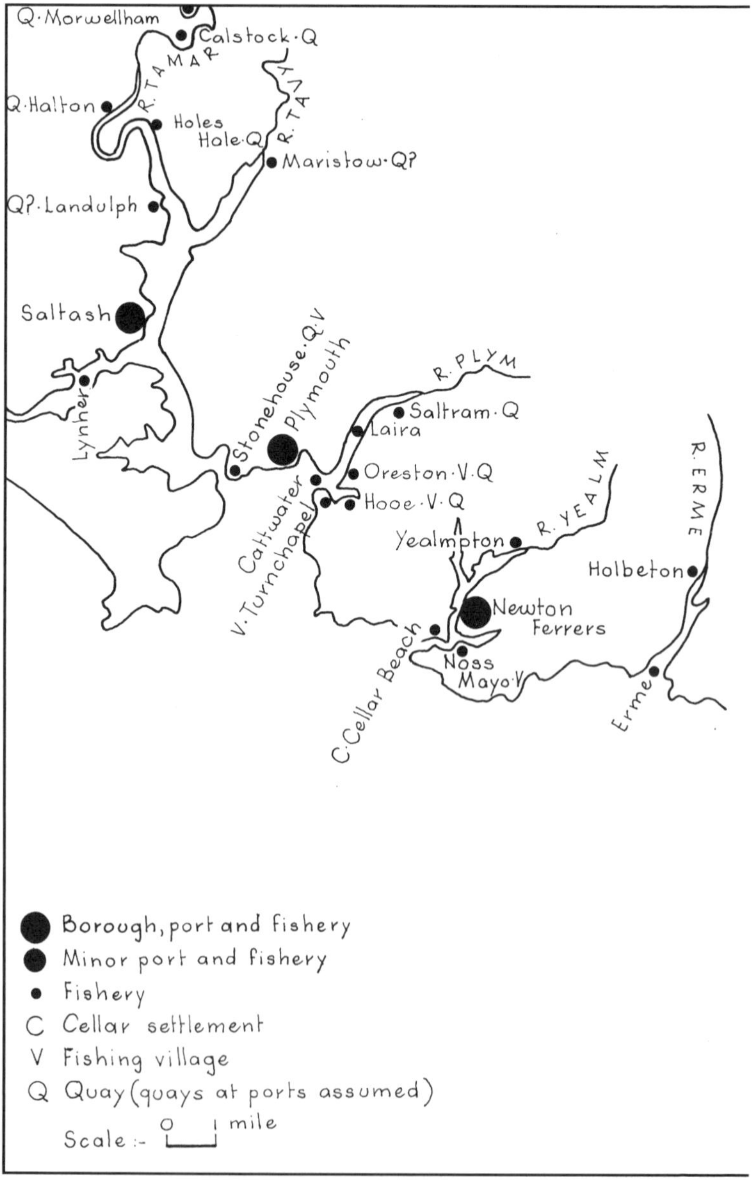
Q·Morwellham
Calstock·Q
R. TAMAR
R. TAVY
Q·Halton
Holes Hole·Q
Maristow·Q?
Q?·Landulph
Saltash
Lynher
Stonehouse·Q·V
Plymouth
R. PLYM
Saltram·Q
Laira
Oreston·V·Q
Hooe·V·Q
Cattwater
V·Turnchapel
R. YEALM
Yealmpton
R. ERME
Holbeton
Newton Ferrers
Noss Mayo·V
C·Cellar Beach
Erme
Borough, port and fishery
Minor port and fishery
Fishery
C Cellar settlement
V Fishing village
Q Quay (quays at ports assumed)
Scale :- 0 1 mile

The Coast

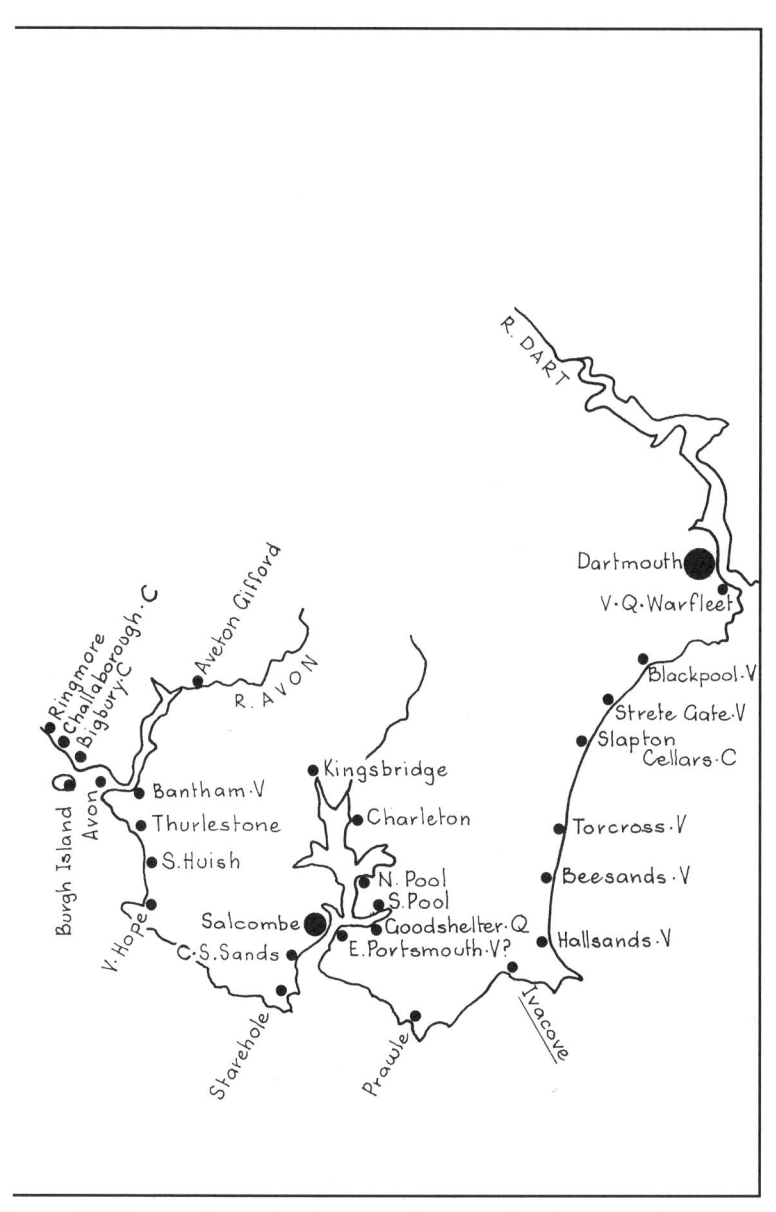

Figure 2.4 Fisheries and coastal settlement in the sixteenth and seventeenth centuries: from Dartmouth to the Tamar. In cases where a fishing place has no known name, it is given the name of the manor to which it belonged, as in the documents.

Of the coastal boroughs on this stretch, one – Plymouth – comes very near the top of the league according to statistical indications of port size: 29% of all Devon ships in royal service during the fourteenth century and 47 ships according to the survey of 1619 (compare Dartmouth's figures of 45% and 57). At the very end of the seventeenth century, Plymouth was about to have added to it the entirely new settlement of Dock, developed as a new dockyard town and eventually to rival the old port in size.[74] The other port and borough was Newton Ferrers, with a fair complement of mariners in the seventeenth century. Newton was asked to contribute only moderate numbers of craft to royal levies in the fourteenth century yet it had inhabitants who might own 'boats, barges and ships', who might wish to sell goods anywhere in the borough and to carry 'merchandise below and above the shoreline'; these words are from the *inspeximus* of an unusual charter of Reginald de Ferrers, in favour of a merchant, showing that the lord was keen to develop his port by granting maximum privileges to individuals.[75] One other port on this stretch was never a borough: Salcombe, set just inside the mouth of the Kingsbridge Estuary on a site almost identical to Dartmouth's inside the mouth of the Dart. Here was a port with a fleet of respectable size both in the fourteenth century and the seventeenth, a place important and wealthy enough to attract the unwelcome attentions of a Breton and Norman force in 1403. Yet in terms of lordship and institutions it was a forgotten settlement. It was not a Domesday manor; it was not a separate vill for taxation purpose; it had no ancient parish church; it straddled manorial boundaries; its inhabitants at first had no courts or other formal institutions of their own.[76] Salcombe therefore takes its place alongside other relatively minor ports which were never boroughs, like Exmouth, Kingswear and Brixham (see above, previous sub-sections). These places would benefit from further research as a group or sub-type: did they fail to develop as great ports because their lords lacked much interest in them or was it the case that some physical characteristic of site or channel held them back and prevented the development experienced by some of their rivals?[77]

Shortage of space prevents much discussion of the very numerous places along this stretch of coast where fishing took place on purely rural manors (Fig. 2.4), but a few general points should be made. First, the sea coast itself is devoid of quays whereas the River Tamar has many. In many places the cliffs are too high and steep to encourage construction of quays at their feet; moreover, unlike Tor Bay (discussed above, in the sub-section on quays), this coast, especially westwards of Start Point, takes the full blast of south-westerly gales and it may be that no quay could survive for that reason. There is one anomaly, for the fishing village of Hope is called *Hope-key* by the chorographer Tristram Risdon, writing in the seventeenth century. The only earlier reference to this quay is on Saxton's printed county map of 1575, and it is not shown on the two detailed estate maps of Hope made in the eighteenth century.[78] The quay at Hope may possibly be an invention of Saxton which was then borrowed from his map by Risdon. Riverine quays, by contrast, were very numerous especially on the Tamar and Fig. 2.4 may well under-estimate their number in the sixteenth and seventeenth centuries. In the nineteenth century there were around twenty quays on this river[79] and some may certainly be traced back to the Middle Ages: Halton Quay (later fourteenth century), Morwellham Quay (around 1230), and quays at Calstock (1462) and possibly at Landulph (in the fifteenth century?). There may also have been a quay at Maristow on the River Tavy, 2 miles beyond its junction with the Tamar.[80] Of all these quays, Morwellham is the best documented, for it belonged to Tavistock Abbey. It is also the earliest known of the Tamar quays, being the subject of a charter of the 1230s which mentions a *portus* (the quay itself?), a house associated with it, and a furnace (*clibanus*), possibly a lime kiln. Tavistock Abbey used this quay for imports of wine, fish and sea-sand.[81]

A second general point to be made about this coastline is that it is the only one of the three stretches discussed in this monograph which can claim deserted fishing villages, perhaps, again, because of its very exposed character. One of these, Hallsands, was certainly battered away by storms, in 1903, 1904 and 1917, its fishing families being eventually re-housed in homes set well back from the cliff edge; this was not entirely a natural disaster, for the village had been made vulnerable after dredging in Start Bay caused changes in the level of the pebble beach which had formerly protected the settlement.[82] Another deserted site which was a casualty of storms was Strete Gate or *Undercliff*, below the cliffs at the northern end of Slapton Ley. Little is known precisely either about the beginning or about the ending of this village. It is first recorded in print on the coastal map of Greenvile Collins, dated 1693, whence it was probably copied by Herman Moll who shows the name (*Startgate*) on his county map of 1724.[83] Earlier, Blackawton's burial register mentions people who had died at *Under Cliffe* or *Streate Under Clift*, the earliest reference being in 1658.[84] We do not know how old the village then was; if it originated at around the same time as some other fishing villages on Start Bay, we should probably place its beginnings as an inhabited place in the early sixteenth century. A survey of the middle of the eighteenth century mentions 19 dwellings here, only one with a garden, and a few cellars – a typical fishing village divorced from the land.[85] The demise of the village was romanticized increasingly as writers became more and more distant from the event. A guidebook of 1933 writes of 'fishermen's cottages clinging to the cliffs like swallows' nests . . . [then] swept into the sea'. When the Lysons brothers were collecting information for their *Magna Britannia* they were told (1818) of 'a large village . . . where a herring fishery was carried out but the sea has so encroached on that part that not a vestige of it now remains'. A little earlier, Thomas Brice wrote in 1802 of houses and land 'carried away by the sea' within the past 20 years. This would put the loss of Strete Gate at around 1780.[86]

Another deserted fishing station may possibly lie near Starehole Cove at the mouth of the Kingsbridge Estuary, and was investigated by the amateur antiquarian John Cranch and others in 1799. Unfortunately the romantic nature of the scenery affected their young imaginations and they saw tumuli and ramparts at every turn, their minds wandering at random from Phoenician, to Roman, to Danish antiquities. What is certain is that the folklore of the neighbourhood claimed that there had been a settlement here and that its remains had been recently ploughed away. In the middle of the eighteenth century the incumbent was told the same kind of story which had been recounted to Cranch – of 'a town as appeared by the ruins and foundations of the houses', of one large building which was, by old people, called a church and of the tearing up of the settlement remains to provide stones for enclosure of a common. The descriptions of Cranch and of the incumbent are independent of one another but their similarity suggests that they have a common folkloric source. A single manorial account, dated 1534-5, records huge rents, and large increases of rents, for what can only have been rough ground adjacent to Starehole Bay and these may conceal some kind of activity by the sea shore, perhaps the construction of cellars or cottages which later for some reason became disused and were destroyed by the activities mentioned above. We are on more certain ground with a deserted fishing site in East Portlemouth parish, on the banks of the Kingsbridge Estuary, where the minister in 1791 reported 'the remains of some cottages which tradition … says were inhabited by fishermen'.[87]

2.3 Conclusion

The classifications adopted here for the coastal settlements of South Devon as they appear to have been in the sixteenth and seventeenth centuries provide a rough and ready guide to that period but not to earlier or later ones. For example, in the late eighteenth and nineteenth centuries, at some fishing villages, the number of people who could be counted as belonging to fishing families became out-numbered, if not dwarfed, by those who catered for, or were catered for in, the coast's rapidly growing resort industry. Then again, in the High Middle Ages (say, thirteenth century), there were far fewer fishing villages than there were in the seventeenth century and more cellar settlements; in other words, outside the port towns, most fishing was still firmly in the hands of farmers who fished on a part-time basis, although there may be a few exceptions to this generalization.[88] Moreover, there were certainly places which did not fall neatly into any one of the classes which are introduced in this chapter, a few of which will be discussed by way of conclusion. These cannot be called misfits, because that would be to malign their innocent inhabitants for breach of an academic classification made many years later; rather they were places which showed some of the characteristics of more than one of the levels in our classification, thus neatly demonstrating its imperfections.

One example is Kenton, a large parish and manor on the western shore of the Exe Estuary. In the period between the fourteenth and sixteenth centuries, many Kenton people were employed in the fishery of the Exe, in the nurture of mussels, in the ferry business, in the gathering of rushes and, to a small degree, in the unloading of cargoes. Most were primarily farmers or labourers, as a very detailed sixteenth-century survey shows, their maritime occupations being secondary. The maritime settlement was originally a collection of storage huts called Starcross, which is also very well documented; then, in the seventeenth century, the cellars at Starcross began to be converted into cottages for habitation and a permanently occupied shoreline settlement developed.[89]

At first sight, classification seems simple. Inland there were rural settlements – the loose nucleation of Kenton itself and many hamlets and isolated farms – while on the shore was a cellar settlement later to become a village. But closer examination reveals some of the characteristics of a port. At least twice in the early fourteenth century, royal orders were directed to Kenton (along with other places, mostly established ports) asking for ships to help with the Scottish or French wars; in the sixteenth and seventeenth centuries royal surveys of shipping name vessels 'of Kenton', some relatively large (50 tons and over), and we know from other sources that Kenton men or ships were engaged in foreign trade.[90] That Kenton parish was home to masters and mariners, some of whom were also farmers, does not of itself make the place a port, because, as Todd Gray has shown, maritime occupations spread to many of South Devon's *inland* parishes where masters and men resided between voyages and, if they had agricultural land, used family or servants for farmwork while they were away.[91] Kenton had ships attributed to it, but presumably all that this means is that it was the parish of residence of their owners. The ships would not have traded there with overseas cargoes and may not even have lain there between voyages: we know for certain that ships from some of the exposed Tor Bay parishes regularly sheltered in the Dart Estuary.[92] But we cannot call Kenton a port because it had no foreign trade (which, for the whole of the Exe Estuary, was normally permitted only at Topsham, unless, under some special circumstance, it was allowed elsewhere), it had little coastal trade and, moreover, had no quay or other port facilities, only mudbanks and two shallow creeks. Above all, people with maritime occupations were greatly out-numbered by those involved solely in farming (rather than *vice versa* as in a port town) and may well have lived in settlements scattered over the face of the parish (rather than in a concentration). Constant exposure to a view of great ships from exotic places as they sailed in the deep channel of the Exe, which curved close to Kenton's shore, would have enticed some of the people of the parish to aspire to be mariners, masters or shipowners, while others, not Kenton born, would have regarded property in the parish as an investment and a rural retreat between voyages, in view of the shipping but distant from port authority.

Another type of place which does not fit easily into the classification suggested in this chapter is the fishing station which lacked structures of any kind, being neither a cellar settlement nor a fishing village. A Victorian description of an inlet in the rocks on the coast of Chivelstone parish sets the scene. It was 'a small basin in which some half-dozen fishing boats may float, surrounded by rocks … The fishermen, however, turn it to account … and use it as a harbour; and in the hollows of the big rock close by they find storerooms for their tackle, and vaults for their fish.'[93] The storage cellars of a cellar settlement provided convenience, security and safety, but the inlet just described, made all by nature, gave none of those. We shall never be able to say why no cellars were built here: because of a lack of space for their foundations, perhaps, or because of relatively infrequent use? Nor can we tell how many sites such as these once served the fisheries of the South Devon coast.

---

[1] BL, Cott. Aug. I i; G. Collins, *Great Britain's Coasting Pilot* (1693). Parts (but not all) of the Devon section of the map of around 1540 are redrawn, quite accurately, in D. and S. Lysons, *Magna Britannia*, vol. 6, *Devonshire* (1822), pt 2, plates opposite pp. 155, 320, 399. The *Coasting Pilot* (edition of 1753) has been reprinted. For Collins, see W. Ravenhill, 'The maritime cartography of south-west England from Elizabethan to modern times', *NMHD*, vol. 1, pp. 157-8.

[2] A useful collection, including many coastal charts, is E. Stuart, *Lost Landscapes of Plymouth: Maps, Charts and Plans to 1800* (1991).

[3] T. Gray, *Early-Stuart Mariners and Shipping: the Maritime Surveys of Devon and Cornwall, 1619-35* (DCRS, new ser., 33, 1990).

[4] DRO, glebe terriers, Blackawton perambulation of 1613; DRO, 48/13/2/3/2. The Cockington inventories are rare survivals because most Devon documents of this type were destroyed in World War II.

[5] W. R. Lee, 'The socio-economic and demographic characteristics of port cities: a typology for comparative analysis?', *Urban History* 25 (1998), pp. 147-72 is a very useful discussion of the demographic and sociological characteristics of port towns in the modern period. Similar work needs to be done for the Middle Ages.

[6] A. Fox, 'Some evidence for a Dark Age trading site at Bantham', *Antiquaries Jnl* 35 (1955), pp. 55-67.

[7] Principal sources are (in chronological order of publication) H. R. Watkin, *Dartmouth*, vol. 1, *Pre-Reformation* (1935) for abstracts of records; P. Russell, *Dartmouth: a History of the Port and Town* (1950); R. Freeman, *Dartmouth and its Neighbours* (1990); M. Kowaleski, 'The port towns of fourteenth-century Devon', *NMHD*, vol. 1, pp. 63-4; T. Gray, 'Fishing and the commercial world of early Stuart Dartmouth', in T. Gray, M. Rowe and A. Erskine, eds, *Tudor and Stuart Devon: the Common Estate and Government* (1992), pp. 173-99. For privateering see S. P. Pistono, 'Henry V and John Hawley, privateer, 1399-1408', *TDA* 111 (1979), pp. 145-63.

[8] DRO, SM 1989, cited by Gray, 'Fishing and the commercial world', p. 184.

[9] Watkin, *Dartmouth*, pp. 44, 47; *ibid.*, frontispiece for the map; W. G. Hoskins, *Devon* (1954), p. 383; Gray, *E-SMS*, p. 18 (shipwrights of Stoke Fleming who would have worked at South Town – part of the town of Dartmouth, though in Stoke Fleming parish) and p. 22; I. Friel, *The Good Ship: Ships, Shipbuilding and Technology in England, 1200-1520* (1995), p. 42.

[10] Names from Watkin, *Dartmouth* and M. Kowaleski, 'The 1377 Dartmouth poll tax', *DCNQ* 35 (1985), pp. 286-95.

[11] Kowaleski, 'Markets', p. 362; Watkin, *Dartmouth*, pp. 9-10; *ibid.*, pp. 38-41 and *Cal. Ch. Rolls*, vol. 5, pp. 3-4 for the charter. Dartmouth was not separately represented at the eyres of 1238 and 1244 but at that of 1249 was amerced for sending a jury of its own instead of coming with the Hundred of Coleridge as before: D. Crook, *Records of the General Eyre* (1982), p. 206; M. W. Beresford and H. P. R. Finberg, *English Medieval Boroughs: a Hand-List* (1973), p. 90. This may suggest that Dartmouth became a borough between 1244 and 1249.

[12] Gray, *E-SMS*, pp. 19-22. For the conflation of fishermen and mariners in this document, *ibid.*, p. xvi and T. Gray, 'Devon's coastal and overseas fisheries and New England migration' (unpublished Ph.D. thesis, University of Exeter, 1988), p. 134. The maritime survey of 1565 (under Dorset) explicitly notes the conflation: 'The same mariners are also fishermen and when they return from any voyage of merchandise they occupy themselves in fishing': PRO, SP12/37-9 (quotation and reference kindly supplied by Dr Simon Pawley). See also A. L. Rowse, *Tudor Cornwall: Portrait of a Society* (1941), p. 70.

[13] Leland, *Itinerary*, vol. 1, p. 220; Watkin, *Dartmouth*, p. 196; Kowaleski, 'The 1377 Dartmouth poll tax', p. 292; PRO, E179/95/126; *Rotuli Hundredorum*, vol. 1, p. 90;

Watkin, *Dartmouth*, p. 353; *ibid.*, caption to plate xii.

[14] *Cal. Inq. Misc.*, vol. 4, p. 148; D. M. Gardiner, ed., *A Calendar of Early Chancery Proceedings Relating to West-Country Shipping, 1388-1493* (DCRS, new ser., 21, 1976), p. 51; below, Section 3.3 for Topsham.

[15] DRO, Exeter City Archives book 57; M. Kowaleski, 'The expansion of the southwestern fisheries in late medieval England', *Ec. Hist. Rev.*, 2nd ser., 53 (2000), pp. 435-44.

[16] Photographs in R. P. Chope, *The Book of Hartland* (1940), opposite p. 113 and in N. Orme, ed., *Nicholas Roscarrock's Lives of the Saints: Cornwall and Devon* (DCRS, new ser., 35, 1992), plate 3. For pirates, see T. Gray, 'Turkish piracy and early Stuart Devon', *TDA* 121 (1989), pp. 159-71 and S. Bhanji, 'The involvement of Exeter and the Exe Estuary in piracy', *TDA* 130 (1998), pp. 23-49.

[17] 1851 census enumerators' returns.

[18] PRO, SC6 827/28, Dittisham account of 17-18 Edw. IV; DRO, 346M/M/264 (*apud les Chesills*, i.e. shingle, at Lympstone); DRO, 1334M/M/4 (Sidmouth).

[19] DRO, 1508M/Devon/surveys/Kenton/5.

[20] There is some useful material in C. R. S. Kilpatrick, 'The development of harbour and dock engineering', reprinted in A. Jarvis, ed., *Port and Harbour Engineering* (1998), pp. 1-43. The same collection, pp. 45-74, has details of the harbour works of the Mediterranean in classical times. Some leads may be found in B. Hobley, 'The London waterfront – the exception or the rule?', P. Marsden, 'Early shipping and the waterfronts of London' and A. G. Dyson, 'The terms "quay" and "wharf" and the early medieval London waterfront', all in G. Milne and B. Hobley, eds, *Waterfront Archaeology in Britain and Northern Europe* (1981). Also useful is the chapter on ports in G. Hutchinson, *Medieval Ships and Shipping* (1994), pp. 104-16.

[21] PRO, SC6 827/28, Dittisham account of 13-14 Edw. IV.

[22] Above, n. 9; below n. 42. For quays at ports in the sixteenth century, see J. Youings and P. W. Cornford, 'Seafaring and maritime trade in sixteenth-century Devon', *NMHD*, vol. 1, pp. 98-100.

[23] Evidence for a quay at Warfleet (*Welflut, temp.* Edw. 1) comes from the name. The second element is *fleot*, referring to the small creek here, and the first seems to be *weall*, 'wall', which bemused the editors of *PND* (vol. 1, p. 321), but must surely have been a riverine quay. Morwellham: DRO, W1258M/D/39/5, charter of about 1240 and H. P. R. Finberg, 'Morwell', in W. G. Hoskins and H. P. R. Finberg, *Devonshire Studies* (1952), pp. 158-61. For Halton, see n. 31 below.

[24] *VCH Cornwall*, vol. 1, p. 483; Gardiner, ed., *Calendar*, p. 15.

[25] For examples of early references which use the name Tor Bay to cover an area far larger than the sea in the vicinity of Torre, see *PND*, vol. 1, p. 20; DRO, W1258M/D/39/5, e.g. court of 18 Dec. 14 Hen. VII; Saxton's map of Devonshire, 1575.

[26] Henry VIII's map of the southern coastline (BL, Cott. Aug. I i) shows quays at Brixham, Paignton and Torquay. In addition to the Chancery reference in 1412, there is another, possible, mention of the quay at Paignton in 1523: DRO, W1258M/D/39/5, court of 21 Jan. 14 Hen. VIII. The doubt is because the reference is to a 'causey' – vernacular for causeway – so there could either have been a causeway (as well as a quay?) at Paignton

at that time, or else the word was being used in the sense of quay. The latter explanation is possible, because what was almost certainly a quay at Mousehole was referred to as a causeway (*calcetum*) in 1435: G. R. Dunstan, ed., *The Register of Edmund Lacy* (5 vols, DCRS, new ser., 7, 10, 13, 16, 18, 1963-72), vol. 1, p. 306. The fourth quay in Torbay was at Livermead: H. H. Walker, 'Livermead Harbour, Torquay', *TDA* 99 (1967), pp. 287-8 and plate; P. Russell, *A History of Torquay*, plate 1, engraving of 1662, attributed to Wenceslaus Hollar.

[27] Dunstan, ed., *Register*, vol. 1, p. 126; *ibid.*, p. 263; vol. 2, p. 45; *ibid.*, p. 176. Vol. 1, p. 306 refers to a quay at Mousehole.

[28] Leland, *Itinerary*, vol. 1, pp. 317-8 noted 'quays or piers' at these last three places. For St Ives there is an earlier reference, from the 1470s: J. H. Harvey, *William Worcestre Itineraries* (1969), p. 35.

[29] M. Nix and M. R. Myres, *Hartland Quay: the Story of a Vanished Port* (1982), pp. 6-7; T. Risdon, *The Chorographical Description or Survey of the County of Devon* (1811), p. 242.

[30] *Cal. Inq. Misc.*, vol. 1, p. 473.

[31] PRO, SC6 822/23, account of 13-14 Hen. VI. The full range of industrial and commercial developments at Halton Quay may be reconstructed from accounts at SC6 822/15-823/12, between the reigns of Hen. IV and Edw. IV and therefore spanning the fifteenth century. There are further accounts from the reign of Hen. VII and one from the reign of Hen. VIII. For the lime kiln see also R. W. Dunning, ed., *The Hylle Cartulary* (Som. Rec. Soc., 68, 1968), p. 90. Nix and Myres, *Hartland Quay*, pp. 8-13 for trade at Hartland Quay.

[32] Dunstan, ed., *Register*, vol. 1, p. 126; *Cal. Inq. Misc.*, vol. 4, p. 30, where the Cobb is said to have been 'constructed at the cost of the burgesses'.

[33] N. Orme, 'Indulgences in the Diocese of Exeter 1100-1536', *TDA* 120 (1988), pp. 15-32.

[34] PRO, SC6 827/28, account of 17-18 Edw. IV.

[35] PRO, SC6 823/4, account of 13-14 Edw. IV; Nix and Myres, *Hartland Quay*, pp. 9, 24-9.

[36] Mousehole was more of a fishing village than a port. Considerable fishing activity is recorded there in inquisitions (miscellaneous and *post mortem*) of 1322 and 1327 and many of the 40 recorded 'burgesses' were probably fishermen; the quay does not seem to have been built until 1392: PRO C145/87 and C135/3; *VCH Cornwall*, vol. 1, p. 483. For capitalistic organization of fishing at Mousehole in the fourteenth century, see *Register of Edward the Black Prince*, pt 2, pp. 93-4.

[37] C. A. R. Radford, 'The Roman site of Topsham', *PDAES* 3 (1937-47), pp. 6-17; Kowaleski, *LCAPE*, p. 1, citing the royal pipe roll of 1178-9; *ibid.*, pp. 2-3 and A. M. Jackson, 'Medieval Exeter, the Exe and the Earldom of Devon', *TDA* 104 (1972), pp. 57-79 for conflict between the earls of Devon and the city of Exeter.

[38] W. G. Hoskins, *Industry, Trade and People in Exeter 1688-1800* (1935), p. 154; E. A. G. Clark, *The Ports of the Exe Estuary, 1660-1860* (1960), *passim*; W. B. Stephens, *Seventeenth-Century Exeter* (1958), *passim*.

[39] Occupations (largely seventeenth and eighteenth centuries) taken from Clark, *Ports*, pp. 51-5 which also contains much else of interest on the town at this time.

[40] Gray, *E-SMS*, p. 46.

[41] R. Bearman, ed., *Charters of the Redvers Family and the Earldom of Devon, 1090-1217* (DCRS, new ser., 37, 1994), pp. 77-8; W. White, *History, Gazetteer and Directory of Devonshire* (1850), p. 210. Oddly, White does not mention the thriving salmon fishery. For details of the seigneurial fishery here in the thirteenth century, below Section 3.3.

[42] Clark, *Ports*, p. 51 and D. M. Bradbeer, *The Story of the Manor and Town of Topsham in Devon* (1968), p. 39 for references to the quay in 1316; Kowaleski, *LCAPE*, p. 3; DRO W1258M/G/6/50, account of 31-2 Hen. VI.

[43] Kowaleski, *LMRTE*, pp. 224-32, 239; eadem, *LCAPE*, pp. 24-6.

[44] Kowaleski, *LCAPE*, pp. 55, 58, 62, 65, 66. Ireland was said to be 'of Topsham' (p. 65).

[45] Kowaleski, *LCAPE*, pp. 24-6; Leland, *Itinerary*, vol. 1, p. 232.

[46] Kowaleski, *LCAPE*, pp. 1, 3; DRO, W1258M/G/6/50, account of 31-2 Hen. VI, for the substantial sum brought in by burgage rents.

[47] 'Little more than a village': Clark, *Ports*, p. 51. 'The size and importance of Exmouth in medieval times has been much exaggerated': R. Bush, *The Book of Exmouth* (1978), p. 23.

[48] Bush, *Exmouth*, p. 25; Gray, *E-SMS*, p. 45; Clark, *Ports*, p. 59; DRO, 96M/box 6/5b, a survey which lists at least 105 dwellings at Exmouth, giving a minimum population of about 400 if one takes the (very low) figure of 4 people per house.

[49] M. M. Oppenheim, *The Maritime History of Devon* (1968), p. 10; *Cal. Close Rolls, 1323-1327*, pp. 183-4 and 641-2. The corrupt spelling given there is *Lulham*: this can only be for Littleham. See also *LCAPE*, p. 47 for a ship of *Pratteshide*.

[50] A. H. Smith, *English Place-Name Elements* (2 vols, 1956), vol. 1, p. 278.

[51] Kowaleski, *LCAPE*, p. 8.

[52] Bush, *Exmouth*, p. 15 (ferry first mentioned in 1265-6 and mill around 1240). Compare the mill, a tide mill, on the shore at Dartmouth, which is very prominent in the early records of the port: Watkin, *Dartmouth*, pp. 9, 16, 19.

[53] See below, Section 3.1.

[54] P. Weddell, 'The excavation of medieval and later houses and St Margaret's chapel at Exmouth 1982-1984', *PDAS* 44 (1986), p. 128; BL, Cott. Faust. A II, f. 69-72; *Cal. Inq. Post Mortem Hen. VII*, vol. 2, p. 228.

[55] BL, Cott. Faust. A II, f. 69-72; PRO, E179/95/126; Weddell, 'The excavation', p. 138.

[56] Bush, *Exmouth*, p. 16 and Kowaleski, *LCAPE*, p. 5; Kowaleski, 'The expansion', p. 444.

[57] Kowaleski, 'Markets', p. 363; Kowaleski, *LCAPE*, p. 5; Jackson, 'Medieval Exeter', p. 64.

[58] Statement on the number of chapels based upon a conflation of opinions in Bush, *Exmouth*, pp. 95-6; Weddell, 'The excavation', pp. 115-16; N. Orme, *English Church Dedications with a Survey of Cornwall and Devon* (1996), p. 163; J. James, 'Medieval

chapels in Devon' (unpublished M.Phil. thesis, University of Exeter, 1977), gazetteer. There is not much agreement among these works about the number of chapels in medieval Exmouth. The statement that there may have been five (R. Bush, 'The origins of Exmouth', *TDA* 98 (1966), p. 73) is a result of confusion caused by changing dedications and by chapels projected but not built. Proliferation of chapels was partly a result of the fact that the maritime settlement straddled two parishes, Littleham and Withycombe Raleigh, the earliest reference (1329) being to a building in the latter parish (not in Widecombe in the Moor as surmised in the printed bishop's register: Weddell, 'The excavation', p. 115, citing the register). The petition is *Cal. Papal Letters*, vol. 6, pp. 487-8; see also p. 508.

[59] C. Dyer, 'The hidden trade of the Middle Ages: evidence from the West Midlands of England', *Jnl Historical Geography* 18 (1992), pp. 151-2.

[60] Leland, *Itinerary*, vol. 1, p. 232.

[61] ECA, DC 3684 and BL, Cott. Aug. I i for the Cockwoods; DRO, 1508M/Devon/surveys/Kenton/5 for Starcross; DRO, 96add.M/E/11 (map of 1743), W. L. D. Ravenhill, ed., *Benjamin Donn. A Map of the County of Devon 1765* (DCRS, new ser., 9, 1965) and DRO, 346M/M/264 for Lympstone. Another survey of Lympstone (Antony House MSS, PE/C4/1A) mentions cottages but is also unhelpful topographically. For more detail on the Cockwoods, below Section 6.1 and on Starcross, below Section 5.1.

[62] DRO, Z17/3/19, survey of Dinham lands; DRO, 1508M/Devon/surveys/vol. 3, Courtenay estate survey; ECA, VC 3370.

[63] Kowaleski, 'Port towns', p. 68; Gray, *E-SMS*, pp. 24-5, 38; Kowaleski, *LCAPE*, p. 17.

[64] E. M. Thompson, ed., *Adae Murimuth Continuatio Chronicarum* (Rolls Series, 1889), p. 109 n. 6 for the raid of 1340. H. J. Trump, *Westcountry Harbour: the Port of Teignmouth* (1976), pp. 28-30 for the raid of 1690. Some of the main sources for the silting of West-Country harbours, the result of tin-working on upper reaches of rivers, are H. P. R. Finberg, *Tavistock Abbey: a Study in the Social and Economic History of Devon* (1951), p. 186 (order in the Great Court of the Stannaries compelling tin workers to deposit detritus away from water courses); Leland, *Itinerary*, vol. 1, p. 215 (choking of a tributary of the Plym); *Statutes of the Realm*, vol. 3, pp. 375-6 (act of 23 Hen. VIII on the decay of south-coast ports); Trump, *Westcountry Harbour*, p. 25 (parliamentary debate on the same); PRO, E178 2880 (reference, in a survey of ports, to Teignmouth harbour's having been 'much decayed by tin-works').

[65] Gray, *E-SMS*, pp. 27-8; DRO, Exeter City Archives book 57.

[66] DRO, 1962B/W/M/3/2, Kingswear court of 20 Oct. 5 & 6 Phil. & Mary for warehouses called 'pallaces';*Cal. Close Rolls, 1364-1368*, p. 163 for the ferry; *Cal. Inq. Post Mortem Hen. VII*, vol. 1, p. 471 and G. Yorke and P. Russell, 'Kingswear and its neighbourhood', *TDA* 85 (1953), p. 65 for quays. This last paper provides much useful background.

[67] No ships 'of Kingswear' are recorded in the customs accounts of the late thirteenth century and the early fourteenth, although it is possible, indeed probable, that some ships 'of Dartmouth' belonged to the port of Kingswear: Kowaleski, *LCAPE*. By the

1460s, however, a few ships from this settlement appear in the customs accounts, bringing fish to the port of Exeter: information kindly supplied by Maryanne Kowaleski. For royal levies in 1325, 1398 and 1386 see Oppenheim, *Maritime History*, pp. 11, 16, 17.

[68] H. R. Watkin, *The History of Totnes Priory and Medieval Town* (3 vols, 1914-17), vol. 1, pp. 94-6; D. Seymour, *Torre Abbey* (1977), p. 214.

[69] Hoskins, *Devon*, p. 212 for the tithes (which, as Hoskins states, probably included Kingswear, a chapelry dependent on Brixham); BL, Cott. Aug. I i. For the poor showing of Brixham in early records see J. R. Pike, *Brixham* (1993), *passim,* and P. Russell, 'Some historical notes on the Brixham fisheries', *TDA* 83 (1951), pp. 278-97. For an early reference to the port of Brixham, see Watkin, *Totnes Priory*, pp. 256-7.

[70] Kowaleski, *LCAPE*, p. 51; Gardiner, ed., *Calendar*, pp. 7-8; *ibid.*, pp. 54-5; information from customs accounts of the 1460s supplied by Maryanne Kowaleski; I. Friel, 'Devon shipping from the Middle Ages to *c*.1600', *NMHD*, vol. 1, p. 75.

[71] PRO, C139/122. This is a survey of one-third part of the manor, with 30 cottages, so I have assumed 90 as a total; the total number of farm holdings was only 30, so it is not likely that the 90 cottagers were farm labourers.

[72] G. Oliver, *Monasticon Dioecesis Exoniensis* (1846), p. 183, charter granting Torre Abbey the right to draw nets into Livermead and to dry them there; DRO, 48/13/4/1/2, account of 16-17 Hen. VI, and subsequent accounts in this file, for various references to the fishery at Livermead. The account for 1439-40 has been printed: H. S. A. Fox, 'Fishing in Cockington documents', in T. Gray, ed., *Devon Documents in Honour of Mrs Margery Rowe* (1996), pp. 76-82.

[73] DRO, 48/13/4/2/4 (survey); 4/1/7-8 (accounts of 1528 and 1529); 2/3/2 (inventories); 3/1/16 and 3/1/78 (leases). Oddly, the surveyor was sometimes rather vague about whether a structure on the shore was a cellar or a cottage, perhaps because so much conversion was going on.

[74] Kowaleski, 'Port towns', p. 68; Gray, *E-SMS*, pp. 5-6, 24-5; C. Gill, *Plymouth: a New History, 1603 to the Present Day* (1979), pp. 49-61; J. Coad, 'The development and organisation of Plymouth dockyard, 1689-1915', *NMHD*, vol. 1, pp. 192-200.

[75] Oppenheim, *Maritime History*, p. 14, showing that 'Yealm' (= Newton Ferrers) contributed 2 ships in the Crécy campaign, compared to Plymouth's 26; DRO, 1392M/title deeds/Newton Ferrers.

[76] Oppenheim, *Maritime History*, p. 18 for the raid. The place was recognised by the Crown to some degree because some of the ships 'of Portlemouth' (*ibid.*, pp. 10-11, 13-14, 16) which were pressed into royal service almost certainly came from Salcombe: the town lay close to the manor of West Portlemouth. Part of the town came to be reckoned as a separate manor but, like Exmouth, it was very much of a boundary settlement, the built-up area spilling over into the territory of the Domesday manor of Batson. Ecclesiastically, Salcombe was a chapelry, license for a chapel having been granted in 1420: Dunstan, ed., *Register*, vol. 1, p. 6. Salcombe either escaped royal taxation or was subsumed within the combined payment for the vills of Batson and Bolberry: R. E. Glasscock, ed., *The Lay Subsidy of 1334* (British Academy Records of Social and Economic History, new ser., 2, 1975), p. 51 where the relatively high sum paid by those vills could

possibly indicate inclusion of some of the urban area of Salcombe. The place was not, therefore, taxed separately, despite having a market: T. Collings, 'Which Portlemouth?' *Devon Historian* 56 (1998), pp. 36-7.

[77] Stonehouse, very close to Plymouth, was probably another port of this kind, at least by the fifteenth century.

[78] Risdon, *Chorographical Description*, p. 177; DRO, 1508M/Devon/estate/surveys/vol. 3.

[79] A. Patrick, 'Tamar traffic in the nineteenth century', *NMHD*, vol. 2, p. 60; *eadem*, 'Tamar traffic, 1836-1900', in S. Fisher, ed., *Studies in British Privateering, Trading Enterprise and Seamen's Welfare* (1987), pp. 41-78.

[80] PRO, SC6 822/15, Halton account of 2-3 Hen. IV and subsequent accounts in this collection; Finberg, 'Morwell', especially pp. 158-61; F. Booker, *The Industrial Archaeology of the Tamar Valley* (1967), p. 35 (for Calstock); J. H. Adams, 'The port of Landhelp', *DCNQ* 32 (1973), pp. 210-15. Sand was brought to Maristow by barges in the fourteenth century and silver was shipped from there in the 1290s, both suggesting, but not proving, the existence of a quay: WDRO, 70/92, *Martinstow* (i.e. Maristow) account of 3-4 Ric. II and 70/93, account of 16-17 Ric. II, and later accounts in the same collection for the landing of sand there; L. F. Salzman, *English Industries of the Middle Ages* (1923 edn), p. 61 and Gill, *Plymouth*, p. 68. An interesting account for Morwell manor, with some details of traffic at the quay, is DRO, W1258M/D/52/2, for 12-13 Hen. VII.

[81] DRO, W1258M/D/39/5, charter; Finberg, 'Morwell'.

[82] 'Midnight of Friday 26th [January 1917] saw the abandonment of the village': R. H. Worth, 'Hallsands and Start Bay', *TDA* 55 (1924), p. 132. This paper (pp. 131-47) is the last of Worth's three remarkable (and illustrated) scientific accounts of coastal changes at Hallsands. The other two are in *TDA* 36 (1904), pp. 302-46 and 41 (1909), pp. 301-8.

[83] Collins, *Coasting Pilot*; map by Moll, reproduced in K. Batten and F. Bennett, *The Printed Maps of Devon* (1996), p. 53. Moll's coastal names owe much to Collins, e.g. Babbacombe is spelled *Barbican* on both maps.

[84] DRO, Blackawton parish register kindly inspected for me by Tony Collings. Some of the surnames of *Under Cliffe* people are to be found among the Blackawton men listed in the maritime survey of 1619: Gray, *E-SMS*, pp. 16-17.

[85] DRO, CR 20048. In this survey the name of the settlement is *Streate Sands*.

[86] M. F. Smithies, *Strete, Past and Present* (1933), p. 6; BL, Add. Ms. 9426, f. 49 (Lysons correspondence); T. Brice, *The History and Description, Ancient and Modern, of the City of Exeter* (1802), p. 132.

[87] *Kingsbridge and Salcombe, with the Immediate Estuary, Historically and Topographically Depicted* (1819), pp. 119-209; Bodleian Library, Top. Devon b. 2, Milles questionnaires; PRO, SC6 Hen.VIII/537, account of Malborough with Sewer, 26-7 Hen. VIII; R. Polwhele, *The History of Devonshire* (3 vols, 1793-1806), vol. 3, p. 475. There are no clues about the nature of the fishing station at Starehole on an eighteenth-century map: DRO, 1508M/Devon/estate/surveys/vol. 3.

[88] One may be the shoreline borough of Noss Mayo quite close to the mouth of the

Yealm. Although a coastal settlement and a borough, of thirteenth-century creation, it does not seem to have had any of the attributes of a port. Its inhabitants were described in a fifteenth-century petition as for the most part 'fishermen and labourers' (with no reference to farmers), having no spare time for long journeys to a mother church: Dunstan, *Register*, vol. 4, pp. 314-8 (note that this is a petition by the parish of Revelstoke, but the description of the inhabitants would mainly apply to Noss Mayo, which was by far the largest nucleation in that parish). In terms of its borough status and the occupations of its people, Noss was an unusual type of settlement along the South Devon coast, although a parallel may perhaps be found in Mousehole, Cornwall, for which see above, n. 36. A planted fishing village perhaps? Or a spontaneous growth whose people were given the status of burgesses in order to free their time for fishing?

[89] This is a summary of the relevant part of Section 5.1 below.

[90] Oppenheim, *Maritime History*, pp. 10-11 for royal orders; *ibid.*, p. 40 and Gray, *E-SMS*, p. 43 for listings of ships of Kenton, some of which were bound for foreign parts; J. Youings, 'Raleigh's country and the sea', *Procs British Academy* 75 (1989), pp. 288-9; Kowaleski, *LCAPE*, p. 166 for a Kenton mariner working on a wine ship in 1318 and claiming portage (the right to freight a small cargo free of charge in place of wages).

[91] Gray, *E-SM*, pp. xvii, xxvi.

[92] *Ibid.*, p. 25.

[93] W. White, *A Londoner's Walk to the Land's End* (1855), p. 137, another reference kindly supplied by Tony Collings.

Chapter Three

THE FISHERIES AND THE FORESHORE

3.1 Early evidence for fisheries

With one exception (see below), the earliest written references to Devon's fisheries come from Domesday Book. There was, for example, one on the Exe Estuary, at Exminster, and three on the Dart, at Dartington, Cornworthy and Ashprington. But, all in all, the Domesday references to fisheries in Devon are pretty meagre, as they are for some other coastal counties such as Dorset, and we can be fairly sure that this is because the record is incomplete.[1] Thus Richard de Redvers granted the fishery at Axmouth to Montebourg Abbey at some date probably in the late eleventh century (certainly before 1107, the date of his death); it is therefore likely that this fishery existed in 1086, yet it is not recorded in Domesday Book. Then again, we know of a fishery at Braunton, on the North Devon coast, as early as the mid-ninth century when King Ethelwulf granted the manor to Glastonbury specifically so that it could supply fish to the abbey, but no fishery is recorded there in Domesday Book.[2]

There are other suggestions of fisheries probably in existence in 1086 yet not recorded in Domesday Book. Exmouth people were much engaged in fishing, ferrying and other commercial activities according to documents from the thirteenth century onwards. This coastal place lies in the manor of Littleham whose manorial centre and church were situated inland about 1½ miles away. The manor was a small one, as its name implies, yet its Domesday record suggests considerable activity within it. It was valued at 40*s.*, a far higher figure than for many other small manors in the same hundred, as Table 3.1 shows. What activity lay behind this high valuation? A possible clue is provided by the

Table 3.1 Littleham and other small manors (E. Budleigh Hundred) in 1086

	Hides	Value	Slaves	Villeins	Bordars
Littleham	0.5	40*s.*	0	15	20
Brightston	1	20*s.*	0	3	6
Dotton	0.4	7*s.*	1	0	2
Nutwell	1.5	20*s.*	2	7	4

Source: C. and F. Thorn, eds, *Domesday Book, Devon* (2 vols, 1985), vol. 1, sections 7/1, 2/17, 16/135, 52/35.

information which Domesday Book gives about the population here: there were 20 *bordarii*, far more than on many other small manors (Table 3.1) and far more than on some huge inland manors east of the Exe, Colyton, for example, with ten, Sidbury with five.[3] Some historians have regarded *bordarii* as smallholders living literally 'at the edge'[4] – although this view is not universally accepted – and it is tempting to suggest that those on Littleham manor dwelt near the shore and were fishing farmers engaged partly in operating a fishery which existed in 1086, hidden as it were within the high Domesday valuation; and to suggest also that they were the ancestors of the abnormally large population of cottagers recorded in later rentals for the manor.[5]

Parishes with detached coastal portions are highly interesting and this evidence may also be hinting at pre-Conquest activity on the shoreline. The parish of Haccombe with Combe, with a good stretch of low estuarine shore along the River Teign, had a minute detached portion comprising a small cliff-girt cove looking out to the open sea of Babbacombe Bay; likewise, the parish of Kenton, with a largely estuarine shoreline, had a detached portion called Week which gave it access to the open sea (Fig. 3.1). With Stokenham parish the situation was reversed: most of its shoreline faced the sea in Start Bay but there was

Figure 3.1 Detached parts of the parishes of Haccombe with Combe and Kenton

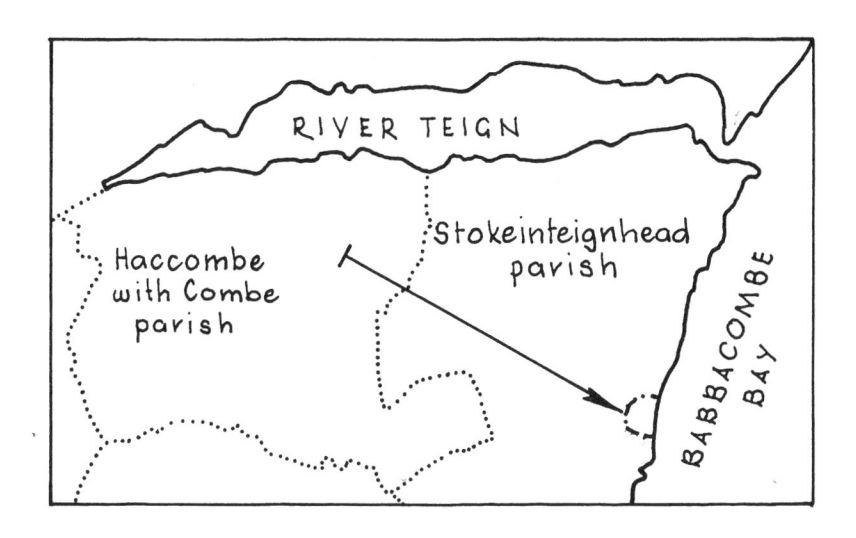

RIVER TEIGN

Haccombe with Combe parish

Stokeinteignhead parish

BABBACOMBE BAY

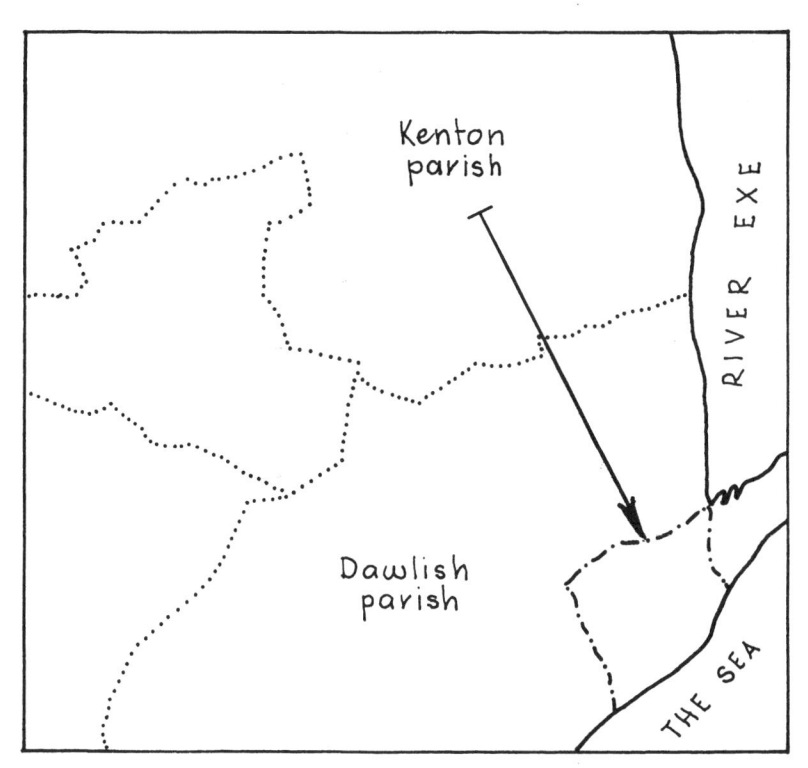

Kenton parish

RIVER EXE

Dawlish parish

THE SEA

also a small detached portion with a shore in the placid Kingsbridge Estuary (Fig. 3.2).[6] One may reasonably surmise that people desired access to shorelines of different kinds because each type was suitable for a different type of activity: cliff coastlines with beaches or small coves for sea fishing, estuarine shorelines for sand gathering, salt making and exploitation of oysters and salmon. The dating of the detached portions, and all that they may imply, is of course difficult because historians are understandably reluctant to commit themselves to a broad date band for the formation of parishes and parish boundaries. All we can say is that if parish development took place before the Norman Conquest (as many would regard to be highly likely) then the coastal activities, including fishing, which the boundary patterns suggest must be at least that old. It seems very unlikely that the communities, incumbents and patrons associated with churches would have submitted to the loss of a portion of land to neighbours *after* parishes and their boundaries had become established.

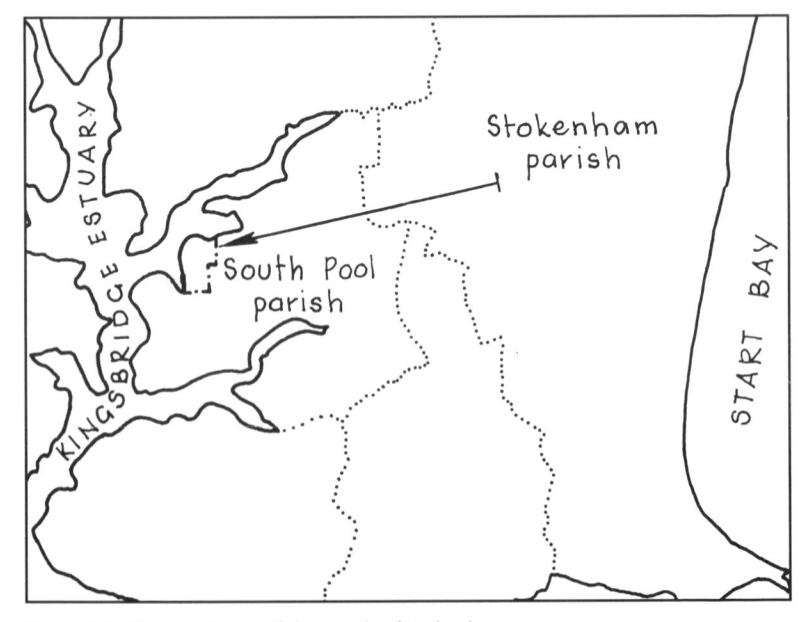

Figure 3.2 Detached part of the parish of Stokenham

How much further back this kind of evidence may take us is a matter for conjecture. For Kenton, certainly, there is very good evidence to show that the pattern of parochial boundaries mirrors the manorial pattern and we would expect this to have been the case for Haccombe with Combe and Stokenham also.[7] Indeed, Domesday Book for Devon has one explicit reference to a detached coastal manorial offshoot, Ottery St Mary (over 5 miles inland) owning a salt-pan on the coast near Otterton.[8] Manorial boundaries with intermingled and detached portions were often produced during the fragmentation of a larger unit into two or more smaller ones later to be called manors, but it would be a rash historian who would attempt to date that process in the three cases discussed here. All we can say is that it had certainly occurred by 1086 because Domesday Book names and records both the manors with detached portions and also the manors within which those portions lay. None of the three places discussed in this and the preceding paragraph is recorded in Domesday Book as having a fishery; if the evidence and reasoning put forward here is accepted, they further illustrate the deficiencies of that document in its recording of fishing.[9]

During the century or so after the Norman Conquest almost all references to fisheries in Devon come in grants to religious houses. For example, in 1088, as part of the foundation endowment of Totnes Priory, Juhel of Totnes gave the Saturday yield of his two fisheries of Ashprington and Cornworthy both, as we have seen, recorded in Domesday Book; no doubt he had in mind the monks' abstinence from meat on Sunday. At some time before 1107 Richard de Redvers granted the fishery of Axmouth to Montebourg Abbey. A few decades later his son Baldwin granted the tithe of a fishery at Topsham to the Priory of St James in Exeter. In 1196 the foundation charter of Torre Abbey gave the new monks there freedom 'to fish and to draw their nets in the sea of Torre' (Tor Bay).[10]

3.2 'Thirty shillings from the fishery this year'

From the thirteenth century onwards references to fisheries become more numerous, especially in manorial surveys and in the financial account rolls of manors. It is the historian's very good fortune that lords expropriated what they thought of as their share of their tenants' fisheries; because of this financial interest by lords, fisheries are mentioned in relatively common seigneurial documents. Some of the thirteenth-century and later references are rather laconic but others contain better detail from which a good picture of medieval fisheries may be reconstructed. 'Thirty shillings from the fishery this year' runs an entry in an account roll for Yealmpton, from 1395.[11] What lies behind that bald statement? In answer to this question we look first at the ways in which fisheries were managed and, more briefly, at the technology of fishing, leaving the people who fished, their settlements and the disposal of their catches to later chapters.

By the later fourteenth century the most common way in which lords with coastal manors took profits from fisheries was to impose a charge on the fishers, just as it was common seigneurial policy to impose small levies on men and women engaged in other non-agricultural activities, such as brewing, baking, digging fullers' earth, making pottery or burning turf into charcoal.[12] For example, at Ermington the Stonors drew 26s. 8d. from their tenants' two fisheries in 1384, the bailiff nostalgically recording that the sum should have been £3 which was probably its value before the Black Death. One may put these sums into context by adding that the mill of this largely arable manor was let at £4 in 1384 and had previously been let at £4 6s. 8d. At Plympton the fisheries brought in 15s. to the lord in 1422 (probably a low point) and 18s. 4d. yearly at the end of the century.[13] These references show that on some manors the profits which lords drew from fisheries were 'mobile' (to use the term employed in manorial accounts): they were adjusted upwards or downwards according to fluctuations in the fortunes of the craft. On other manors lords seem to have submitted to ancient custom, never claiming more from a fishery than a sum fixed at an earlier date. Such was the fixed 'farm' paid by the fishers of Kenton for fishing in the Exe and in the sea beyond the river mouth, which was set at 4s. at some date before 1296 and remained at 4s. in the reign of Henry VIII and indeed later.[14] By the sixteenth century this was therefore a modest sum for such a valuable fishery. The fact that it became frozen at an early date warns us that we cannot always take the stated value of a fishery at its face value, because it could be an anachronism, antique and out of date when first recorded.

The cash which lords took from the fisheries of their tenants may perhaps be seen as commutation of ancient payments in kind. It so happens that the earliest detailed reference to a fishery anywhere in England, from the Tidenham custumal (probably tenth century), refers to fish rents in kind. There, on the rivers Severn and Wye, 'at every weir . . . every alternate fish belongs to the lord of the estate and each rare fish'. In other words, the tenants of Tidenham were the fishers and paid the lord a share in kind in return for the privilege of fishing from his shores.[15] From the South Devon coast the best evidence for this system – which we can call the requisition system – comes from the manor of Stokenham. It is mentioned in a number of fourteenth-century documents, the most concise being a manorial survey of 1309: 'the lord has the option of taking one-third of the mullet which they [the bondmen] catch'.[16] Slightly different is what can be termed a purveyance system (purveyance in the sense of 'buying for a fixed price'): no fish may be sold on a manor without the lord having first choice as a buyer at an agreed price. This system operated on the Tidenham estate in the tenth century alongside the requisition system, for even after the tenants had had 'every alternate fish' taken away from them in dues, the other half could still be diverted to the lord's table: 'no one may sell fish for money when the lord is on the estate without informing him of it'.[17] The purveyance system is also in evidence in Devon. A thirteenth-century custumal of Otterton Priory states that the house 'should by right buy fish before all others and at the keenest price' at Sidmouth market; the lord of Stokenham, according to fourteenth-century extents and custumals, not only requisitioned one-third of the mullet but was also 'entitled to buy every porpoise his men take at 1s. apiece' while people selling fish (other than mullet) from their boats must first, if asked, 'provide for the lord at a fixed price'.[18] The terms 'keenest price' and 'fixed price' provide the key words here: in these cases seigneurial privilege was exercised not through expropriation of the product itself but through reduction of the cash profit which the tenants might expect to make through fishing.

The emphasis in the Tidenham custumal on payments in fish (whether requisitioned or paid for by cash) is entirely understandable, for they come from an age when, in the agricultural sphere, there was a greater emphasis on rents in kind than there was to be later. Domesday Book is full of references to fisheries which paid in kind to the lord of the manor: for example, the great herring renders of coastal places in East Anglia and the eel renders of places along the Thames, in the eastern Fens, along Yorkshire's rivers and in the Somerset Levels. In South Devon the Domesday fisheries of Dartington and Cornworthy, both on the Dart, paid renders to their lord in salmon, and we have a further reference to the latter two years later when the Saturday yield of the fishery (presumably still in kind) was granted to Totnes Priory.[19] Post-Domesday references to requisitions and purveyance may be found elsewhere in England. For example, in the early thirteenth century Tynemouth Priory allowed fishermen at North Shields to operate a fishery in return for part of the catch, which was to go to the larder of the monks. The charter for the borough of Dunster in Somerset, in the middle of the thirteenth century, stipulated that the lord should be able to buy at the port or in the borough market (in part a fish market, as the charter states) before all other competition.[20]

In the 1240s, the Bishop of Lincoln's 'Rules' for the better running of the life of the Countess of Lincoln instruct her to plan her travels at Michaelmas 'for the whole of the coming year and for how many weeks in each place according to the seasons of the year and the advantages of the land in flesh and fish'.[21] This reference hints at payments in kind still; later, especially in the fourteenth century, the requisition and purveyance systems tended to be replaced by payments in cash from those who operated the fisheries. A potent catalyst in this decline was the tendency for lords to reduce peripatetic living; according to Christopher Dyer this was 'the most radical change in aristocratic domestic life' to take place in the fourteenth century.[22] No lord wanted basket-loads of fish piling up outside the kitchen door of a coastal manor if there was no resident household to consume it and no resident kitchen staff to salt it away. As lords cut down on the number of manors which they visited (many never completely abolished visitations), they were likely to prefer cash rather than renders in kind from their tenants' fisheries, although there were always exceptions. The fishery at Stokenham, already mentioned in this chapter, provides an interesting example, for the lords of the manor there, by the early fourteenth century, gave themselves the option either of taking fish (by the requisition and purveyance systems) *or* of taking cash: this is probably a case of the transition from renders in kind to payment in cash. The transition may also be seen in an account for Yealmpton in 1395 which implies that previous accounts had included references for fish in kind, and states that the fishery was now 'let for cash' (without, unfortunately, giving the date of the transition).[23] To all of the generalizations given above, the exceptions are payments made by the fishers (many of them full-time) of port towns. The 'shares' or 'doles' in cash paid at Dunwich, Winchelsea and Rye, for example, seem to have replaced renders in kind at an early date, the earliest reference (for Rye) being from the twelfth century. These places had large fleets and large catches so that the sheer volume of the fish, if requisitioned, would have been inconvenient to manage; moreover, the recipients were usually the governing bodies of the towns, not individuals.[24]

Many of the documentary references to profits in cash which lords made from their tenants' fisheries provide no detail at all about how levies were made. A few, however, are more informative. Where tenants used boats in their fishing a levy on each boat was an easy and straightforward means of raising cash: boats were highly visible and could not be concealed, unlike the act of fishing which might be carried out surreptitiously when a lord's officers were not present to observe the catch. At Kenton in the fifteenth century lords took 6*d.* yearly from each of nine boats used for 'dragging and taking mussels and oysters' and they also levied separate payments on boats employed in the salmon fishery there. At Sutton an inquisition relating to the profits of the fishery, perhaps in the early thirteenth century, describes various levies, one being a tax on every fishing boat which came ashore. Fishermen at Penzance and Mousehole in Cornwall paid 'rent for [permission to own] boats'.[25] Almost as simple and effective as a levy on each boat was one on each net, where large nets were used. At Ringmore on the Teign estuary lords took profit from 'sayndrayth', a word which seems to be made up of seine (a large net) plus an archaic ending formed from 'drag'; the charge was on each net which might be dragged ashore with its catch. On the western bank of the Tamar at Saltash, just beyond the stretch of coast surveyed here, the great survey made in 1337 upon the foundation of the Duchy of Cornwall records that 12*d.* was levied yearly on each seine taken out to sea.[26]

To raise cash from each person who fished was another means employed in the seigneurial exploitation of fisheries. The method was certainly used by some tithe-owners who collected tithes in cash from those who fished, as will be shown later in this monograph.[27] Of all the medieval sources scoured for evidence of fishing, the court rolls of Newton Ferrers are the most informative about personal payments made by fishers to their lords for they list the people concerned and the sums which they paid 'for fish taken from the sea'.[28] The sums varied from person to person according to size of catch so that, for example, in October 1427 John Banning paid 10*d.* while John Cock paid 6*d.* Precisely how these sums were calculated is not stated in the sources. At other places where there is evidence of personal taxes on those who fished the levy was a proportion of the price of the fish when sold – one-third of the price of mullet sold on the manor of Stokenham around 1360, 1*d.* on each load of fish sold at Sutton in the early thirteenth century.[29] At Newton Ferrers the levies are invariably termed *nonnys* in the court rolls, a word not recorded in dictionaries but almost certainly related to the figure 9, so we can say that the rate there was one-ninth of the price of the catch. The levy must have been difficult to collect, because it was not a one-off yearly payment but was probably calculated for each of the weeks in which fishing was practised, while to escape payment must have been relatively easy, for people could fish or sell fish out of sight of the lord's officials: presentments before the manor court of Newton Ferrers show that some surreptitious fishers were apprehended but, by the nature of the record, we have no means of knowing how many people escaped notice. It was probably for all of these reasons that, in 1434, the 'fishers . . . within the lord's lordship made a fine with the bailiff', agreeing to pay between them a lump sum of 8*s.* 6*d.* For the bailiff the new single payment was an advantage in that he no longer had to police each catch; assuming that the collective fine remained fixed for several years, as was often the case with such payments, the fishers would have gained in years when the catch was especially good.

3.3 Seigneurial fisheries

Relatively few examples have come to light of lords who managed fisheries with their own boats and nets and labour force – what may be called 'direct management', borrowing the term which historians apply to cultivation of demesnes by their lords. This is not particularly surprising because early on they had access to plentiful supplies of fish through the requisition and purveyance systems described above, while, during the fourteenth and fifteenth centuries, they could obtain fish at relatively low prices on the market and did so, as their household accounts demonstrate. To this generalization a few exceptions have been discovered. First, religious houses were granted not only the profits from fisheries, or the tithe from fisheries, but also rights to fish: for example, in 1196 the foundation charter of Torre Abbey gave the new monks freedom 'to fish and to draw their nets in the sea of Torre' (Tor Bay) and the brethren there certainly made use of the rights granted to them, for in 1327-8 we find them dragging in their nets to the shore at Livermead Sands (part of Tor Bay) and drying them, for which they needed permission from a neighbouring lord; no mention is made of the involvement of tenants so presumably this was a fishery operated by the brethren themselves and their servants.[30] The enterprise takes its place alongside other examples of monastic management of fisheries elsewhere in England (for example, the management of inland fishponds).[31]

Another example of direct seigneurial management of a fishery is the earl of Devon's exploitation of the Exe at Topsham. Here the tidal waters of South Devon's second largest river narrow considerably, presenting opportunities for the partial blocking of the channel. Such an enterprise would be all the easier if approached from both banks and the earls, by lucky chance, held the manor of Exminster which faced

Topsham across the river. At Exminster there may already have been some kind of weir in 1086, for Domesday Book values the manor's fishery at 20*s.*, one of the most profitable recorded Devon fisheries of its time.[32] Baldwin de Redvers, sixth earl of Devon, constructed (or reconstructed) a weir at this point but it was torn down in 1263 by irate citizens of Exeter, anxious about access to the city by water. It was rebuilt of stone in 1284 by Countess Isabella de Fortibus, sister of the seventh earl (hence the place-name Countess Wear, which still survives), and thenceforth the value of the fishery was much increased 'because of a certain weir' as a document puts it.[33] An account for 1295-6, when the estate of the earldom was in Crown hands following Isabella's death, records that £8 3*s.* 4*d.* was received from the sale of salmon, trout and mullet; the reeve paid for the refitting of the fishing boat, for purchase of six nets with their ropes, and for repairs to the weir. This was clearly a seigneurial fishery, the lord or lady, through their reeve, providing the capital and taking profits through the sale of fish, perhaps at Topsham market.[34] As for the labour force, it seems that local people with expertise in fishing were paid for operating the boat and nets.

A final example of a seigneurial fishery comes from Livermead Sands (Tor Bay) in the fifteenth century. There the Cary family, lords of Cockington, kept a boat for which the oars cost 3*s.* according to a manorial account of 1439-40 and ropes, one for mooring and the other for the nets, cost 2*s.* The Carys owned at least two seine nets and, once the fish were caught, they were stored in barrels packed with salt bought at the port of Dartmouth, a little way westwards along the coast. A proportion of the fish was sold but the price received, and the month in which the sale took place, suggest that an equal or greater quantity was used by the family at Cockington and, perhaps, at its other residences inland. The labour force seems to have comprised local men who had shares in the nets (and perhaps the boat) and who presumably received shares of the catch.[35]

Direct management by the earls of Devon of their Topsham fishery at the end of the thirteenth century may be explained not so much as a malicious attempt to damage the city of Exeter by obstructing the river (a story current in the sixteenth century) but rather as a reaction to especial local circumstances. The family had the good fortune to own the manors on either side of the channel when, in the last half of the thirteenth century, direct management of lords' demesnes was at its most profitable and fashionable; so here, at this place and time, there was an opportunity to exploit one of the most fruitful of all the South Devon fisheries. The decision was a wise one, for the yield in 1295-6 – over £8 – would probably not have been matched if the family had simply exploited a tenants' fishery. Direct management of a fishery by the Carys near their residence of Cockington in the fifteenth century may be seen as a small landlord's endeavour to exploit an 'alternative' source of income (in both cash and kind) at a time when traditional incomes for the gentry – from rents, profits of courts and sale of agricultural produce – were typically at a low ebb.[36]

3.4 The technology of the fisheries

In 1309 a custumal for Stokenham listed the types of fish which the lord could buy from his tenants at a preferential price, while towards the end of the fourteenth century a dispute about rights on the tidal river Erme mentioned the species which were expected to be caught there; other lists come in those sections of household or manorial accounts which record purchases of fish for the kitchens of lords and consumption at their tables. From sources such as these it is possible to specify some of the types of fish (and shellfish and porpoise) which were taken off the South Devon coastline during the Middle Ages (Table 3.2). The table demonstrates the great range of fish to be found off south-western shores, a range which contrasts with the more restricted number of species found off the eastern coasts of England.[37] Because of this range, fishing could be carried out at many times of the year, weather permitting: for example, mullet visited the coast of South Devon in February while hake were commonest in late spring and summer. In addition, a variety of technologies would have been used to capture all the varieties listed, some being pelagic (swimming close to the surface), others being creatures of the sea bed, some being easier to take in the estuaries, others offshore.

Table 3.2 The species which were caught

	1	2	3	4	5	6	7	8
Bass				x				x
Cockles				x				
Cod								x
Conger		x	x			x	x	x
Hake	x		x		x	x	x	x
Herring	x		x		x		x	x
Ling			x		x	x	x	x
Mackerel	x							x
Mullett		x		x				
Mussels				x		x		
Oysters							x	
Pilchard	x							x
Plaice		x						
Porpoise	x	x						
Prawns	x							
Salmon		x	x	x	x	x	x	
Skate		x						
Whiting			x		x	x	x	

Sources and details of sources: 1. Longleat House MSS, 11251, 11271-2, purchases for Glastonbury Abbey at Lyme Regis, 1300-05. 2. PRO, C134/16/9, fish which the lord could purchase at a preferential price on Stokenham manor, 1309. 3. CRO, AR12/25, household consumption of Thomas Courtenay staying at South Pool, 1341-2. 4. M. Kowaleski, *Local Markets and Regional Trade in Medieval Exeter* (1995), p. 34, citing an enquiry into riverine rights on the Erme, 1389. 5. DRO, CR 535, purchases, at places not specified, for Edward Courtenay, residing at Tiverton, 1383. 6. PRO, SC6 830/29, household purchases at Yealmpton, 1395-6. 7. PRO E36/223, household consumption of the Countess of Devon at her East Devon residences, 1523-4, selected weeks only. 8. H. P. R. Finberg, 'A cellarer's account-book', in W. G. Hoskins and H. P. R. Finberg, *Devonshire Studies* (1952), p. 262, consumption at Tavistock Abbey, 1536-7. Note that it is not possible to prove that all of the fish consumed by a household was purchased locally. 'Prawns' is a guess for the Latin *scorpio*. The *Medieval Latin Word-List* has 'stickleback'. I first proposed 'lobster', but since 2000 were purchased on one occasion, I changed this to 'prawns'.

In his thesis on the Lincolnshire coast in the Middle Ages, Simon Pawley neatly divides fishermen into 'trappers' who set up snaring devices (fixed nets) on the shore and waited for the fish to swim into them and 'hunters' who set out with moveable nets in pursuit of a quarry. From the South-West there are many references to seine nets, for example from Tor Bay in which the Abbey of Torre was permitted to have a seine (*sagena*) in 1196, from the coastal parish of St Goran (Cornwall) where they are mentioned in an allocation of tithe in 1271, and from Plympton where the 'saynying' of the Cattewater is referred to in various financial accounts from the fifteenth and sixteenth centuries.[38] Seines might be taken to sea in boats – hence the 'sea seines' of Saltash, mentioned in a survey of 1337 – but they could also be operated from the shore, again with the help of boats: at Dawlish in 1566 the seines were described as 'on land or sea'.[39] There are no sources to tell us whether or not these medieval seines for encircling the shoals were around 150 fathoms (300 yards) in length and could drop to a depth of 13 fathoms (26 yards) – like those reported, at the traditional seine beach of Hallsands, to the Commission into the Sea Fisheries of the United Kingdom (1866) and which needed a good deal of teamwork for their operation.[40] By the sixteenth century we hear also of tuck nets which are listed alongside seines[41] and which were possibly drag nets to scour the sea bottom for species such as plaice or whiting, possibly subsidiary nets used for dredging fish from the seine.[42]

Snaring devices, that is fixed nets, are frequently referred to in the sources, an early reference, from 1296, being to a rent paid on Kenton manor for permission to 'fix up' nets on a mudbank in the Exe Estuary. Later references include mention of payments for 'stakes upon the lord's soil' at Newton Ferrers in 1427, to a 'haknett ... pitched upon stakes', again at Newton Ferrers (1566), and to the 'poles for fixing nets to take fish at high water' which the Reverend John Swete observed, and painted, at Sidmouth towards the end of the eighteenth century.[43] These devices were very simple ones, the stakes being arranged in the shape of a V and hung with nets to trap fish by stranding them as the tide ebbed and flowed. It may be that, in Devon, this technology was restricted to estuaries at the end of the eleventh century, because all of the fisheries recorded in Domesday Book are estuarine;[44] Reginald Lennard, always perceptive, considered that a 'fishery' in Domesday must mean 'a fixed contrivance of some kind', for there are references to 'new' and 'waste' fisheries and to the 'sites' of fisheries.[45] Later on, nets on stakes also came to be set up on coasts facing the open sea – where the shore did not shelve too steeply, as at Sidmouth referred to above, and on the northern coasts of Devon and Somerset where they were especially common. Later on, too, lords were drawing profits from fisheries of all kinds, not just from fixed traps – as we have seen in an earlier section of this chapter.

Fixed V-shaped traps have been discovered by archaeologists in the Severn, where the arms of the V were about 10 feet long, and also in the estuaries around Foulness Island, Essex.[46] In their excellent discussion of the Severn fishtraps, S. Godbold and R. C. Turner miss one very important reference to these structures, namely Carew's description written in the late sixteenth century and referring to Cornwall: 'certain stakes are pitched in the ooze [of an estuary] at low water, athwart from the creek … to whose feet they fasten a net, and at full sea draw the upper part thereof to their stops, that the fish may not retire with the ebb'.[47] Carew calls this contrivance a 'haking', which helps to explain several medieval references from Devon, almost all of them from manors with an estuary shore. Thus on the manor of North Pool, which bordered Frogmore Creek (Kingsbridge Estuary), 'the water called the hakying' brought in the large sum of 103s. 4d. in 1534. Similar terminology is used in financial accounts of Ermington and Yealmpton in the fifteenth century and we have already referred above to a 'haknett' at Newton Ferrers.[48] From Kingsteignton manor, at the top of the Teign Estuary, an inquisition *post mortem* of 1422 refers to 'a fishery in the water of the Teign called *Hakyng*' while another inquisition, of 1497, refers to a fishery called *le Hayken* on the Dart in Berry Pomeroy manor. At both places the name Hackney survives today although, as the editors of *The Place-names of Devon* confess, 'the derivation from haking is obscure'.[49] The word haking itself may derive from the hooks by which nets were attached to stakes, and probably has no direct connection with fish of the hake species.

As for boats, there are numerous medieval references to them in connection with fishing along the South Devon coast. For example, from the fifteenth and early sixteenth centuries there is mention of 'sandleave' on boats at North Pool, that is, a payment to drag craft up on to the sand when they were out of use; of the salmon and oyster boats at Kenton whose owners paid the lord a small sum for permission to fish; of the fishermen at Newton Ferrers 'who tie up their boats along the shore on the lord's land'.[50] That some fishing boats had sails is clear from a thirteenth-century reference to Plymouth fishermen who used the shore for the drying of nets and sails, while the fishing farmers of Stokenham manor were obliged to go to Totnes and Dartmouth to fetch their lord's wine, a highly arduous journey had not sails been available.[51] About the sizes of medieval fishing boats the sources remain forever silent. In the nineteenth century the traditional mackerel and pilchard fishery at Hallsands was worked by boats of about 20 feet long, while the fishery at Sidmouth, lovingly observed by Stephen Reynolds in the early years of the twentieth century, was worked by boats of a similar size. Reynolds frequently makes the point that, if they had been larger, the craft could not have been hauled on to the shingle, which was common practice at Sidmouth where there was no quay and, apparently, capstans were not in use.[52] Under the system of official registration in the nineteenth century, these would have been classified as 'third-class' boats, of 1 or 2 tons only.[53] Craft of similar size were used in traditional inshore fisheries along all the coasts of Britain, for example, the double-ended 'lerrets' (around 20 feet) of Chesil Beach, Dorest, built thus so that they could be rapidly launched from the pebbles when a shoal was spotted, or the Hastings 'punts' (around 15 feet).[54]

There is every reason to suppose that the people of the inshore fisheries of medieval Devon used boats of a size similar to those mentioned in the previous paragraphs, for, after all, their cellars were of a length which could easily accommodate them (Chapter 5). Management of such a boat and its seine net might easily (from nineteenth-century evidence) occupy the hands of a team of five males (men and boys) and, sure enough, a unique fifteenth-century tithe documents from Dawlish parish mentions six fishing boats each with a crew of four or five.[55]

3.5 The foreshore; hunting and gathering

Important though fishing in distant seas was to become for Devon people, this monograph concentrates on coastal waters and estuaries, and on local, inshore, fisheries which probably yielded far more, in terms of the value of the catches, than did the distant ones, at least until the sixteenth century. Coastal and estuarine fishing involved a good deal of activity on the foreshore, as when stakes for nets were driven into the mud of estuaries, when boats were moored close to the high tide mark, and when seines were drawn on to beaches, then dried. The foreshore – the area between high and low water marks – is of variable width, depending largely on how steeply the land shelves towards sea or estuary channel. Wide expanses of foreshore, of mud ('ooze' on the coastal maps of Greenvile Collins and on an eighteenth-century map of the Exe Estuary)[56] and, more occasionally, salt-marsh nearer dry land, are to be found in many of the estuaries. Where the shore shelves very steeply, as in Start Bay, the foreshore is of far more limited extent. From the late sixteenth century onwards, cases were made for the Crown's ownership of the foreshores of all England and this view still slightly colours the legal position today,[57] but in the Middle Ages it is clear that a particular foreshore was regarded as the property of the lord of the manor which it bordered; it was not the Crown's unless the manor happened to be in royal hands.

Landwards of the foreshore there might be a beach, raised up in past time or, in some cases, more recently by an exceptional storm. In some cliff coastlines a few yards of fallen rock and rubble lie beyond the high water mark, before the cliffs begin to rise; in others the sea laps and sucks at the cliff foot and the only space, measured horizontally, between the water line and the cultivated fields above is a bevelled cliff-top edge, characteristic of many south-western coasts, too steep for cultivation but supporting rough pasture, bracken and gorse; rights 'on the . . . cliff for pasture and fuel' are mentioned in one eighteenth-century document.[58] The foreshore – sand, shingle, mud, marsh – and the usually narrow band between the high-tide mark and the beginnings of improved land were all described as 'the waste soil of the manor'. The word 'waste'

The Fisheries and the Foreshore 65

here does not mean 'useless' or 'unwanted' but was applied in the Middle Ages to land not in use as arable, meadow or good pasture; thus rough pasture, moorland and heath were so described in medieval sources. Rough pastures and most of the plants growing upon them had very productive uses, and so too did the overflown mudbanks of estuary foreshores, the sand of beaches, the salt marshes, the steeply-sloping bevelled edges of cliff-tops, haunt of seagull and cormorant, as I well know from dangerous expeditions made alone many years ago.

The foreshore, the cliffs, the cliff-top: all were 'waste soil of the manor' and all, therefore, were the property of the lord. Thus those who drove stakes (to support nets) into the mud at Newton Ferrers in 1425 were said to have done so 'upon the lord's soil' while those who moved sand at Yealmpton in 1506 were removing what was described as 'the lord's soil'; at Newton Ferrers, again, fishermen who moored boats did so 'to the land of the lords of the manor' while a survey of Nutwell explicitly states that some of the cottages were 'next the sea shore and therefore on the lord's land'.[59] Tenants might have customary rights on wastes, but, increasingly one suspects in the twelfth and thirteenth centuries, lords made charges for their use. For example, most of those people with customary rights of grazing on Dartmoor in the Middle Ages were charged a head-tax on cattle put out to graze there; the same practice existed in the great inter-commonable wastes of East Fen and West Fen in Lincolnshire.[60] Other uses of 'the lord's soil' came to be sources of income for lords: throughout England local potters were charged for extracting clay; those who dug for fuller's earth on the manor of Minchinhampton were charged for their digging; most people who took turves to make peat-charcoal on Dartmoor (beyond a few moorside tenants with ancient, perhaps untouchable, customary rights) were charged likewise.[61] All of this helps explain the charges which lords imposed on people who made use of fisheries, discussed in an earlier section of this chapter. They were constantly 'interfering' with the lord's soil. They drove stakes into it, they drew boats and nets on to it, they hung their nets out to dry above it. Therefore they must pay. Today the law still argues that 'fisheries are in their nature mere profits of the soil over which the water flows and . . . the title to the fishery arises from the right to the soil'.[62] Boats which had fished at sea beyond the limits of the foreshore still had to cross the lord's soil in order to reach land, so there was no escape.

The soils and ecology of the foreshore varied between estuary and sea-coast and between one type of coast and another. There were many species and commodities to be hunted and gathered and these enriched the lives of men and women who had access to them. The terms fishing farmer, fisher, fisherman and fishing village are used as convenient shorthand terms throughout this monograph but we must always remember that those who caught fish and shellfish were lucky in the diversity of other things which the shore had to offer and were highly inventive and skilful in their uses.

Among the commodities which were gathered on the shore, sand itself probably gave more employment than any other. Sand lightened soils and, containing pulverized shells, it helped to counter acidity. When Richard, earl of Cornwall, around the middle of the thirteenth century, granted that sea-sand could be taken freely from the coasts of the county, he not only provided what is probably the earliest written reference to the practice in the South-West, but also testified to a contemporary perception among farmers of the utility of sanding, because presumably he was reacting to a petition from the people. When a steward of one of the Tamar-side manors attempted to interfere with the traffic of sand in barges, all the people of the hundreds of Tavistock and Plympton complained bitterly before the great royal inquiry of 1275 which has given us the hundred rolls. We hear, in a court roll, of Devon tenants who obtained a reduction in rent because of the expenses of sanding, and, in a petition of 1357, of the farmers of Helston in western Cornwall who complained to the Black Prince that their lands laid untilled because of interference with the carriage of sand. These documents testify to the belief among medieval farmers that sanding was beneficial to cultivation, while from a later age we have comments such as that from a surveyor at Churchstow, who wrote that the tenants there 'do bestow the sand upon their several grounds which increases the goodness . . . very much'.[63]

All of these references – and others in pleas of debt relating to sanding – indicate that it was regular practice on tenants' holdings.[64]

For more detail we have to turn to the demesnes of lords because only for these lands are there financial accounts relating to expenditure on sanding. Thus from the end of the thirteenth century a demesne account for Plympton shows that two specialist sanders were employed on the demesne, which comprised about 300 acres of arable, and from the end of the fourteenth century an account of the manor of Maristow shows that one-third as much money was spent on sand and sanding as on wage labour for reaping the whole demesne. Because the account rolls of Tavistock Abbey's demesne of Hurdwick are so reasonably continuous, Finberg was able to chart fluctuations in the rate of sanding there and found one increase in the 1490s and another early in the sixteenth century.[65]

Sand was carried to inland farms by two means, packhorse and barge. It is rather surprising that lords did not charge for the actual removal of sand from sea beach or estuary, because this was, after all, removal of the most fundamental aspect of a manor – its 'soil' and therefore its land. Instead, and perhaps because the method was easier to supervise, they took a toll from each packhorse which left a beach to begin its laborious inland journey along tracks known as a sandways. The best documented sandway along the coast of South Devon is that belonging to the Stonors, lords of Ermington, on which the toll paid by each packhorse was 2*d*. In the early fifteenth century, the owners of the manor seemed disturbed about loss of jurisdiction over this lucrative sandway and, sending an official to investigate, found that around 300 pack-horses were expected to use it each year.[66] These details are exceptional. More usually we simply read, in a manorial survey or account, that 'the sandway is worth 2*s*. yearly' (Yealmpton, 1309), or that a certain sum of money had been paid by one lord to another for right of passage with sand, like the 16*d*. paid by the lord of North Huish to the lord of coastal Kingston in 1365.[67]

Over many centuries, movement of sand from the shore to farms inland was bound to leave its mark in the landscape in the form of tracks, some of them deeply incised and determined in their direction, leading down to the beaches. In Ireland a small amount of research has been carried out on these land-sea links, known there as 'wrack roads' after the seaweed which was the main commodity carried on them;[68] for the South-West the discovery and documentation of similar tracks is a research topic crying to be taken up. Preliminary inspection of maps reveals that there are many hundreds of tracks linking small coastal coves and estuarine beaches and mudflats to settlements inland, like those of the coast between Brixham and Kingswear and those leading inland from Gerrans Bay, Cornwall; along them would have travelled fishing farmers and fish carriers, but sand was probably the heaviest commodity, leading to the deep incision of some of these tracks into the landscape. Just south of Brixham is a cove called Man Sands, the first element in the name being Old English *(ge)maene*, 'common'; two tracks lead down to it, suggesting that the name means that the beach was shared by two manors, in all probability Woodhuish and Upton. Many of the smaller coves and sandways served single farms and hamlets, like the 'necessary sandway' which went with properties in the parish of Newton Ferrers, or the little sunken track which still leads from the mudbanks of the Avon Estuary to the farm of Aunemouth.[69] At larger coves and stretches of sand there began more widely used sandways resorted to by farmers from further afield, like that at Ermington, mentioned above. There are occasional references to sandways in inland manors without a coastline, such as one in Broadhembury, but these may have been so named because packhorses laden with sand were frequently to be seen upon them (compare the naming of the 'saltways' found in many English inland counties) and were not devices for levying toll as the coastal ones were.[70]

Traffic in sand by barge is best known from the River Tamar.[71] By the end of the thirteenth century both the water of the Tamar and jurisdiction over the water of Sutton (that is the mouth of the Tamar and Plym combined) were in the hands of the earls of Cornwall whose officials were therefore in a good position to impose a toll on sand barges as they passed in sight of their forbidding castle keep at Trematon. The 'custom from every barge carrying sand' brought in 11*s.* 4*d.* in 1296 and about 8*s.* (1*s.* for each barge) in 1337.[72] We can trace these barges further upstream through documents from manors on either side of the river. At Maristow barges were unladen for Plympton Priory's demesne, conveniently situated close to the water's edge. At Halton on the Cornish side the enterprising Hylle family built a quay and levied tolls on, among other things, sand brought by barges; they also made profits from sale of pasture for packhorses waiting near the quay before carrying the sand inland.[73] Further up-river on the Devon side was the Abbot of Tavistock's quay at Morwellham which was in existence as early as the 1230s. An entry in an account roll, relating to the Abbey's demesne of Leigh in Milton Abbot in 1496, records the expenses of 'one barge-load of sand' which would have arrived at this quay, and the more continuous accounts for the manor of Hurdwick near Tavistock, analyzed by Finberg, show that between one and four barge-loads yearly were being used on the demesne there in the early fifteenth century.[74] Having begun this paragraph near the mouth of the Tamar, we are now deep inland: Morwellham is about 11 miles from the mouth as the crow flies, but the barge journeys would have been much longer than that because of the lovely curving course of the river. Leigh and Hurdwick lie 6 miles and 4 miles respectively from Morwellham over hilly ground, the last stretch of the journey being by packhorse.

The typically south-western practice of spreading sand on the soil gave livelihoods, in whole or in part, to people dwelling near coast or river shore. Men with barges plied their trade up-river from the coastal beaches and dank mudflats which provided their sources of income. Generally they are nameless individuals, for the manorial officials who charged them tolls for passage, or who paid them for their services, recorded sums, not names, in their account rolls. One bargeman, however, comes to life, because he found his way before a manorial court whose records name him and give good detail about his activities. John Scott worked a North Devon river, the Torridge, and in 1452 was distrained by the bailiff of the manor of Monkleigh. His offence was that his rent was in arrears for a plot on the riverside where, for 16 years, he had been boat-building as well as making piles of sand which he had dug downstream. Scott had been before the manor court of Monkleigh 4 years earlier when he failed to honour a contract for carrying sand on behalf of another tenant – an interesting case because it tells us that some farmers employed specialists to bring in their sand.[75] The court rolls unfortunately do not ascribe an occupation to John Scott, but local farmers would probably have called him a sander, whence, possibly, the surname Sander, Saunder or the like, which is common in Devon (the name could also become attached to the specialist spreader of sand employed on large demesnes, the *zabulaterius* of manorial accounts).[76]

Carrying and spreading sand were summer occupations: John Scott should have carried for his farmer-employer 'through the whole summer' and demesne accounts also show that sanders were employed at that season.[77] The reason is that sanding was part of the complicated Devonshire method of preparing the soil for a spell of cultivation after it had lain for several years under grass ley: the grass sod was pared, piled and then burnt, an operation which required dry summer weather, the ashes were then scattered on the soil and at this point the sand was also applied.[78] The summer sands of coast and estuary would have seen bargemen and the leaders of packhorses at work, and probably ancillary workers to speed up the processes of piling and loading the sand. Who these last people were, we do not know: youths, women and others needing casual work perhaps, as on the northern coast of Cornwall in the nineteenth century, but the medieval documents do not descend that far.[79]

Devon's two coastlines, and her many estuaries stretching deep inland, bring a good deal of the land area of the county close to the coast or to a navigable river. Sand was carried some distance inland from the shores where it was gathered or from quays where it arrived by the barge-load, John Norden, always interested in local custom, noting in the early seventeenth century that it was fetched 'on horseback above 12 miles in many places'.[80] If, for the sake of argument, we use a figure of 10 miles, then simple inspection of a map shows that only about one-third of the county of Devon was beyond that distance from seashore or navigable river and this means that demand for sand must have been considerable. There would have been fluctuations in demand over time. We hear in 1405 of a beach to which 'no sanders' came, presumably because of a local decline in sanding at a time of low population and high labour costs.[81] However, the sources do not suggest a complete cessation of the practice during the later fourteenth century and the fifteenth: sanding continued, although its intensity slackened and, almost certainly, the number of acres treated declined as the acreage under cultivation contracted. One would expect an increase in sanding activity, and therefore more activity on the foreshore, when cultivation picked up again towards the end of the Middle Ages and, sure enough, statistics for the number of barge-loads used on Tavistock Abbey's demesne at Hurdwick show an increase in the 1490s and another one in the first two decades of the sixteenth century.[82]

Of all the things gathered along coast and estuary the evidence is best about sand and, after sand, about wreck. Wreck – that is, ships or boats on which no live bodies remained and parts of their structures, their equipment and cargoes – belonged to the Crown and was therefore likely to be the subject of royal enquiries. Details of wreck are also found in private documents because some lords owned hundreds (which were originally royal jurisdictions) or owned manors to which hundredal rights had become attached. A good chance to survey wreck in a single year is provided by the presentments made to the royal eyre (high court) held in Devon in 1238, 'Of wrecks at sea' being one of the articles to be enquired about by this type of court. It so happens that no major wrecks occurred off the South Devon coast in 1238. The eyre was told, for example, of a tun of wine washed up at Sidmouth and of part of a ship's bow which had been found on the shore of Littleham and had been concealed by the people there; at Wembury a tunic and a net had come ashore and at Paignton two casks of wine, spoiled because salted.[83] Other cases were brought before the court, but all were of minor items, like those cited above. It was the same when a survey of the coast was made in 1566 on behalf of the Vice-Admiral when it was claimed that a few anchors had been discovered on the shore but nothing of much more consequence, though how much was concealed we shall never know.[84] On occasion, more valuable items might be cast ashore. Thus the lord of the manor and hundred of Hartland, on the North Devon coast, sent an official to value a wreck stranded at the foot of a cliff in 1386. He found that the cargo was largely of wax, worth over £23 but some value was also put on ropes, sails and various items in the mens' quarters; the coffers, if they had ever contained coin, had already been rifled, broken and left without locks. Along the same dangerous coast, in 1418, a carrack of Genoa, laden with a cargo of some value, apparently became wrecked on Lundy Island and was abandoned by her crew. That at least was one version of the story, perhaps invented by the people of the locality in order to try and cover up the truth, because other versions claimed that the ship was set upon at sea or was ransacked when she put into the wild North Devon port of Ilfracombe. Another example of a valuable wreck was that brought ashore somewhere on the long sands of Stokenham manor in the late sixteenth century. Here the lord was not so lucky for he claimed in 1588 that, although he had indisputable right of wreck, canvas bags 'being of the bigness of a hundred pounds' and containing 'money or bullion of gold or silver or both' had been taken away before his officials were able to reach the wreck. Given the date, this ship could well have been part of the scattered Spanish Armada.[85]

Items from wrecks were so commonly noticed and gathered up because people living near the coast made frequent visits to the water's edge. They sought fish and shellfish and they helped in the gathering of sand. In addition there were many other minor products to be had near the waters, each one of small value in itself but, taken together, enriching the lives of those people with access to them. The collection of these minor products, like much hunting and gathering, is virtually invisible as far as the record of the landscape goes, but just an occasional documentary reference to them hints at activities which were almost certainly widespread, as is shown by the example of the trapping of seagulls. A household account of the countess of Devon, for 1523-4, from time to time mentions 'golles' served at table at her East Devon houses, yet from only one Devon manor has record been found of the trapping of gulls: when Richard Beauchamp died in 1439 his manor of Langdon contained 'a certain place called *Meweston* where there are . . . birds called gulles', from which he made a small profit, presumably through a levy on tenants who trapped them.[86] Great Mew Stone (the name being from 'mew', vernacular for seagull) is still shown on the Ordnance Survey 1-inch map, near the mouth of the Yealm. Other birds are sometimes mentioned. A firkin of puffins (possibly shearwaters) was part of a cargo imported at Topsham in 1492,[87] two cormorants were received as a special gift by the countess of Devon in 1523-4 and in 1272-3 Sir John Dinham at Hartland purchased 27 gannets from Lundy Island, six being sent as gifts to a member of the Pomeroy family.[88] Both these last species may have been rather unusual catches for they were being used in the gift-giving of rare items by which landed families bound themselves together. At a more humble level, Hooker, writing in the sixteenth century, had seen farmers 'near the seasides . . . [gathering] a weed called oar and this . . . they do carry into their grounds and it does much good for the time'. No documentary record has been found of the gathering of seaweed from the coast of South Devon in the Middle Ages but there are later references and also many records relating to it in North Devon and North Somerset.[89] The 'sea coal' (*carbo maris*) gathered in the fifteenth century from the shores near Budleigh Salterton is something of a mystery still. It was almost certainly what we call coal today but how it arrived at that spot is not clear.[90]

In this discussion of the products of the shore, salt has been left until last, because salt-making was of minimal importance along the South Devon coast between the thirteenth century and the sixteenth, despite the large demand for this commodity in the processing of fish. This state of affairs had not always been so, for Domesday Book records 58 salt-pans in Devon, most of them along the stretch of coast surveyed in this monograph, and salt-workers were also recorded.[91] The figures no doubt omit some pans[92] but even so, when compared with those from other counties, indicate a salt-making industry of only moderate proportions: Sussex had about 309 salt-pans according to Domesday and Norfolk had about 290.[93] Salt-making in Devon was largely an estuarine occupation at this time, for manors with only a sea coast tended not to have pans, while most of those which did were on estuaries or had small creeks.

There are no descriptions of saltworks from the eleventh century, but the account of Celia Fiennes, who acutely observed the industry at Lymington in the seventeenth century, is perhaps relevant with small changes in detail. Sea water, she writes, 'they draw into trenches and so into several ponds . . . and it stands for the sun to exhale the watery fresh part of it . . .; they draw off the water from the ponds by pipes which convey it into a house full of large square iron and copper pans . . . under which is a furnace that burns fiercely to keep these pans boiling apace'. She adds that the evaporation and boiling were carried out only in four or five months during the summer.[94] Construction of the 'ponds' used for the initial evaporation with heat from the sun would be feasible in shallow estuaries but not where sands shelved steeply away into the open sea: hence the estuarine distribution of the Devon industry at the time of Domesday Book.

From the end of the eleventh century onwards there was a sharp decline in salt-making. Because it took place on the waste soil of the manor, it yielded profits to lords, as the valuations in Domesday Book indicate, so that salt-works, had they still existed, should have been recorded in thirteenth-century charters and fines and in later manorial accounts, yet no references have been found to them in such sources. Local studies make the same point. For example, salt-workers at Kenton were recorded in Domesday Book but by the late thirteenth century and the fourteenth the manor's relatively good documentation contains no references at all to the industry, although it gives good details about many other shore-line activities.[95] On the great manor of Otterton, which stretched in 1086 between the Rivers Otter and Sid, and included what is now Sidmouth, 33 salt-workers toiled in 1086, yet by the thirteenth century the industry there was dead according to detailed surveys (a rental and a custumal) made by the priors of Otterton, who did not let much escape them.[96] The collapse of the Devon industry contrasts sharply with the survival of salt-making on the east coast of England, in Norfolk and in Lincolnshire for example.[97]

One reason for the demise of the South Devon salt industry may have been a collapse in supplies of the fuel which it consumed in such quantity. This is a conjecture but some support for it comes from an examination of manors having a shoreline north of the River Teign and west of the River Exe. Eight manors recorded in Domesday Book had a stretch of this shoreline but only four of these contained salt-works: Kenton, Holcombe in Dawlish parish (where salt-working is also recorded in a charter of 1044), Bishopsteignton and Whiteway in Kingsteignton parish.[98] Most of these four probably had land or rights extending up into the hills of Haldon whereas coastal manors with no hill-land had no salt-works either. The explanation of the correlation between hill-land and salt-works probably lies in the presence, in the late Saxon period, of woods on the slopes of the Haldon Hills, these providing fuel for the boiling process. Domesday Book itself and the evidence of place-names give ominous hints on the fate of much of this woodland. The former records many pig-men in the hills – and pigs can damage wood if they are not controlled – while the area has many place-names of the type Woodhouse, Charlwood, Newhouse, Kenwood and Southwood which are typical of new farms established in woodland clearings during the two centuries following the Norman Conquest.[99] By the late thirteenth century, it may be suggested, woodland had become much diminished. The shores of the Exe and Teign did not have large supplies of peat such as those which sustained the salt-making industry in Norfolk, where many of the salt pans were in the Broads, and in Lincolnshire.[100]

A second reason for the demise of the South Devon salt industry has to do with the relative location of the English salt-producing coastlines on the one hand and those of southern Europe on the other. In his definitive monograph, *England and the Salt Trade*, Bridbury repeatedly makes the point that salt may be produced more easily, and therefore more cheaply, the further south one goes in Europe, simply because southern suns work more quickly in evaporating the brine and less fuel needs to be used – or none at all.[101] The southern coasts of Devon and Cornwall are relatively close to the famous salines of the northern parts of the Bay of Biscay, so much so that cheap and superior salt from the Bay could flood the markets of south-west England; the salt-making industries of the coasts of Lincolnshire and Norfolk, being more distant, were safer from this competition.

The salt trade from the Bay of Biscay to the ports of south-west England was probably associated with the wine trade, as Bridbury surmised.[102] Both were certainly flourishing in the late thirteenth and early fourteenth centuries. Occasional general references to both trades (though south-western ports are not specified) may be pushed back to the early decades of the thirteenth century when English merchants and ships were given licences of safe passage to Gascony, to Poitou and to Oléron in order to buy salt. Similar licences were granted to wine merchants, and Gascon wine and purchases from Bordeaux merchants are frequently mentioned in the pipe rolls of King John, from around 1214 onwards.[103] Moving backwards, the earliest reference to import of wine to the port of Exeter is from 1178, though the origin of the cargoes is not known. The earliest reference to import of salt to south-western England is from 1202 when several merchants of Bayonne paid the Crown for the privilege of having first option on the purchase of congers and mullet off the Cornish coast and for drying and salting these fish.[104] Other Gascon merchants had probably plied the same trade earlier on because the licence stipulates that no other Gascony men, except those named, were henceforth to be involved. Most historians have assumed that the trades in salt and wine commenced soon after Henry II, in 1152, married the unhappy Eleanor of Aquitaine who brought with her some of the salines of the Bay of Biscay and the incipient Gascon vineyards whose produce was eventually to displace that of Anjou in English taverns and on English tables. At some time in the twelfth century or early thirteenth the fate of the South Devon salt-works was thereby sealed. Occasional references to salt-working are to be found later on, but they are sporadic and widely scattered.[105]

---

[1] Domesday, 1/4, 20/15, 17/48, 1/71; H. C. Darby and R. Welldon Finn, eds, *The Domesday Geography of South-West England* (1967), pp. 269-71 (Devon) and pp. 110-111 (Dorset).
[2] R. Bearman, ed., *Charters of the Redvers Family and the Earldom of Devon, 1090-1217* (DCRS, new ser., 37, 1994), pp. 73-4; P. H. Sawyer, *Anglo-Saxon Charters: an Annotated List and Bibliography* (1968), no. 1695.
[3] Domesday, 7/1, 1/13, 2/15. The Domesday entry for Beer (7/4) is also very instructive. This was another half-hide manor but was valued at the large sum of 60s. Here there were 20 bordars, far outnumbering the villeins of whom there were 6; the bordars, it may be suggested, could have been smallholders working partly on the land and partly at a fishery (not recorded in Domesday) and its associated salt-works, which are recorded.
[4] S. P. J. Harvey, 'Evidence for settlement study: Domesday Book', in P. H. Sawyer, ed., *Medieval Settlement: Continuity and Change* (1976), pp. 197-9. See also S. P. J. Harvey, 'Domesday England', in H. E. Hallam, ed., *The Agrarian History of England and Wales*,

vol. 2, *1042-1350*, pp. 59-60 where there is also a mention of bordars with specialist non-agrarian occupations, e.g. cobblers and market gardeners. S. H. Rigby, *Medieval Grimsby: Growth and Decline* (1993), p. 7 suggests that the Grimsby bordars of Domesday Book had non-agrarian occupations.

[5] For the large cottage population of Exmouth in the fourteenth century, above Section 2.2.

[6] Evidence for Combeinteignhead and Kenton from the Ordnance Survey 1-inch edition called 'Index to the tithe survey'; for Stokenham from the tithe map at DRO.

[7] DRO, 1508M/Devon/maps/Powderham/2, a map which shows the detached part of Kenton manor.

[8] Domesday, 10/1 where Ottery St Mary's salt-pan is said to be at Sidmouth. For similar patterns in Lincolnshire and Norfolk, H. C. Darby, *The Domesday Geography of Eastern England* (1952), pp. 69, 71 and T. Williamson, *The Norfolk Broads: a Landscape History* (1997), p. 45.

[9] The narrow tongue of Stoke Fleming parish, thrown out to the shore of the Dart (as recorded on the tithe map), and the narrow tongue of Towednack parish (western Cornwall) probably also represent coastal toe-holds for fishing or salt-making, or for both.

[10] H. R. Watkin, *The History of Totnes Priory and Medieval Town* (3 vols, 1914-17), vol. 1, p. 3; Bearman, ed., *Charters*, pp. 73-4; *ibid.*, pp. 77-8; G. Oliver, *Monasticon Dioecesis Exoniensis* (1846), p. 172.

[11] PRO, SC6 830/29, account of Yealmpton, 19-20 Ric. II.

[12] J. M. Bennett, *Ale, Beer and Brewsters in England: Woman's Work in a Changing World* (1996), p. 4; below, n. 60 and n. 61.

[13] PRO, SC6 827/34, account of Ermington, 7-8 Ric. II; PRO, SC6 1118/6, account of lands in the hands of the King during the minority of Thomas, earl of Devon, 10 Hen. V; DRO, CR 496, Plympton account of 5-6 Hen. VII (my value includes a small 'failure of rent').

[14] L. M. Midgley, ed., *Ministers' Accounts of the Earldom of Cornwall, 1296-1297* (2 vols, Camden Soc., 3rd ser., 66, 68, 1942-5), vol. 2, p. 216 (and compare PRO, SC6 827/38, undated account of Kenton, close in time to that printed by Midgley); PRO, SC6 Hen.VIII/513, account beginning 24 Hen. VII. The first account, printed by Midgley, describes the fishery as that of 'the men of Geoffrey de Albemarle' (i.e. the men of Woodbury, Albemarle's manor, on the opposite shore of the Exe) but that seems to be an error for most later documents say or imply that the 4s. came from Kenton's inhabitants and the fishery is described as 'of the sea' or 'of Exmouth', i.e. the Exe Estuary. Post-medieval reference to the value of the fishery: DRO, 1508M/Lon./manor/Kenton/6, survey of 1578.

[15] A. J. Robertson, *Anglo-Saxon Charters* (1956), pp. 205-7. The text of the Tidenham custumal is also to be found in W. de Gray Birch, *Cartularium Saxonicum* (3 vols, 1885-93), vol. 3, pp. 102-3. For a recent commentary see R. Faith, 'Tidenham, Gloucestershire and the history of the manor in England', *Landscape History* 16 (1994), pp. 39-51.

[16] PRO, C134 16/9.

[17] Robertson, *Charters*, p. 207.
[18] Oliver, *Monasticon*, p. 255; PRO, C134 16/9 and Huntington Library, San Marino, California, HAM box 64, rental of '1577'.
[19] R. Lennard, *Rural England, 1086-1135: a Study of Social and Agrarian Conditions* (1959), pp. 250-1; references to Dartington and Cornworthy as in note 1 above.
[20] H. H. E. Craster, *History of Northumberland*, vol. 8, *The Parish of Tynemouth* (1907), p. 285; H. C. Maxwell Lyte, *A History of Dunster* (2 vols, 1909), vol 1, pp. 278-9. The lords of Dunster certainly exercised their privilege of buying fish at a cheaper price than the market price: C. Dyer, *Standards of Living in the Later Middle Ages: Social Change in England, c. 1200-1520* (1989), p. 69.
[21] D. Oschinsky, *Walter of Henley and other Treatises on Estate Management and Accounting* (1971), p. 397.
[22] Dyer, *Standards of Living*, p. 99.
[23] PRO, C134 16/9; SC6 830/29, Yealmpton account of 19-20 Ric. II.
[24] M. Bailey, 'Coastal fishing off south east Suffolk in the century after the Black Death', *Procs Suffolk Inst. of Archaeology and History* 37 (1990), p. 106 (Dunwich); A. J. F. Dulley, 'The early history of the Rye fishing industry', *Sussex Archaeological Collections* 107 (1969), pp. 37, 39 (Rye and Winchelsea); J. H. Round, 'Some early Sussex charters', *Sussex Archaeological Collections* 42 (1899), pp. 78-9.
[25] PRO, SC6 828/5; R. N. Worth, *Calendar of Plymouth Municipal Records* (1893), p. 36; PRO, C145 87/1.
[26] PRO, SC6 827/40, Ringmore account of 28-9 Hen. VI; P. L. Hull, ed., *The Caption of Seisin of the Duchy of Cornwall (1377)* (DCRS, new ser., 17, 1971), p. 118.
[27] See below, Section 5.1 (Woodbury).
[28] The court rolls for Newton Ferrers are in PRO C116/37-40. They must have been overlooked when the PRO made its great 'Special collection' of court rolls (SC2) and they remained in this obscure class of 'Masters' exhibits'. I would never have found them had not Richard Smith drawn them to my attention, now many years ago. Most of my notes are from roll 37, containing many courts from the reign of Hen. VI (1420s-50s). Almost all of the early courts in this roll contain information on personal payments from fishermen; the agreement with the bailiff is in the court near the Conversion of St Paul, 12 Hen. VI.
[29] PRO, C134 16/9; Worth, *Calendar*, p. 36.
[30] Below, Section 4.4 for examples of household accounts; Oliver, *Monasticon*, p. 172; D. Seymour, *Torre Abbey* (1977), p. 252.
[31] There are many examples in M. Aston, ed., *Medieval Fish, Fisheries and Fishponds in England* (2 vols, British Archaeological Reports, British Series, 182, i and ii, 1988) and in J. McDonnell, *Inland Fisheries in Medieval Yorkshire* (Borthwick Papers, 60, 1981).
[32] Domesday, 1/4.
[33] Background in A. M. Jackson, 'Medieval Exeter, the Exe and the Earldom of Devon', *TDA* 104 (1972), pp. 57-79; also Kowaleski, *LCAPE*, pp. 1-4. The explanation 'because of a certain weir' is from an extent cited by Jackson in his note 52.
[34] The account of 1295-6 is PRO SC6 829/27, a document which also contains accounts

from the previous and following years, both with more information about the fishery. Details about works on the weir on the Exminster side of the channel are in PRO SC6 827/39, account of lands late of Isabella de Fortibus.

[35] The best run of Cockington manorial accounts is in DRO 48/13/4/1/2, for the 1430s and 50s. Most of the detail I give in this paragraph is from the account of 18-19 Hen. VI (1439-40) printed in H. S. A. Fox, 'Fishing in Cockington documents', in T. Gray, ed., *Devon Documents in Honour of Mrs Margery Rowe* (1996), pp. 76-82.

[36] C. Dyer, 'A small landowner in the fifteenth century', *Midland History* 1 (1972), p. 9.

[37] M. Kowaleski, 'The expansion of the south-western fisheries in late medieval England', *Ec. Hist. Rev.*, 2nd ser., 53 (2000), p. 447.

[38] Oliver, *Monasticon*, p. 172; F. C. Hingeston-Randolph, *The Registers of Walter Bronescombe and Peter Quivil* (1889), p. 249; BL, Add. roll 64683, Plympton account probably around the reign of Hen. VII, and DRO, CR 532, Plympton account of 1534-5.

[39] Hull, ed., *Caption of Seisin*, p. 118; DRO, Exeter City Archives book 57.

[40] Cited in M. Firestone, 'The traditional Start Bay crab fishery', *Folk Life* 20 (1981-2), p. 67.

[41] DRO, Exeter City Archives book 57.

[42] C. Noall, *Cornish Seines and Seiners: a History of the Pilchard Fishing Industry* (1972), p. 30.

[43] Midgley, ed., *Ministers' Accounts*, vol. 2, p. 216; PRO, C116/37; DRO, Exeter City Archives book 57; T. Gray and M. Rowe, eds, *Travels in Georgian Devon* (4 vols, 1997-2000), vol. 2, pp. 137-8.

[44] I am very grateful to John Blair for pointing this out to me.

[45] Lennard, *Rural England*, p. 248 n. 2.

[46] S. Godbold and R. C. Turner, 'Medieval fish traps in the Severn Estuary', *Medieval Archaeology* 38 (1994), pp. 19-54; B. Crump and S. Wallis, 'Kiddles and the Foulness fishing industry', *Essex Jnl* 27 (1992), pp. 38-42.

[47] F. E. Halliday, ed., *Richard Carew of Antony: the Survey of Cornwall* (1953), p. 115.

[48] PRO, SC6 Hen. VIII/537, North Pool account of 26-7 Hen. VIII; PRO, SC6 827/34, Ermington account of 7-9 Hen. V; PRO, SC6 830/29, Yealmpton account of 19-20 Ric. II ('le hakyn'). At South Pool there was a fishery called 'la haukyna': CRO, Arundell MSS, South Pool account of 28-9 Hen. VI.

[49] *PND*, vol. 2, pp. 479, 505.

[50] PRO, SC6 Hen. VIII/537, North Pool account of 26-7 Hen. VIII; PRO, SC6 828/5, Kenton account of 1-2 Hen. VI; PRO, C116/37, court near the Conversion of St Paul, 6 Hen. VI.

[51] Worth, *Calendar*, p. 36; PRO, C134/16, Stokenham extent.

[52] Firestone, 'Start Bay', p. 74; S. Reynolds, *A Poor Man's House* (paperback edn, 1982), *passim*.

[53] A. M. Northway, 'Devon fishing vessels and their ownership, 1760-1880', in H. E. S. Fisher and W. E. Minchinton, eds, *Transport and Shipowning in the Westcountry* (Exeter Papers in Economic History, 7, 1973), pp. 22-6.

[54] E. W. White, *British Fishing-Boats and Coastal Craft* (1973) for these and other dimensions. For other details of small medieval fishing craft, see G. Hutchinson, *Medieval Ships and Shipping* (1994), pp. 139-45.
[55] ECA, DC 957.
[56] G. Collins, *Great Britain's Coasting Pilot* (1693), *passim*; DRO, 96add.M/E/11.
[57] S. A. Moore, *A History of the Foreshore and the Law Relating thereto* (1888) which prints, among much else, the arguments of Thomas Digges, in the late 1560s, attempting to claim that much of the foreshore was in royal ownership; Halsbury's *Laws of England* (latest edn), *s. v.* foreshore.
[58] R. Potts, ed., *Calendar of Cornish Glebe Terriers* (DCRS, new ser., 19, 1974), p. 177 (Zennor in Cornwall).
[59] PRO, C116/37, court near Michaelmas, 5 Hen. VI; Huntington Library, HAM box 74, account of 'Salisbury's lands', 22-3 Hen. VII; PRO, C116/37, court near the Ascension, 8 Edw. IV; DRO, Z17/3/19.
[60] H. S. A. Fox, 'Medieval Dartmoor as seen through its account rolls', *PDAS* 52 (1994), pp. 156-62; N. Neilson, ed., *A Terrier of Fleet, Lincolnshire* (British Academy Records of the Social and Economic History of England and Wales, 4, 1920), pp. x-xiii.
[61] M. Chibnall, ed., *Charters and Custumals of the Abbey of Holy Trinity, Caen* (British Academy Records of Social and Economic History, new ser., 5, 1982), pp. 115-6, 136; H. E. J. le Patourel, 'Documentary evidence and the medieval pottery industry', *Medieval Archaeology* 12 (1968), pp. 113-5; Fox, 'Medieval Dartmoor', pp. 162-3.
[62] Halsbury's *Laws of England* (latest edn), *s. v.* fishery.
[63] *Cal. Charter Rolls*, vol. 1, *1257-1300*, p. 36; *Rotuli Hundredorum*, vol. 1, pp. 76, 81; DRO, CR 1144, Monkleigh court roll; *Register of Edward the Black Prince*, pt 2, pp. 130-1; DRO, 123M/E/31, sixteenth-century survey.
[64] DRO, Cary MSS, Ashwater court near St Barnabas, 10 Hen. VI; DRO, W1258M/D/70, Werrington court near St Mathias the Apostle, 40 Edw. III.
[65] K. Ugawa, 'The economic development of some Devon manors in the thirteenth century', *TDA* 94 (1962), p. 635; WDRO, 70/93, account of *Martinstow*, 16-17 Ric. II; H. P. R. Finberg, *Tavistock Abbey: a Study in the Social and Economic History of Devon* (1951) p. 91.
[66] *Cal. Inq. Misc.*, vol. 1, p. 521; PRO, SC6 827/34, account of 7-9 Hen. V.
[67] PRO, C134/6; DRO, 158M/M/11, account of 39-40 Edw. III.
[68] E. Evans, *Irish Folk Ways* (1957), pp. 22, 223. See also, for Cornwall, N. J. G. Pounds, 'Sandingways to the Sea', *DCNQ* 22 (1942-6), pp. 289-91, especially for post-medieval references.
[69] PRO, C116/37, court near the Annunciation, 9 Hen. VI; inspection of Aunemouth sandway made with Frank Meeres in December 1997. For what was probably another 'private' sandway, to Pulsack in Philleigh, see H. S. A. Fox and O. J. Padel, eds, *The Cornish Lands of the Arundells of Lanherne, Fourteenth to Sixteenth Centuries* (DCRS, new ser., 41, 2000), pp. 90, 134.
[70] O. J. Reichel, ed., *Devon Feet of Fines*, vol. 1 (DCRS, 6, 1912), pp. 87-8 for a way called *Sandweie* in Broadhembury, a good distance inland from the coast.

The Fisheries and the Foreshore 81

[71] In North Devon there was significant traffic in sand on the Taw: see references in H. S. A. Fox, 'Devon and Cornwall: farming practice and techniques', in E. Miller, ed., *The Agrarian History of England and Wales*, vol, 3, *1348-1500* (1991), p. 311, n. 320.

[72] Midgley, ed., *Ministers' Accounts*, vol. 2, p. 238; Hull, ed., *Caption of Seisin*, p. 118. For references to this traffic in the hundred rolls, see above, n. 63.

[73] WDRO, 70/92, *Martinstow* account of 3-4 Ric. II and 70/93, account of 16-17 Ric. II; PRO, SC6 822/15, account of 2-3 Hen. IV for the earliest reference to sand landed at Halton Quay (other references in later accounts in this collection); PRO, SC6 822/17, account of 9-10 Hen. IV (for packhorses).

[74] Above, Section 2.1 for the quay at Morwellham; DRO, W1258M/D/52/2, Leigh account of 12-13 Hen. VII; Finberg, *Tavistock Abbey*, p. 91.

[75] DRO, CR 1097, court of near the Apostles Peter and Paul, 30 Hen. VI; 1096, court near Easter, 26 Hen. VI.

[76] PRO, SC6 830/29, account of Yealmpton, 19-20 Ric. II for an example of *zabulaterius*. In his *Surnames of Devon* (1995), pp. 172-3 and n. 165, David Postles considers that for most people with the surname Sander and the like, it is derived from the forename Alexander; however, he does cite one William le Sonder (1302), where the name certainly seems to have been occupational. The name was very common in medieval Devon: A. M. Erskine, ed., *The Devonshire Lay Subsidy of 1332* (DRCS, new ser. 14, 1969), index s. v. Saundre.

[77] DRO, CR 1096, Monkleigh court near Easter, 26 Hen. VI; DRO, W1258M/E/24, account of Cargoll, beginning in 23 Ric. I.

[78] Finberg, *Tavistock Abbey*, pp. 91-4; R. Stanes, *The Old Farm: a History of Farming Life in the West Country* (1990), pp. 107-12.

[79] J. Maclean, *The Parochial and Family History of the Deanery of Trigg Minor* (3 vols, 1873-9), vol. 1, p. 481.

[80] C. E. Welch, 'A survey of some Duchy manors', *DCNQ* 30 (1965-7), p. 35.

[81] CRO, AR2/542, Hartland account 6-7 Hen. IV.

[82] Finberg, *Tavistock Abbey*, p. 91.

[83] H. Summerson, ed., *Crown Pleas of the Devon Eyre of 1238* (DCRS, new ser., 28, 1985), pp. 38, 40, 89, 105; pp. 128-9 for the articles.

[84] DRO, Exeter City Archives book 57.

[85] CRO, AR MSS, account of Hartland wreck; *Cal. Inq. Misc.*, vol. 7, pp. 313-17; W. A. Roberts, 'Wreck of the sea', in his *Stokenham Occasional Papers*, 1 (1980), pp.13-17, based upon PRO REQ2 168/28.

[86] PRO, E36/223; PRO, C139/94, survey of Langdon.

[87] Notes from Exeter local customs accounts kindly made available by Maryanne Kowaleski. Katherine, countess of Devon also served up 'puffys'.

[88] PRO, E36/223; CRO, AR2/727/1, printed in C. M. Woolgar, ed., *Household Accounts from Medieval England* (2 pts, British Academy Records of Social and Economic History, new ser., 17-18, 1992-3), pt 2, p. 502.

[89] W. J. Blake, 'Hooker's Synopsis Chorographical of Devonshire', *TDA* 47 (1915), p. 343. There are post-medieval references to the gathering of oar or seaweed on the shore

of Kenton manor (Exe Estuary) and of Ringmore (Teign Estuary): DRO, 1508M/Lon./manor/Kenton/2, e.g. water court of 11 Apl 1608; DRO, Carew of Haccombe MSS, MR/31, court of 1645. Oddly, references from the north coasts of Devon and Somerset are, by contrast, very numerous: *VCH Somerset*, vol. 5, p. 47 (mid-sixteenth century onwards at Old Cleeve), p. 93 (rights to seaweed on the beach at Kilton, sixteenth century), p. 100 (seaweed burned for bottle manufacture or manure at Kilve, sixteenth century), p. 105 (share in seaweed in a Lilstock lease of 1706), p. 125 (burning of seaweed at East Quantoxhead); F. Hancock, *Minehead in the County of Somerset* (1903), pp. 34-5; T. Risdon, *Chorographical Description or Survey of the County of Devon* (1811), p. 242 (medieval deed granting a right of way to carry sea-oar and sea-sand near Buck's Mills in Woolfardisworthy); DRO, CR 951, Lincombe court of 1848 (agreement between manors about the gathering of seaweed).

[90] DRO, CR 1448. L. F. Salzman, in *English Industries of the Middle Ages* (1923 edn), pp. 2-3, notes how common the term 'sea coal' was in the Middle Ages; he considers that it implied either coal washed up from seams exposed on the sea bed or coal which had been brought southwards in the coastal trade from the North-East towards London. Neither of these explanations is really appropriate to Budleigh Salterton. The entry in the *Oxford English Dictionary* does not clear up this matter.

[91] Darby and Welldon Finn, eds, *Domesday Geography*, pp. 269-72.

[92] Thus Domesday mentions no salt pans near Salcombe ('salt valley', Kingsbridge Estuary) nor at Salcombe Regis; the latter place-name, certainly, was in existence in 1086.

[93] H. C. Darby and E. M. J. Campbell, eds, *Domesday Geography of South-East England* (1962), pp. 455-7; Darby, *Domesday Geography of Eastern England*, pp. 134-6.

[94] C. Morris, ed., *The Journeys of Celia Fiennes* (1949), pp. 49-50.

[95] Domesday, 1/26; Kenton documents cited above, n. 14. For the numerous types of medieval documents relating to salt-making which we should expect from an area where the industry was flourishing, see H. E. Hallam, 'Salt making in the Lincolnshire Fenland during the Middle Ages', *Lincs. Architectural and Archaeological Soc. Reports and Papers* 8 (1960), pp. 85-112.

[96] Domesday, 11/1; PRO, SC 11/171; Oliver, *Monasticon*, pp. 254-5.

[97] For the industry's survival in Lincolnshire, at least until the seventeenth century, see E. L. Rudkin and D. M. Owen, 'The medieval salt industry in the Lindsey marshland', *Lincs. Architectural and Archaeological Soc. Reports and Papers* 8 (1960), pp. 76-84; A. E. B. Owen, 'Medieval salting and the coastline in Cambridgeshire and north-west Norfolk', in K. W. de Brisay and K. A. Evans, *Salt: the Study of an Ancient Industry* (1975), pp. 42-5.

[98] Domesday, 1/26, 34/11, 2/4, 16/157; J. B. Davidson, 'On the early history of Dawlish', *TDA* 13 (1881), pp. 109, 112.

[99] For the pig-men of Kenton and Bishopsteignton, for example, see Domesday, 1/26 and 2/4.

[100] There were hill turbaries on the Haldon Hills: PRO, C133 95/2; BL, Harl. ch. 48 I 21. But they were not so deep and nowhere near so extensive as the medieval turbaries

of Norfolk, for example, for which see Williamson, *Broads*, pp. 81-4.

[101] A. R. Bridbury, *England and the Salt Trade in the Later Middle Ages* (1955), for example p. 46.

[102] *Ibid.*, p. 43.

[103] See, for example, the sources cited *ibid.*, p. 44, many of them licences for safe passage of ships; P. M. Barnes, ed., *Great Roll of the Pipe for the Fourteenth Year . . . of King John* (Pipe Roll Soc., new ser., 30), p. 45; A. L. Simon, *The History of the Wine Trade in England* (2 vols, 1964 reprint), vol. 1, pp. 73-86.

[104] Kowaleski, *LCAPE*, p. 1; *Rotuli de Oblatis et Finibus*, p. 191. For another reference to Gascons drying fish in Cornwall, see S. F. Hockey, ed., *The Beaulieu Cartulary* (Southampton Record Series, 17, 1974), p. 217.

[105] For example, the salt-making works at Seaton, begun in 1704 and, according to the excellent researches of Margaret Parkinson, 'a revival of an industry which appears to have lapsed for nearly six centuries': 'The Axe Estuary and its marshes', *TDA* 117 (1985), especially pp. 42-4. On the western side of the Exe Estuary the two salthouses on Dawlish Warren, shown on a map of 1743, may have been similar revivals: DRO, 96add.M/E/11. However, some late references to salthouses may not relate to the making of salt but to storage of imported salt: examples are ECA, DC 3684 (salthouse at Cofton in Dawlish, 1513) and CRO, ME/1903, m. 3 (saltchambers at Bigbury: reference kindly supplied by Maryanne Kowaleski).

Chapter Four

CONSUMPTION AND DISTRIBUTION

4.1 Consumption

The place of fish in medieval diet has been discussed by Alison Littler. The household accounts of the rich show that huge quantities of fish were consumed in Lent and on many special days outside the Lenten season. Littler also argues that fish, being very cheap, was much consumed by other social groups. Even fresh fish was carried over relatively long distances, a fact which indicates strong demand, while cured fish was a 'convenience food and universal standby'. Littler's basic argument is that very many medieval references to inland fisheries, to fishponds and to coastal fisheries must imply a national consumption on a considerable scale.[1]

Consumption of fish in medieval Devon was probably even greater *per capita* than that in England at large, not only because of the county's two long coastlines which made this item of diet especially abundant and cheap,[2] but also because the county contained considerable numbers of people who had little or no access to agricultural land and who were not therefore producers of meat; among these groups fish would have been an especially attractive source of food. Devon was a highly urbanized county from the thirteenth century onwards on account of its diversified and commercialized economy, its two coastlines, on which port towns developed, and its broken landscape in which numerous estuaries and hill ranges made movement difficult, thereby multiplying the opportunities for town foundation. By the end of the thirteenth century there were over 70 boroughs and although some have been described by historians as 'still born' or 'failures', it can be shown that most, even the smallest, functioned as truly urban places at this time.³ Calculations based upon urban rentals and surveys, or upon backward extrapolation from the poll tax of 1377, indicate that the urban component probably comprised 26% of the total population of the county at this time.⁴ Some town dwellers had access to generous burgage plots on which animals were kept, but many, especially the poorest, would not have been able to produce any foodstuffs and for these the plentiful supply of cheap fish must have been particularly welcome. It is highly unlikely that the size of the county's urban population declined overall between 1300 and 1500; it almost certainly grew, and along with that growth there was probably a rise in urban demand for fish.⁵ Devon supported other groups who did not produce their own foodstuffs, especially those among the labourers in the stannaries who had no agricultural land, a group which may have grown in size during the later fourteenth century and the fifteenth.⁶ Post-medieval accounts stress the importance of fish in the tinners' diet.

From these general points we may turn to specific examples of consumption, beginning with lordly households. Lords of manors had easy access to supplies of fish. If a lord owned a coastal manor with a fishery he could, if he wished, use it to supply his kitchens through the requisition system described in Chapter 3.⁷ A lord residing inland could use his manors to provide a network of purchase and carriage of fish to his residence: for example, in the 1390s the Dinhams, then residing at Kingskerswell, employed the reeve of their far western property of Gurlyn to purchase fish at St Michael's Mount and were accustomed to use their tenants at Bodardle (about half way home) to provide free customary carrying services to bring it to their kitchen.⁸ Once acquired by such means, fish was consumed in large quantities, as shown by the household accounts of lordly residences. When Sir William Courtenay was residing 'with his family' at South Pool, very close to the Kingsbridge Estuary, his account for 1341-2 shows that consumption of large quantities of fish began around Christmas time, then increased through Lent to Easter week when two salmon, six conger, three ling, 52 hake, 98 buckhorns (dried whiting), 180 red herrings and 166 white were prepared in the kitchen. In late spring and during the summer and early autumn the Courtenays consumed less fish.⁹ The household accounts of Katherine, countess of Devon, residing largely at Columbjohn, 5 miles north of Exeter and 8 miles from Topsham where she made purchases of fish, reveal the same pattern, with relatively little fish eaten at some times of the year and large quantities, and great variety, consumed in Lent. For example, the account for the week beginning October 22nd indicates a diversified diet of meat and fowl – a piece of beef 'to boil', veal, pork, rabbits, woodcock, mutton and chicken. By contrast a week in Lent saw the lady and her household sitting down to about ten types of fish in all, including salted salmon, white herrings and dried conger; no meat at all was eaten, except two puffins (possibly shearwaters), perhaps allowed at this time of abstinence because of their fishy taste.[10] In both households almost all of the fish consumed was salt-water fish; because of the abundant supply of fish from the sea, relatively few Devon manor houses had fishponds.

About patterns of consumption in other, lesser, families we have no direct information because we lack documentary evidence such as household accounts. We can only argue along the same lines as those used by Littler for England at large: that the very great number of fisheries recorded along the coastline of South Devon from the eleventh century onwards strongly suggests a high demand. We may also argue that, among the poorest people, fish – which could be had very cheaply and in fresh or preserved forms at all times of the year – was a more consistent item in diet than it was in aristocratic households. One very good type of evidence for a widespread demand for fish comes from the presence of fishmongers in the inland urban centres of medieval Devon who would have supplied townspeople and also, because the towns were market centres for rural hinterlands, the people of the countryside. In the lay subsidy returns of 1332 Walter le Vyshere was taxed 2*s*. 6*d*. in the borough of South Molton; a royal inquisition of 1419, touching the chattels of outlaws and felons, lists William Godynow, 'fyscher' of Holsworthy, while a list of some of the awkward inhabitants of Modbury in 1463, contained within the Stonor papers, includes John Cryspyn, 'fysher'.[11] All of these places were boroughs of moderate size, the first two being 9 and 15 miles respectively from the North Devon coast, the last 4 miles from the South Devon coast. These 'fishers' could just possibly have been fresh-water fishermen working local streams, but the word very often meant 'fishmonger' in the Middle Ages and, given the urban contexts, this is the most likely explanation in all three cases; there is also good independent evidence to show that medieval Holsworthy had a fish market, while a jowter, or fish-hawker, was among the inhabitants of Modbury in 1463.[12] These people, known from scattered sources, take their place alongside the small-town fish traders who frequented Exeter's fish markets in order to make purchases and, through infringements of one kind or another, ended up before the mayor's courts whose records have been systematically analyzed by Maryanne Kowaleski. These defendants, during the late fourteenth century, included 'fishers' (fish traders) from the Devon boroughs or towns of Honiton, Bradninch, Colyford, Tiverton, Kennford, Sampford Peverell, Ottery St Mary and Cullompton, all except Kennford being inland places north or northeast of Exeter.[13] Many of them were plump little towns with some involvement in the cloth industry and they all had formally sanctioned markets which attracted people from their surrounding countrysides. The presence of one or more fishmongers in each testifies, therefore, to a steady urban demand for fish and also to consumption of fish in their hinterlands. The presence of the bones of marine fish among faunal deposits recovered from excavations in towns points in the same direction.[14]

4.2 Marketing

A team of fishers haul their writhing seine on to a remote South Devon beach. Later in the week part of this imagined catch is put on sale by a fishmonger of the borough of Bradninch, just under 50 miles away. How was the commodity marketed, carried and traded from the shore of a manor with a fishery to its consumers inland? This and the following section attempt to answer that question.

If we forget for a moment the world of regulated trade and chartered markets, it would seem that the most obvious place at which to buy fish at its cheapest and freshest was on the beach itself or from boats grounded on the beach. A rental of the manor of Stokenham made in about 1360 states that 'any fisherman of *any neighbourhood* [my italics] coming ashore on the lord's manor . . . must provide to the lord fish from his boat at a fixed price' and then goes on to state the price of porpoise, salmon, ling, cod, bream, plaice, skate, conger and mullet, this being the purveyance system described in the previous chapter.[15] The shore of the manor of Stokenham had several beaches from which its own tenants fished and, presumably, the tenants sold part of their catches at those beaches, which thus came to be known as places where fish could be bought. Because they attracted buyers, the beaches began to be used by people from the fisheries of nearby coastal manors, the 'fishermen of any neighbourhood' of the passage cited above. Another informal fish market on the shore was described by jurors speaking before an inquisition of 1282-3 touching the manor of Sutton Prior (later to become Plymouth) who recalled a time long before, perhaps in the early thirteenth century, when fishing boats would come ashore and their owners would offer catches for sale on a certain piece of 'waste' formed through the 'withdrawal of the sea' (that is, either a reclamation or the foreshore). From Exmouth in 1268 there is a reference to people selling fish from boats, and at Paignton the lord allowed those who fished to sell near the seashore instead of having to take their catches to the manor's official market place inland.[16]

The concept of the beach (or boats grounded there or moored just out to sea) as the most natural place for the selling of fish is worth following up with a few other south-western examples from beyond the stretch of coast surveyed in detail here. In the third quarter of the thirteenth century, Glastonbury Abbey granted out a tenement near the sea at Lyme Regis and a clause in the charter specified that the grantees were not to hinder the abbey's servants from buying 'on the sea shore' (*in littore maris*) as in past time; fish are not specified but they are almost certainly implied, because the abbey used Lyme Regis for bulk purchases of fish.[17] In the fourth decade of the fourteenth century there is a reference to a stall (*selda*) 'next to the strand at Appledore' on the North Devon coast; clearly, some product of the sea was being sold here, almost certainly fish but perhaps salt as well.[18] Finally, a clause in the borough charter (1246) of Saltash, on the Cornish side of the Tamar, mentions the custom of purchases from boats while they were still in the river channel and although the commodities are not stated it is unlikely that fish was not one of them.[19]

At few of the places mentioned in the last two paragraphs was there a legal market, that is a chartered market recognized by the Crown where the owner had formally obtained the right to take tolls and prosecute trading offences. The buying and selling of fish at these places was going on as an ancient custom. The local lord needed to be only moderately astute to realize that he could regulate, and take profit from, this ancient custom by formally instituting the market with a Crown licence, perhaps also moving it a little way from the beach for better supervision. And it so happens that some of the earliest formal markets known in Devon were almost certainly, or certainly, fish markets. The only non-urban market referred to in the Domesday folios for Devon was one recorded under the entry for the manor of Otterton. Otterton at this time included the (later) coastal manor of Sidmouth and, according to subsequent sources, the site of the market was close to the sea there. There was a brisk trade in fish here in later times so it is reasonable to suppose that the Domesday market, eccentrically placed in Otterton manor, also specialized in that commodity.[20] Chronologically the next rural market mentioned in Devon sources was that at Ashprington on the Dart. Between 1134 and 1138 Roger de Nonant gave to Totnes Priory 'the fish market which I made on the land of the monks at Ashprington' and by a separate charter Roger gave the manor of Ashprington to the priory. The two documents are undated and it is not clear which was issued first, nor precisely how they relate to one another. What is not in doubt is the existence at Ashprington of a fishery, mentioned in 1086 (Domesday Book) and 1088, and of the seigneurial institution of a fish market, perhaps not long after.[21] It is worth noting that probably the earliest reference to a market in Cornwall is to what may have been a fish market. In about 1070, Robert count of Mortain, remembering how he had fought safely at Hastings under the banner of St Michael, granted to the monks of Mont St Michel in France a market 'on the fifth day' near the shore opposite St Michael's Mount in Cornwall. It is not specifically stated to have been a fish market but fish could certainly be bought in the vicinity later in the Middle Ages and the day, Thursday, is suggestive (giving the name *Market Jew*, a corruption of Cornish *marghas*, market, plus *yow*, Thursday).[22] These very early references to certain, or probable, fish markets testify to the importance of trade in fish already by the end of the eleventh century.

If we now turn, from these early references, to the thirteenth and fourteenth centuries when the formal establishment of places of trade is relatively well documented, it is possible to discern other places where the trade in fish may have been an important reason for the development of markets and towns. In this connection one rural market and two boroughs will be discussed. The rural market was at Cockington, a manor for which Walter de Wodeland secured a market grant in 1353, shortly after he acquired the property. There are several odd features about this grant: first, the date is strange because it came only five years after the Black Death and at the beginning of a half-century when very few market charters were sought for other places in Devon; second, Cockington was a backwater, neither an important estate centre nor on any much-used medieval routeway; third, as Maryanne Kowaleski points out, the Bishop of Exeter's older and (if longevity is any guide) more successful market at Paignton was less than 2 miles away.[23] The manor of Cockington reaches the sea at Livermead Sands, a small inlet of Tor Bay, and here there is good evidence for a fishery both before and after 1353.[24] In establishing a market at Cockington, Walter de Wodeland may have been seeking to regulate and to profit from the kind of informal buying and selling on the beach which has been described above. If this is the correct interpretation of the grant of 1353, it may be that Wodeland was hoping to develop an additional source of income (from market profits) at a time when the incomes of lords were generally at rather a low ebb.

The two boroughs whose establishment may have had much to do with the marketing of fish, and with activities ancillary to fishing, are Kennford and Chillington. Kennford, very close to Exeter to the south, is a most interesting place. Just over 3 miles from the western shore of the River Exe, the borough (now very decayed) is linked by a pattern of deep lanes to all of the fisheries of that river in the manors of

Exminster, Kenton and Dawlish. Moreover, the borough was strung out along an important medieval routeway (now by-passed), almost certainly the route which would have been taken by fish carriers coming towards Exeter from the coastlines of deep South Devon (a traffic described more fully in the next section of this chapter). The people of Kennford were therefore in an ideal position to buy up, and then sell on, fish from a number of destinations.[25] We are on sure ground here for, although Kennford was a borough of that minute kind which flourished in medieval Devon, with few records of its own, it was relatively close to Exeter and its people are therefore well known to us through offences investigated at the city's mayor's court. In the late fourteenth century several recorded fish dealers from Kennford were active in Exeter; we may infer that their ploy was to buy up (regrate) fish in their own settlement, then to take it to the Exeter fish market where they sold it at a higher price. A pretty penny could be turned in this way as regrating could double the price of mackerel from ½d. to 1d. apiece.[26] And Kennford was notorious for illegal trade in fish, illegal, that is, in the eyes of the civic authorities of Exeter who considered that they had the right to toll fish sales in a wide arc of territory to the south of the city. Men from as far away as Sidmouth came there to buy up fish to the detriment of Exeter's market. Moreover, the brave people of the borough sold wine at its market, again contrary to Exeter regulations which specified that wine should be sold only in the city.[27] In short, the place was a thorough nuisance. Probably founded in 1300 by the Courtenays, the existence of the borough may have added to the grievances felt by Exeter towards that family.[28]

The origins of Chillington, another borough situated just behind the coast, may also have been tied up with activities relating to fishing. It was planted less than 2 miles from the sea in the manor of Stokenham whose people we have already encountered in discussions of lords' profits from fisheries and of selling on the beach, and who will be met once again in the following chapter as fishing farmers.[29] No doubt the borough served as a local market and as a place for simple commodity production for a small rural hinterland, filling a gap as it did in the pattern of markets, between the older towns of Dartmouth and Kingsbridge. No doubt, also, the place functioned as a minor medieval 'thoroughfare' – to use a term from a later age – because it was situated on a routeway, although not on the main overland route between Dartmouth and Plymouth, which ran to the north.[30] The fishery of the manor of Stokenham was very active during the Middle Ages, custumals indicating that many of the tenants owned boats or shares in boats and, as we have seen, fish was brought to the manor's beaches by people from adjacent places. Fish not immediately sold on the shore would have been traded in the borough, bought up by 'fishers' who then distributed it inland, for Stokenham's fishery, although we cannot measure its volume, must have produced more than could have been consumed on the manor and in the borough of Chillington. From the people of the manor, fishing farmers, there would have been a greater demand for smiths,[31] coopers, dealers in salt and iron, makers of anchors, tackle and ropes, than on a manor whose people had purely agricultural occupations. All of these activities, in both marketing and manufacturing, would have given sources of income to the petty burgesses of the borough. Chillington's oldest fair was on the vigil, feast and morrow of saints Philip and James (at the beginning of May) and, later on, a 'well frequented' fair is recorded here on Good Friday.[32]

As well as boroughs situated a little way behind the coast, the port towns themselves were ideally placed as fish markets. As explained in an earlier chapter, most ports were the homes of some specialist, full-time fishermen.[33] Like other types of town, they were concentrations of demand for foodstuffs, including fish. Moreover, victualling and provision of cargoes of dried fish for export introduced additional demands. Most (but not all) ports had good connections with a hinterland and this made the inland distribution of fish relatively easy. For all of these reasons ports attracted both outsider fishers (in addition to residents) with their catches to sell and fish traders in search of those catches. Almost the earliest glimpse which we have of the port of Plymouth is through the memories of certain inhabitants of the locality, testifying to an inquisition of 1282-3 and looking back, they said, 'before the foundation of the town of Sutton'. By this they probably meant 'before the establishment of the borough of Sutton Prior' which, together with adjacent land, eventually (in 1439) became the incorporated port town of Plymouth. The time to which their memories ran is not precisely known, but it was certainly before the 1250s and possibly as early as the first quarter of the thirteenth century. Then, they remembered, the principal activity on the foreshore and on the land just behind it, left high and dry perhaps through reclamation, was the beaching of fishing boats, the drying of nets and sails and the selling of fish. No great fleets under royal command yet, yet no barrels of Gascon wine lining the quay.[34] This earliest thumb-nail picture of what was later to become Plymouth shows that it began as a place from which the people of Sutton, and perhaps of adjacent manors, put out in their fishing boats; they may well have been fishing farmers, as described in the following chapter. And from this early time onwards there are frequent references to the marketing of fish at Plymouth. Thus in 1310 the Prior of Plympton, who owned the borough of Sutton, is found trying to restrict the setting up of stalls (fish is the first of the commodities mentioned), which were to be pitched only in his market place, presumably so that the supervision and tolling of transactions would be easier for his officials. In 1384 the owner of the port of Plymouth (i.e. the maritime jurisdiction of the waters from the shore outwards) was still collecting dues from fish catches brought ashore there and was attempting to ensure that sales were not made elsewhere.[35] That lords were prepared to go to some trouble to guard their rights and profits testifies to the volume of trade in fish in the port. Ultimately, they were never completely successful and fish continued to be sold at unlicensed markets in places adjacent to the town. Stonehouse was one of these, being a place for illicit fish marketing in 1384 and, in the fifteenth century, a place where Tavistock Abbey bought fish.[36]

At Dartmouth, another medieval port of much note, a market is recorded as early as 1205 and in 1275, according to the hundred rolls, local customs dues were levied on conger, on herring and on other kinds of fish: these may have been dues on catches brought to the port by fishers from up-river or from nearby coasts or on exports coastwise or overseas. After fish had been exchanged in Dartmouth's market, much of it probably left by sea, because routes out of the town by land were steep and hazardous and the hinterland restricted as a consequence. Later on, at the end of the fifteenth century, we read of sellers of fish at Dartmouth who infringed regulations concerning freshness.[37]

Ports of a smaller size than Plymouth or Dartmouth also had active fish markets. We know, for example, that there were covered market houses at the ports of Teignmouth and Sidmouth, because the manorial owners of these places expended money on their repair and recorded these expenses in their accounts: thus in the middle of the fifteenth century the 'schamel' of the latter place was frequently repaired while at the former in 1438 the Dean and Chapter of Exeter laid out a large sum of money to repair 'le chypehous' (vernacular for market house).[38] During the summer a fish market needs a roof and the practice of dowsing, to make the product appear fresh, does not compensate for shade.

4.3 Distribution and redistribution

Having considered places on or near the coast at which fishers first offered their catches for sale, we turn to distribution further inland. On the coastal manor of Stoke Fleming there was a track called *le Fishway*, referred to in a medieval court roll and no doubt a route used by those who took the catches to market. Because of the efforts of Exeter's civic authorities to control the trade in fish well beyond the walls there, we have a glimpse, in one of the city's financial documents, of traffic by packhorse along the eastern shore of the River Exe, 520 horseloads being recorded on their way to the city in 1411. One post-medieval reference to the carriage of fish is so graphic that it must be quoted here: a sixteenth-century surveyor at Colyford (just over one mile from Seaton Bay) noted that farmland was very profitable there because fish carriers 'do stay . . . and eat the grasses . . . with their travelling horses'. Close by, in the parish of Sidbury, was a track named *Fisherne Path* 'because', according to a local deponent before an equity case, 'the fishermen used to pass that way'.[39]

The destinations of some of the packhorse journeys which began on or near the South Devon coast were the inland towns south of the great barrier of Dartmoor: Modbury, for example, where there was at least one fishmonger and a jowter (fish hawker) in the 1460s. Many other journeys were to Exeter, partly because the city by virtue of its size was an important centre of consumption, partly because it was a major redistribution centre for this and other commodities. One of the most remarkable achievements of Maryanne Kowaleski's *Local Markets and Regional Trade in Medieval Exeter* (1994) was her accurate delimitation of the city's hinterlands, a picture more comprehensive perhaps than has been provided for any other English medieval town apart from London. Analysis of disputes between buyers and sellers, and of other pleas, before Exeter's mayor's court, detailed scrutiny of the city's local port customs accounts which record the names of importers, time-consuming work on cases of debt in the court of common pleas – through use of all these sources, and many more, combined, she has given us an unexpectedly rich picture of the local trade of a medieval city. The following paragraphs, based almost wholly on this work, should really be dedicated to her powers of insight and imagination.

Exeter was exceptionally well placed as a redistributive centre in the fish trade. Medieval routeways from South Devon coastal manors converged on Exeter, the lowest bridging point on the Exe and, although hilly, the journey was not an excessively long one, for example about 30 miles as the crow flies from the Start Bay fisheries centred on the manor of Stokenham. Cargoes could also reach Exeter from the South Devon coast by sea, a voyage of about the same length. The city stood at the head of the Exe estuary with its fruitful fisheries while eastwards was the coast of East Devon, also with many fishing stations. For the inland redistribution of fish, routes radiated out of Exeter to the north and north-west into a spacious, largely rural, tract of country with few market towns and here it was probably not until a distance of 15 to 20 miles from the city that the hinterland of the North Devon fisheries would have been met. Eastwards from Exeter routes radiate out into the East Devon countryside, relatively densely populated in the Later Middle Ages and containing many towns connected with the cloth industry. The same routes continue into parts of Somerset and Dorset which were also relatively well populated and urbanized at this time. In short, the centrality of Exeter was like a magnet, attracting both those with fish to sell and those wishing to make a profit by buying and selling on again.

Fish was carried to Exeter from the South Devon fisheries both by packhorse and by ship. In the last decades of the fourteenth century (to which Maryanne Kowaleski's book largely relates) fish traders came to Exeter by overland routes from Brixham, Slapton, Yealmpton and Plympton (Fig. 4.1); the last two of these places demonstrate the remarkable pull of the Exeter market, for they were only a few miles from a rival market at Plymouth. Once in Exeter fish traders found

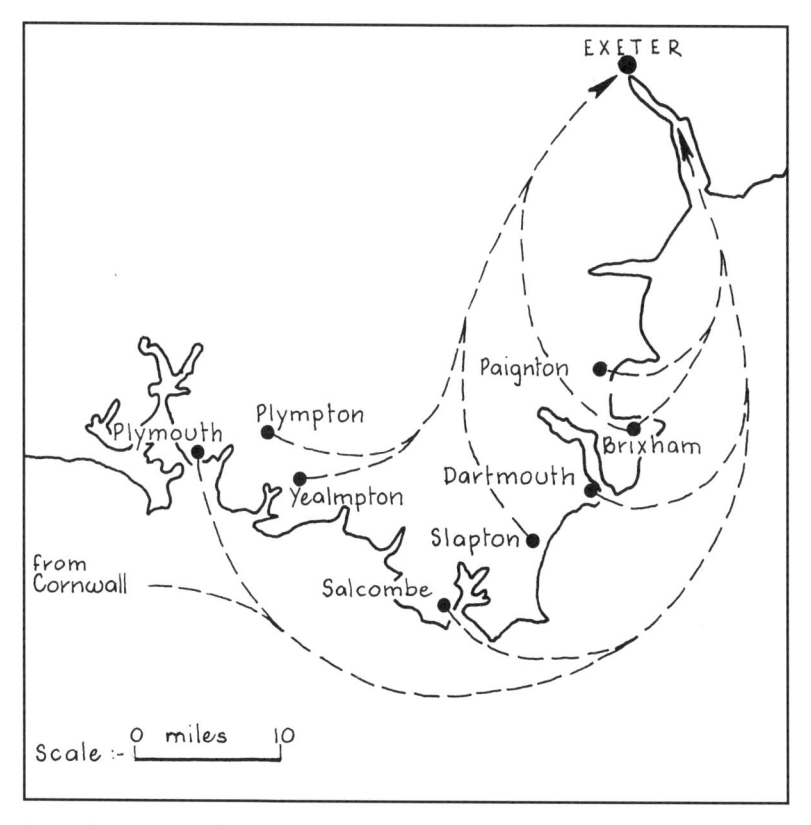

Figure 4.1 Carriage of fish by land and sea from South Devon to Exeter, late fourteenth century

themselves frequently before the mayor's court for some genuine infringement or another, or because fines made by the court became a kind of licensing fee to sell fish.[40] Maryanne Kowaleski suggests, after a good deal of searching for the names of these fish traders in sources relating to coastal manors, that they were not the catchers of the fish they carried; rather that they were 'middlemen who used their superior knowledge of the market to dominate the local and regional trade' and this argument is supported by the findings of a later chapter here which argues that many of those who fished were farmers much occupied with ways of making a living from agriculture on their home manors.[41] By sea, fish arrived at Exeter from a number of South Devon ports in the last decades of the fourteenth century (Fig. 4.1) to be recorded in the local customs accounts, and a few catches came from the Cornish ports or fishing places of Mousehole, Penzance, Looe and Fowey.[42]

Within Exeter there was a lively exchange of fish on the city's three market days and on numerous fair days, especially, after its establishment in 1374, at the fair on Ash Wednesday. The founding of this fair was an astute move on the part of the city, perhaps simply 'institutionalizing' a traditional fair, for it took place on the first day of Lent; in the fifteenth century it became the most profitable fair in Exeter. At all times of the year there was a brisk trade in fish at markets and fairs and, outside these sanctioned occasions, in private dwellings and inns.[43]

From the mid-Devon market towns of Okehampton and Winkleigh (both about 25 miles away) came fishmongers to buy up their stock in Exeter markets. Likewise, fishmongers from East Devon towns such as Bradninch and Ottery St Mary are found making purchases in the city's markets towards the end of the fourteenth century.[44] Such patterns of redistribution are to be expected, because Exeter was interposed between these towns and the rich fisheries of the South Devon coast. Less expected is Maryanne Kowaleski's finding that Exeter's hinterland for sales of fish extended way beyond the county boundary into Dorset and Somerset. Fishmongers from the north Dorset towns of Sherborne and Shaftesbury came to Exeter, as they also did from the east Somerset towns of Yeovil and Wincanton and from Taunton (especially), Langport, Chard and Crewkerne, also in that county. Finally, fishmongers from three towns in land-locked Wiltshire are to be found buying in Exeter: Warminster, Malmesbury and Salisbury.[45] Clearly, Exeter markets were of wide renown for fish and fish supplies there were either relatively cheap, or especially good and varied, to encourage fish traders to make long westward journeys – of over 80 miles in the case of the Salisbury man – in order to purchase them. The complexity and extent of this trade is even more remarkable when it is remembered that some of the fish purchased in Exeter would have come from the fisheries of the South Devon coast, those of Start Bay, for example, which were 30 miles to the west of the city. We end this chapter by considering the 'westwards reach' in more detail.

4.4 The westwards reach

That a Salisbury fishmonger should travel 80 miles to Exeter to buy fish when Southampton was about 20 miles away; that many Taunton fish dealers should frequent Exeter markets when the sea fisheries of Minehead, Dunster and Watchet, and the fresh-water fisheries of the Levels, were far closer over less difficult terrain – these facts strongly suggest that there was something special about the supplies sold in the city. The 'westwards reach' is to be seen also in the purchasing habits of lords for which there is a good deal of evidence both in seigneurial household accounts and also in manorial accounts where the reeve or bailiff is charged with buying fish and arranging for its carriage (Fig. 4.2).

Some patterns in the purchase and transport of fish for lordly households were dictated by the geography of estates and by seigneurial rights. Thus lords of Stokenham, as we have already described, saw to it that they could requisition one-third of the Lenten mullet catch, that they could purchase other fish from their tenants' fishery at a fixed (i.e. low) price and that they could buy fish from boats belonging to other fisheries, again at a fixed price. They also made sure that some of their Stokenham villeins performed carrying services (specifically for fish) to the headquarters of the estate at Erlestoke in Wiltshire and, if the services were not performed, the villeins had to pay 20s., a large sum which, presumably, could be used to pay others to make the journey. It made sense for lords of Stokenham to use that manor, despite its long distance from Erlestoke, because the fish was free or at the lord's price, and carriage was free. Likewise, the abbess of Syon (Middlesex) did well to supply her kitchens with porpoise from her manor of Sidmouth for it came without charge. The porpoise was, strictly, a royal animal, but as early as the thirteenth century the manorial owners of Sidmouth were regarding the local catch there as their own, presumably by royal grant. By the fifteenth century Syon had retracted a little and the lucky taker of each porpoise was allowed half of the beast (an inducement to hunt it) while the rest was either sold on behalf of the abbey or taken up to Middlesex for the table of the abbess.[46]

More unexpected are westward reaches for fish bought at markets. Lords in Devon often purchased fish in Cornwall (Fig. 4.2). In 1358 Richard Turberville, residing at Sampford Peverell, north of Exeter, bought virtually all of the fish for his household at places *apud Cornubiam*.[47] Tavistock Abbey used the officials of its manor of Plymstock (close to Plymouth) to buy some of its fish supplies and the villeins there to carry it to the larder; but the abbey also owned the manor of Werrington, hard by the Cornish border, and the tenants there were sent far westwards to buy salted fish at St Michael's Mount (near which was a fish market, already mentioned in this chapter), at Probus, near to the River Fal, at Bodinnick opposite Fowey and at Marhamchurch near the north Cornish coast.[48] In the 1390s the Dinham family bought fish at St Michael's Mount and paid for its carriage to their residence at Kingskerswell close to the South Devon coast, because some of their Cornish tenants refused to do the carrying.[49] In 1470 the Arundell family purchased a large quantity of fish from somewhere along the north Cornish coast, then had it carried overland to Penzance, then by sea to Lyme Regis in Dorset; its destination may have been the manor house of Mohun's Ottery quite close to Lyme, for an Arundell was staying there at the time, perhaps with kin.[50]

Besides these forays into Cornwall by Devon households there were westward reaches within Devon itself: for example, in 1451 the Dinham family, then residing at Nutwell on the very shore of the fishful

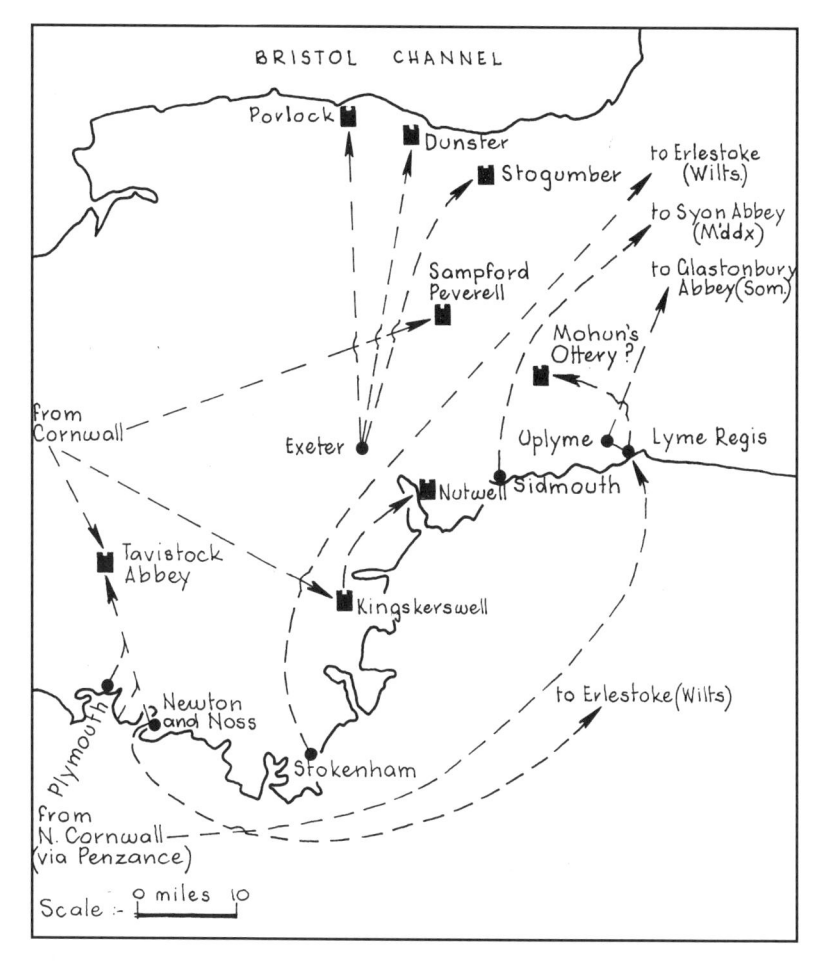

Figure 4.2 Transport of fish to aristocratic households and religious houses

Exe, bought fish at Kingskerswell, produce which had probably been caught in Tor Bay.[51] Somerset lords reached south-westwards to the great fish market at Exeter, from Dunster castle (buckhorn, 1429), from Porlock (ling and conger, 1469) and from Stogumber (herring, 1307).[52] Finally, there is record of a Wiltshire household purchasing fish to the value of 42s., probably at Newton Ferrers or Noss Mayo on the most westerly stretch of the South Devon coast.[53]

Table 4.1 Mileage of coasts and poll tax payers, 1377, by county

	Miles of coastline	Poll tax payers	Tax payers *per* mile of coast
Cornwall	320	34274	107
Devon	197	49250	250
Dorset	78	34241	439
Somerset	80	56075	700

Sources: N. D. and A. R. MacWhirter, *Dunlop Book of Facts* (1966), for lengths of coasts; R. B. Dobson, *The Peasants' Revolt* (1970), pp. 55-7 and M. Kowaleski, *Local Markets and Regional Trade in Medieval Exeter* (1995), p. 71 (poll tax).

An explanation for these purchasing patterns might be that fish was cheaper on the market the further west one went. Why might that have been? A tentative line of argument is introduced by the figures in Table 4.1. The lowest figure – Cornwall's, with fewest people per mile of coast – implies a county in which great quantities of fish could be caught (because of its long coastline) but in which consumption was relatively low (relatively few people per mile of coast). Dorset has a high figure because, although the county had almost exactly the same number of poll tax payers as did Cornwall, its coastline was of no great length, despite some prominent indentations. In Cornwall fish should have been doubly abundant – a long coast, relatively small consumption – and therefore cheap; in Devon fish should have been more expensive, in Somerset and Dorset more expensive still. These figures must of course be subject to many qualifications. Theoretically, with fewer people to fish a long coastline, the labour cost of fishing should have been high; however, as will be shown later in this monograph, many medieval fishers were fishing farmers and their families were without significant labour costs. Then again, the figures assume that all stretches of all coastlines are equally supplied with fish, which would not have been the case:

Consumption and Distribution 103

some stretches may have been frequented by costly fish, others by cheaper species, while some stretches of water were virtually inaccessible from the land (e.g. around Hartland Point in North Devon) although, of course, they could be reached by small craft from nearby landing places. Despite these problems with the figures, they are worth pondering in light of the indisputable westward reach for fish described above. Further work on prices would help to show whether or not these arguments are tenable.

[1] A. S. Littler, 'Fish in English economy and society down to the Reformation' (unpublished Ph.D. thesis, Swansea, 1979), Chapter 1.
[2] For this, see Section 4.4 below.
[3] I develop these themes briefly in 'Medieval urban development', in R. Kain and W. Ravenhill, eds, *Historical Atlas of South-West England* (1999), pp. 402-4; and I hope to return to them in more detail in a future volume in this series of 'Explorations'.
[4] *Ibid.*, p. 406. The figure is higher than in many other parts of England: C. Dyer, 'How urbanized was medieval England?' in J-M Duvosquel and E. Thoen, eds, *Peasants and Townsmen in Medieval Europe* (1995), pp. 173-4.
[5] Fox, 'Medieval urban development', p. 407; below, Section 6.3 for demand from the poor.
[6] Fox, 'Medieval rural industry', in Kain and Ravenhill, eds, *Historical Atlas*, p. 325.
[7] Above, Section 3.2.
[8] Below, n. 49.
[9] CRO, AR12/25.
[10] PRO, E36/223.
[11] A. Erskine, ed., *The Devonshire Lay Subsidy of 1332* (DCRS, new ser., 14, 1969), p. 118; *Cal. Inq. Misc.*, vol. 7, p. 334; C. L. Kingsford, ed., *The Stonor Letters and Papers* (2 vols, Camden Soc. 3rd ser., 29-30, 1919), vol. 1, p. 63.
[12] *O. E. D.*, s. v. fisher, 'a fishmonger'; Kowaleski, *LMRTE*, pp. 309, 314. For the fish market at Holsworthy see Somerset Record Office, DDWO/46/1, account of Whalesborough, 4-5 Hen. IV; for the jowter, Kingsford, ed., *Stonor Letters*, vol. 1, p. 64.
[13] Kowaleski, *LMRTE*, p. 313, n. 161. For inland urban fish stalls in Cornwall, see R. and O. B. Peter, *The Histories of Launceston and Dunheved* (1885), p. 93 and many subsequent references; CRO, AR2/1346, seventeenth-century survey of St Columb Major.
[14] M. Wilkinson, 'The fish remains', in M. Maltby, ed., *Faunal Studies on Urban Sites: the Animal Bones from Exeter* (1979), pp. 74-81.
[15] Huntington Library, San Marino, California, HAM box 64, Stokenham rental of '1577' (really about 1360). For the purveyance system, above Section 3.2; for more

104   *The Evolution of the Fishing Village*

detail on fishing on the shores of Stokenham manor, below Section 5.1.

[16] R. N. Worth, *Calendar of the Plymouth Municipal Records* (1893), p. 36; A. M. Jackson, 'Medieval Exeter, the Exe and the Earldom of Devon', *TDA* 104 (1972), p. 56; C. R. Straton, ed., *Survey of the Lands of William, First Earl of Pembroke* (2 vols, 1909), vol. 2, p. 388.

[17] A. Watkin, ed., *The Great Chartulary of Glastonbury* (3 vols, Som. Rec. Soc., 59, 63, 64, 1947-56), vol. 3, p. 582; Longleat House MSS, nos 11215, 11271, 11272, account rolls for the whole Glastonbury estate, early fourteenth century, for great detail about fish purchases at Lyme Regis.

[18] *Cat. Anc. Deeds*, vol. 6, p. 3. For salt imported at Appledore see B. H. Putnam, ed., *Proceedings before the Justices of the Peace in the Fourteenth and Fifteenth Centuries* (Ames Foundation, 1938), p. 67.

[19] A. Ballard and J. Tait, *British Borough Charters, 1216-1307* (1923), p. 293, referring to named rocks in the river.

[20] Domesday, 11/1. For convincing arguments which show that Otterton's market was at Sidmouth, see Kowaleski, 'Markets', p. 369. For a trade in fish here, see BL, Add. rolls 27288 and 27257, Sidmouth courts of 25 and 29 Edw. III; PRO, SC2 168/24, Sidmouth court near Exaltation of the Holy Cross, 7 Hen. VII, and subsequent courts.

[21] H. R. Watkin, *The History of Totnes Priory and Medieval Town* (3 vols, 1914-17), vol. 1, pp. 27-28, 35-6. For the fishery at Ashprington, *ibid.*, p. 3 and Domesday, 1/71.

[22] P. L. Hull, ed., *The Cartulary of St Michael's Mount* (DCRS, new ser., 5, 1962), pp. 1-2. For the location of the market and the name, *ibid.*, p. xix and n. 7 and O. J. Padel, *Cornish Place-Names* (1988), p. 115. For fish purchases in the vicinity during the Middle Ages, below n. 48 and n. 49.

[23] Kowaleski, 'Markets', p. 362 and *passim*; *eadem*, *LMRTE*, p. 57.

[24] G. Oliver, *Monasticon Dioecesis Exoniensis* (1846), p. 183; Cockington manorial accounts as above, Chapter 2, n. 72.

[25] Kowaleski, *LMRTE*, p. 309 for the illegal selling of fish on the Haldon Hills: this reference confirms that fishers from South Devon used a routeway over the Hills and through the borough of Kennford which is aligned upon it.

[26] *Ibid.*, p. 313, n. 161 (fish dealers) and p. 309 (mackerel).

[27] *Ibid.*, p. 317 (Sidmouth man at Kennford) and p. 267 (wine).

[28] The market charter dates from 1300 (*Cal. Charter Rolls*, vol. 2, *1257-1300*, p. 488) and this may possibly, but not necessarily, date the borough. There is a rather skimpy and late rental for Kennford in PRO SC12 6/61. The excellent little sketch given in M. Beresford, *New Towns of the Middle Ages* (1967), p. 422 is correct apart from its 1340 reference.

[29] For Stokenham, see above Section 3.2, above this section and below Section 5.1. The first mention of the borough of Chillington is in an inquisition *post mortem* of 1309 (PRO, C134 16/9) but this document simply gives the total rental value and the value of the pleas of court, without much detail. Subsequent documents show that the total rental remained more or less the same at around 62*s*. into the sixteenth century: PRO, SC 11/765; Huntington Library, HAM box 64, rental of '1577'; *ibid.*, box 74, accounts

of 1506-7 and 1538-9. At 1s. for each burgage (a rate known from other boroughs but not necessarily applicable to Chillington) this would give 62 property plots.

[30] This was the straightest route, through Moreleigh and over Gara Bridge. The former was a minute borough, not in M. W. Beresford and H. P. R. Finberg, *English Medieval Boroughs: a Handlist* (1973) but indisputably burghal: DRO, 1962B/W/M/3, sixteenth-century court rolls which distinguish manor from borough. For Gara Bridge see C. Henderson and E. Jervoise, *Old Devon Bridges* (1938), p. 27 and plate 8 which makes clear that this was a medieval bridge. Medieval borough and bridge thus help to define this routeway.

[31] See *Cal. Inq. Misc.*, vol. 7, p. 331 for a smith of Chillington with two furnaces.

[32] Kowaleski, 'Markets', p. 361; T. Risdon, *The Chorographical Description or Survey of the County of Devon* (1811), p. 174.

[33] Above Section 2.1.

[34] Worth, *Calendar*, p. 36. The first reference to the borough of Sutton is in 1275: Beresford and Finberg, *English Medieval Boroughs*, p. 98.

[35] Worth, *Calendar*, p. 37; *Cal. Inq. Misc.*, vol. 4, p. 148.

[36] *Ibid.*; DRO, W1258M/D/74/6, Plymstock account of 1-2 Hen. V for purchases at Stonehouse; *ibid.*, account of 20-1 Hen. VI for fish purchased at Stoke Damarel. See Kowaleski, *LMRTE*, p. 72 for other fish markets in the Plymouth vicinity.

[37] Kowaleski, 'Markets', p. 362; *Rotuli Hundredorum*, vol. 1, p. 90; H. R. Watkin, *Dartmouth*, vol. 1, *Pre-Reformation* (1935), p. 196.

[38] PRO, SC6 830/5 and 6, Sidmouth accounts of 8-9 and 21-2 Edw. IV (and other accounts in this series); ECA, DC 5033, Dawlish account of 17-18 Hen. VI which includes details of E. Teignmouth.

[39] DRO, 902M/Stoke Fleming medieval court rolls; Kowaleski, *LMRTE*, p. 308; DRO, 123M/E/31; PRO, E134 5 Jas. I/Mich. 1, depositions in an equity case concerning wasteland in Sidbury.

[40] Kowaleski, *LMRTE*, pp. 284, 309-10 for points of departure of this trade; p. 312, n. 155 for fines.

[41] *Ibid.*, pp. 317-8.

[42] Kowaleski, *LMRTE*, pp. 311, 318; *eadem*, 'The expansion of the south-western fisheries in late medieval England', *Ec. Hist. Rev.*, 2nd. ser., 53 (2000), p. 434 for a great increase in the number of coastal places sending fish to Exeter by the 1460s.

[43] Kowaleski, *LMRTE*, pp. 66-7, 311.

[44] Kowaleski, *LMRTE*, p. 315 (Okehampton and Winkleigh), p. 313, n. 161 (E. Devon towns).

[45] *Ibid.*, pp. 313, 318.

[46] Above, Sections 3.2 and 4.2; PRO, C134/16; PRO, SC2 168/24, Sidmouth court of March, 22 Hen. VII and other courts in this series.

[47] CRO, AR2/727/1, printed in C. M. Woolgar, ed., *Household Accounts from Medieval England* (2 pts, British Academy Records of Social and Economic History, new ser., 17-18, 1992-3), pt. 2, pp. 489-95, at p. 492.

[48] DRO, W1258M/D/74/6, Plymstock accounts from the reigns of Richard II, Henry

V and VI and Edward IV (end of fourteenth century and much of the fifteenth). These indicate purchases of 'fish', salt, 'dried and fresh fish' and 'fresh salt [= sea-water] fish' at Plymouth, Noss Mayo, Stonehouse, Newton Ferrers, Stoke Damarel and possibly Oreston. For the journeys of the Werrington tenants, see H. P. R. Finberg, *Tavistock Abbey: a Study in the Social and Economic History of Devon* (1951), pp. 82-3.

[49] CRO, AR2/481, account of Gurlyn, 18-19 Ric. II.

[50] CRO, AR2/917, receiver's account of the Arundell estate, 10-11 Edw. IV. The same account mentions Katherine Arundell at Mohun's Ottery.

[51] CRO, AR2/568.

[52] H. C. Maxwell Lyte, *A History of Dunster* (2 vols, 1909), vol. 2, p. 111; C. E. H. Chadwyck Healey, *The History of Part of West Somerset* (1901), pp. 495-6; *VCH Somerset*, vol. 5, p. 184.

[53] PRO, SC6 830/29, Yealmpton account of 19-20 Ric. II. The fish were then taken to Plymouth (by land?), then shipped in the *Katerine* to Warblington on the Hampshire coast; their final destination was almost certainly Erlestoke in Wiltshire.

1. Coombe Cellars and the River Teign, watercolour by John Swete, 1795.

2. Sidmouth beach, watercolour by John Swete, 1795, showing what the artist described as 'poles for fixing nets to take fish'.

3. Beer, East Devon, a fishing place with no protection in the form of any creek or quay, drawing of 1807, unsigned.

4. Warfleet, Dartmouth, watercolour by John Swete, 1800, showing a thatched cellar, a cottage and possibly ruins of cellars.

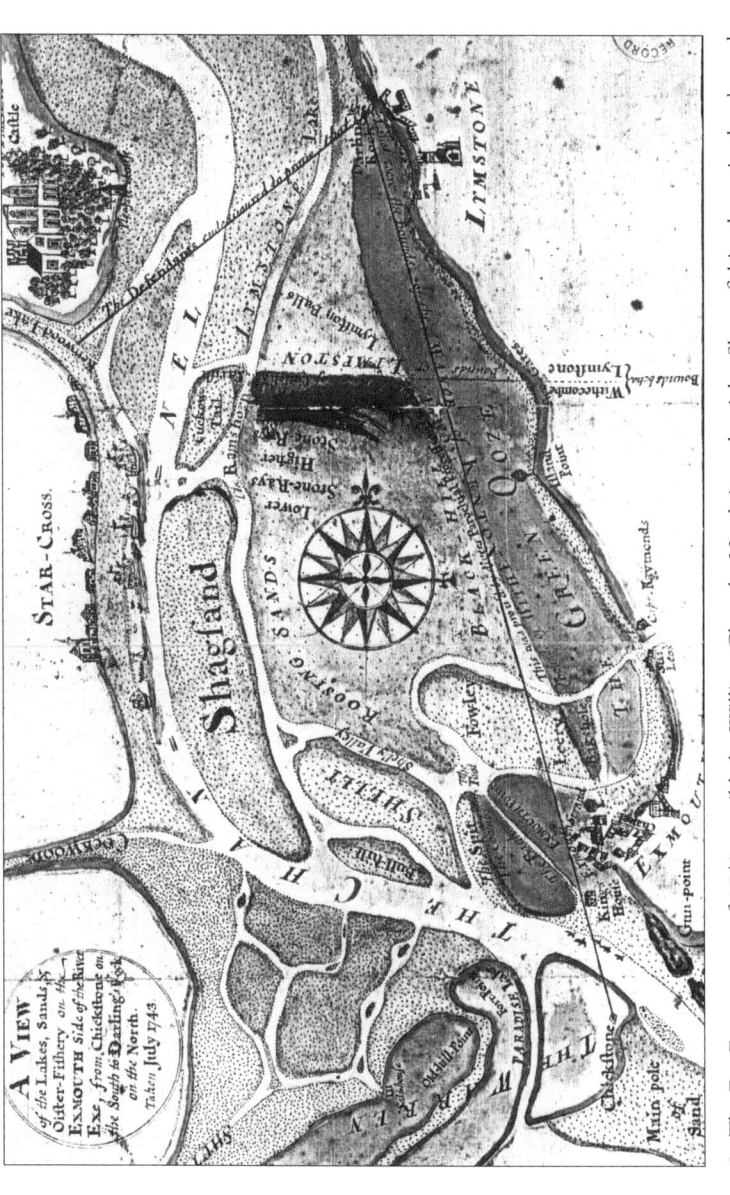

5. The Exe Estuary, map of 1743, possibly by William Chapple. North is to the right. Shows fishing boats in the channel of the Exe, near Exmouth, and several coastal settlements, including Lympstone Strand and Starcross.

6. Barrepta, Carbis Bay, Cornwall, drawing by E. W. Cooke, 1848, showing cellars, boats and capstans – and an ingenious way of protecting boats from storms.

7. (*Above*) Part of a tithe account for the parish of Woodbury, Easter 1432 to Easter 1433. The marginal heading reads 'Tithes of fish and labourers', and the third line from the foot begins *ii s xi d de Willelmo Westecote pro decima pisc* ('2s. 11d. from William Westecote for tithe of fish').

8. (*Right*) Coombe Cellars and the River Teign, photograph of around 1900: a rebuilt inn and the remains of one cottage, possibly that painted by Swete in 1795.

9. Lympstone and the Exe Estuary, watercolour by John Swete, around 1799, showing cellars and a lime kiln on the beach, and inhabited cottages, with chimneys, behind.

10. Minehead, Somerset, watercolour of around 1800, unsigned, showing a net fixed on stakes.

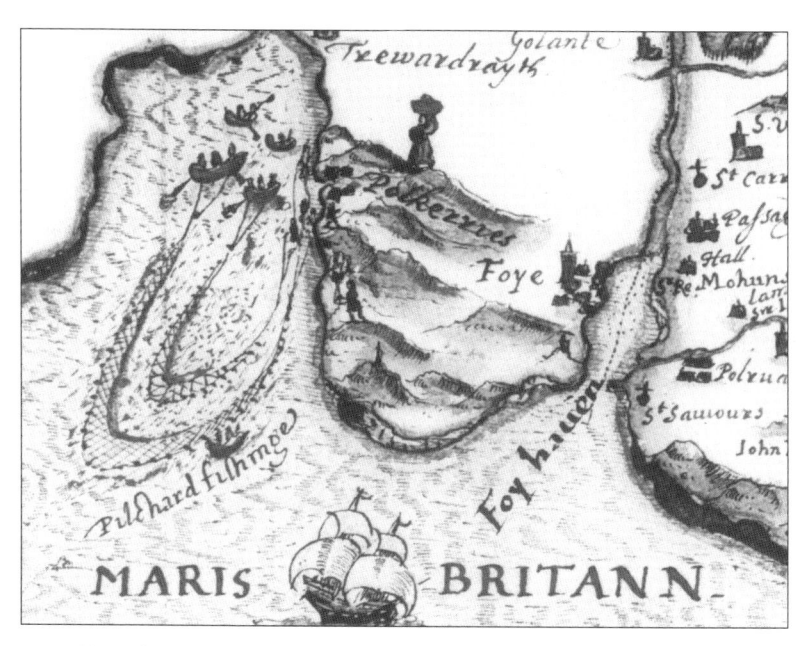

11. Pilchard fishing in St Austell Bay, map of the late sixteenth century by John Norden, showing a seine, a huer (watcher) on the shore and a female fish carrier with a basket on her head.

12. Torcross, watercolour by John Swete, 1793, showing the site of the village on a beach with Start Bay to the left and Slapton Ley on the right.

13. The Exe Estuary, from a map of landing places and defences of around 1540, showing, among other things, Torquay, Cockwood, Powderham Castle, Exeter, Lympstone, Exmouth and Ottermouth.

14. Hooe manor house and fishing village, drawing by Edmund Spoure, 1694, showing crenellated inner and outer courtyards to the house and two types of quay at the village.

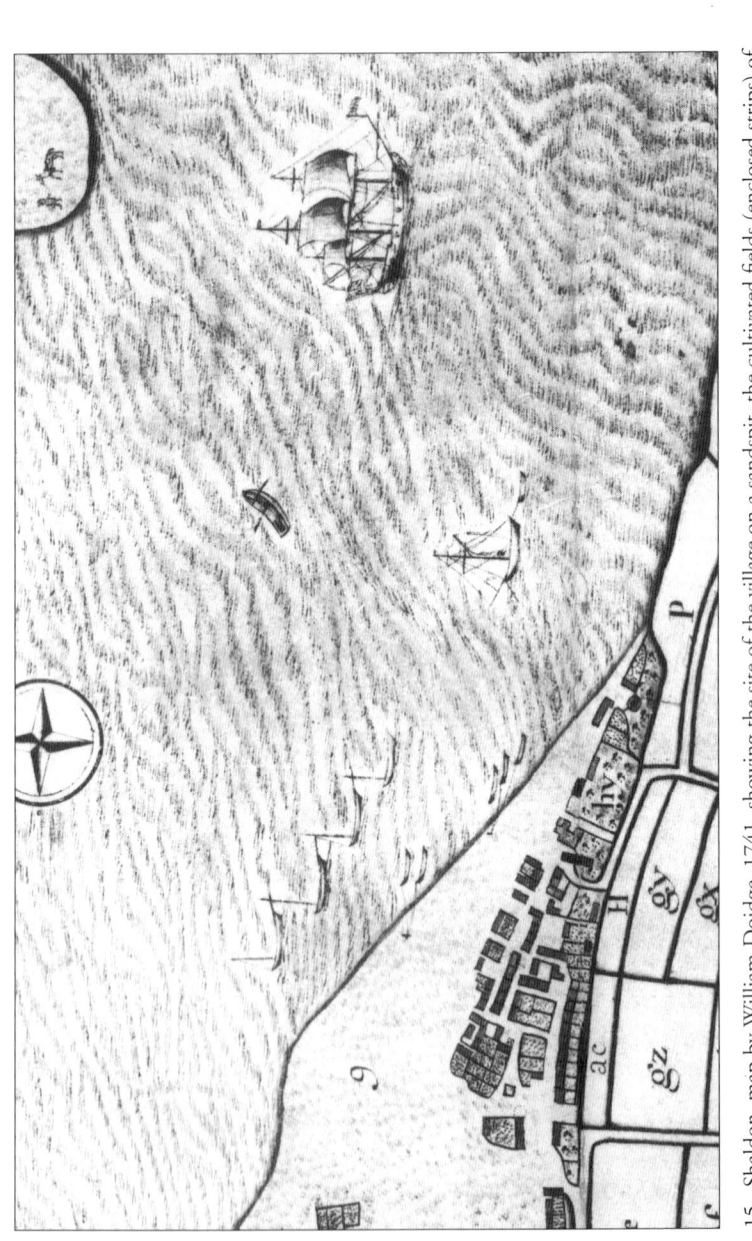

15. Shaldon, map by William Doidge, 1741, showing the site of the village on a sandspit, the cultivated fields (enclosed strips) of Ringmore manor behind, the ferry to Teignmouth and a traveller on the opposite shore.

Chapter Five

FISHING FARMERS AND CELLAR SETTLEMENTS

5.1 Fishing farmers

This chapter deals with the lives of the people who caught fish and who exploited the many resources of the foreshore and with the cellar settlements from which these activities were traditionally directed, sources being drawn largely from the fourteenth, fifteenth and sixteenth centuries. Here we concentrate upon a phase during which fishing on rural manors was largely a by-employment among farmers, the transition to fishing as a single occupation and to the permanently occupied fishing village being discussed in the following chapter.

It is not easy to reconstruct these lives. For many coastal manors there are medieval references to fisheries but usually the sources are not good enough to bring the participants to life or do so only fleetingly and in small numbers. But for three places – Woodbury, Kenton and Stokenham – survival of rare types of source material allows us to meet groups of fishers face to face at last. We begin by dealing with each of these three places in turn.

5.1.i The Woodbury tithe payments
Discovery of the names of those who fished, in the medieval tithe accounts of Woodbury, was a true moment of excitement in the long searching for the evidence on which this monograph is based.[1] The tithes of Woodbury, a parish on the eastern shore of the Exe, were given to the Vicars Choral of Exeter Cathedral in 1205. The Vicars, rarely rich,[2] were ferocious tithers. Very little escaped them. Through their proctor they took their tenth of almost everything: of pears, fish, wax,

honey, hemp and of the more usual items of farm produce and, moreover, much of this was written down in yearly account rolls.

So rare is this type of source material that it is worth describing the account for a single year, that beginning at Easter 1423 and ending at Easter 1424.[3] The account starts with income from rents of the glebe which belonged, with the tithes, to the Vicars. Then comes income from the sale of corn sheaves, hay and lambs taken as tithe (a disappointing section because the names of those who paid are not given). There follows a section headed 'Whitemeats', i.e. dairy produce, also without names. The next section, for wool, is also disappointing in this respect but it is of interest in telling us that the whole of the wool tithe of the parish (worth 66s. 4d.) was sold to Cecilia Yernewey and Joan Hoppyng and two others, who may well have been engaged in putting out wool to female spinners. But then the long and fascinating lists of names begin, for the small and personal tithes, lists of those who paid on geese, calves, piglets, honey, fruit, etc.; and lists of those who paid on the profit of their craft (*ars*) and on the profit from fishing. Other income for the Vicars in 1423-4 came from sale of mortuary beasts from three parishioners who, having been vigilantly tithed for all of their working lives, made their final sacrifice by offering up their second-best beast to the church. All of this amounted to income in cash for the Vicars who either sold off, often in bulk, the farm produce which had been collected or sold the item back to its donor (as in the case of calves for example – simply a paper transaction, the tenth calf having been valued and its value charged to the donor). The expenses of the Vicars, as they are recorded in these accounts generally, include many interesting items connected with their responsibility to provide pastoral care (e.g. stipends of priests, gifts to the poor and expenses around St Swithin's day, the date of the parish feast); the cost of repairs to the priest's house (and to the chancel of the church in some years); and the costs of tithe collection. After these expenses had been taken into account, remaining income went to the Vicars Choral.

The Vicars did not let much pass them by in their parish of Woodbury. For example, a 'stranger woman' died in the parish in 1440, presumably a vagrant on the road; clearly she would have had no animal to be taken as a mortuary payment but she was carrying a pot, so the Vicars took that. Then again, in 1424 and later there was a purge against some parishioners who were evading payment of their tithes in full, especially one John Scorche who was excommunicated and, eventually, prosecuted in the Court of Arches in London.[4] Of course, other parishioners may have avoided making some payments from time to time but internal inspection of the documents and the inclusion among tithe payers even of transients, outsiders and labourers (who paid personal tithes) give much confidence in the source material. In any one year a single individual may be named several times, for example as renting a close of the glebe, being paid by the Vicars for help with the tithe sheaves at harvest time, paying out for tithes of farm produce of various kinds and, if a fisher, being tithed on that craft.

In the following analysis of these tithe accounts we shall first look at aspects of farming in medieval Woodbury and then move on to fit fishing into the picture. The earliest surviving account is from the first decade of the fifteenth century, the latest medieval one is for 1507 and the best run, on which the following is based, is between 1423 and 1435, with some gaps.[5] Given much time and patience, all of the tithe payers of Woodbury could be profiled and put on a scale according to the range and value of their payments. I have not made such an analysis but hope that someone locally may do so in the future. Instead, I shall select some sample names, beginning with Thomas Huntbear who was one of the most substantial farmers in the parish. We know that he had a herd of over ten cows because almost every year the Vicars Choral took a calf from him (i.e. he had at least ten cows producing at least ten calves) rather than levying a sum of money known as 'calf tithe', paid by people with fewer than ten. Surprisingly he was rarely tithed on dairy produce which may possibly suggest that he was principally a beef producer, in which case his herd could have contained at least ten cows, ten calves, ten yearlings, ten two-year-olds and ten three-year olds (say about 40 beasts in all if we deduct those which were culled or which died). His livestock also included pigs, horses and sheep. His farm was probably at the place marked on the 1-inch map as Houndbeare.[6] If his livestock management here was similar to that of other places in the locality in the fifteenth century, the cows would have been kept in enclosed fields around the farmstead, the sheep and younger beasts being allowed to roam on the commons which were very extensive in this parish.[7] Also around the farmhouse, no doubt, were Thomas's orchards planted with apple and pear, while the hives producing the honey and wax on which he was tithed could have been kept near the small woods on the slopes above the farmhouse or on the commons if they were as bright with heather and gorse as they are today. As explained above, we have no details about the tithes of sheaves of individual Woodbury farmers because the accountant valued the tithe corn of the parish *en bloc*. In years when he chose to specify the different crops, these were dominated by oats with lesser amounts of wheat, rye, barley, peas and beans. Thomas Huntbear, with a large farm, would probably have grown all of these. In a survey of the manor of Woodbury made in 1525 one of the largest farms contained 68 enclosed acres and had rights of grazing for 20 beasts and 40 sheep on the commons.[8] Thomas, 100 years earlier, could well have occupied a farm of this type.

The sense of bucolic abundance which emerges from details of tithe payments at Houndbeare does not apply to all of the parishioners. At the other end of the scale of land-holding was a man such as Richard Bond, contrasting with Huntbear in the very number of his entries in the tithe accounts. He owned cows which in some years gave birth to calves but his herd was not large because he always paid in 'calf tithe' (in pence) rather than on the full price of one animal, a type of payment restricted to those with over ten calves. When he died his mortuary payment to the church was indeed a cow, this being his second-best beast, the best having gone to his temporal lord perhaps in the form of another cow, an ox or a horse. He paid tithe on dairy produce but not on many other items, which suggests a smaller, less productive farm. We may call him a smallholder, perhaps occupying one of the 15-acre holdings recorded later in the survey of 1525.

Among those with agricultural occupations in medieval Woodbury, a final group comprised workers with no land at all. One individual who paid tithe on his labour fairly regularly from 1432 into the late 1440s was Robert Colier, his yearly tithe payment declining steadily over this period perhaps because his wages were falling as he approached old age. Another, a little earlier, was Henry Jacob who was regularly tithed on his labour but who also occasionally paid on produce, as in 1434 when he contributed 4*d.* on his wool, one-tenth of the value of the fleeces of about ten sheep which could well have run on the commons. These two men were long-term resident labourers in the parish and almost certainly occupied cottages with little or no agricultural land. In contrast to the settled labourers was John Mape who paid tithe on his labour in only one year (1432) and who bore a surname which was not associated with any of the farming families in the parish. These two small clues – his transience and his alien name – suggest that he was a young immigrant servant in husbandry, arriving in the parish for a year's living-in service and then leaving for a term elsewhere, as was common practice in the Middle Ages.[9] Another of this type is recorded in the account for 1432 under the simple name of 'Phillipus', because the accountant either did not know his name or failed to record it as Philip had no family in the parish.

The men who have been described above – from stout Thomas Huntbear to young John Mape – have been selected because their tithe-paying profiles are especially clear-cut. As it happens, none of them fished. But many of Woodbury's parishioners certainly did fish: of about 300 people recorded as paying tithe between 1423 and 1435, about 55 appear as paying for their fishing. Who were the fishers? Two of the types of men discussed above did not pay tithe on fish: farm servants (who may well have assisted their masters at the nets but who would not have paid fish tithe) and large farmers as exemplified above by Thomas Huntbear. Huntbear never fished, nor did any of the other large farmers like John German, an important grazier-butcher. Those who paid tithe on fishing tended to be in the smallholder or smallholder-craftsmen class. Such was Richard Maister who fished in many years, who was sometimes engaged in dairying and pig-keeping but who did not pay tithe on the great range of produce which we associate with the large farmers of the parish. Quite similar was John Martin, frequently a fisher, owner of a small herd of cows and once tithed on an unspecified craft other than fishing, perhaps labouring – clearly a man with diverse sources of income. Such families would have had spare time in which to fish and no doubt needed the profits from fishing in order to augment incomes. Finally, among the fishers were a few who were the sons of farmers (sons of fishing farmers in some cases), who probably undertook fishing before they entered land; and a few outsiders, people not of the parish apparently, but who occasionally used Woodbury shores for fishing. We shall also encounter outsiders fishing in our next detailed study, of the manor of Kenton.

Were the majority of the people who fished in the parish of Woodbury fishers first and foremost, who practised farming on the side? Or were they the fishing farmers of the title of this chapter, farmers who fished occasionally in order to supplement diet and income? This question may best be answered through an examination of the value of catches, details of which are presented in Table 5.1. The table shows all individual payments of tithe recorded in surviving accounts between 1423 and 1435, so that a person who was tithed, say, in four years over this period enters the right hand column four times. What is quite clear from the figures is that the majority of those who fished did so on a relatively small scale, their contribution to the fish trade lying not in the size of their individual endeavours but in the large number of people involved. For example, John Martin, a fishing smallholder (see above),

Table 5.1 Value of payments of tithes on fishing at Woodbury, 1423-35

Value of tithe payment	Number of tithe payments
Under 11d.	19
1s. – 2s. 11d.	45
3s. – 4s. 11d.	18
5s. – 6s. 11d.	8
7s. – 8s. 11d.	2
9s. – 10s. 11d.	4
11s. – 12s. 11d.	1
13s. – 14s. 11d.	2
15s. – 16s. 11d.	2
17s. and over	2

Source: ECA, VC 3357, 8, 9, 60, 1, 2, 3, 4, 3354.

fished frequently but was never tithed on more than 1s. 11d., his average yearly tithe payment as a fisher being 1s. 2d. If these payments represent one-tenth of the value of catches (the obvious interpretation), then the average yearly value of John Martin's catch was 11s. 8d. He owned, probably, four cows, dairy produce from which might have been valued at about 10s.; if, for the sake of argument, we say that this smallholder had 4 acres under crops, and that these acres were used largely for oats, with some wheat (as the tithe accounts reveal for Woodbury parish at large), then the total value of his crops would have been of the order of 12s. at the least. These are necessarily crude calculations, because they do not take into account the family's consumption of farm produce, nor of fish. But they do place John Martin's fishing in perspective. A relatively large tithe payment for fishing, of 6s. 8d., was handed over in 1433 by Richard Maister, another smallholder whose farming activities are described above. The entry reads 'Richard Maister and his wife for the art of fishing', a nice example of a family team at work. The payment represents a catch value of over 60s. and it is probable that in this year the profits from his fishing were greater than profits from his farming. But this tithe payment is of exceptional size for a single family: a good number of the larger payments recorded in the table are from teams of fishers as for example when Richard Maister 'with five associates' (*cum v sociis*) paid 13s. in 1434. This represents only 2s. 2d. for each person if we assume equal shares. As historians, though, we cannot really divide the spoils in this way because equal shares are not stated and because on many occasions the number of 'associates' is not given. The important fact is that what at first sight appears in the table to be a group of people who did very well out of fishing, with large tithe payments, is an illusion (the group is, in any case, a small one, with 13 payments above 7s. as compared to 90 below that sum). The contribution made by the fishery at Woodbury to the fish trade, the great fish market at Exeter being only 6 miles away, lay in the large number of small catches rather than in any complex capitalistic venture; the same may be said of some of the fishing farmers of Dawlish manor in the fifteenth century, for whom we have tithe payments for one year only – all of them earned far less than a labourer's wage from their fishing and some as little as 6s. 8d.[10]

Rich sources though they are, the tithe accounts for Woodbury contain little information on fishing other than the tithe payments on catches. We can just discern partnerships when two apparently unrelated men pay on a single catch and we can see teams of unnamed 'associates', the largest being a group of six. Behind these arrangements, we can guess, lay the sharing of the costs of nets and boats, for in the era of fishing farmers it was quite normal in coastal parishes for people who were essentially farmers to own boats, or shares in them, as shown for example by documents from Stokenham and East Budleigh.[11] We can also discern sons who first fished with their fathers, then took over from them, perhaps when they inherited nets and boats, or shares in them. The stage was therefore set for the emergence of fishing as a separate occupation but by the 1420s and 1430s that development had not yet taken place, most of those who fished in the parish being farmers also.

The settlement pattern of the manor of Woodbury, as it may be partially reconstructed from a survey of 1525, reinforces this last conclusion: it was one of inland farmers with no permanent dwellings on the shoreline.[12] Woodbury was among those Devon parishes with a large nucleated village, Woodbury itself, at its centre. There were also hamlets such as Exton and Ebford, with eight and six farm holdings respectively according to the survey of 1525, and isolated farms such as Postlake and Heathfield, most of them mentioned in medieval documents. As is usual in Devon parishes, none of these settlements lay on the shoreline, those closest to the coast being typically a little less than half a mile away (Exton and Ebford); Nutwell, which gave its name to a separate manor in the parish, was also set back from the shore. The lists of people who paid tithe on fish do not give details of residence but by chance we can pin-point a few of them. For example, John Scorche – the reluctant tithe payer mentioned above, who sometimes fished – is said to have lived at Hogsbrook Farm, 3 miles from the Exe and well away from ecclesiastical authority at Woodbury village; a fishing farmer called John Westcote lived either at Pilehayes or at Postlake, 2 and 1½ miles respectively from the shore; John Ley, probably a fishing farmer according to the records, is once described as 'of Salterton', a place which, despite its name, was 2 miles from the shore.[13]

The many fishing farmers of Woodbury parish must have had some arrangements for storing nets and boats by the side of the Exe. A single obscure reference from 1495 mentions a 'fish house' or 'fishing house' here, probably a storehouse of some kind. A detailed survey of 1566 for the manor of Nutwell (in Woodbury parish) describes structures called cellars 'lying next the sea shore'; we would expect others for that part of the shoreline which belonged to the manor of Woodbury itself, but the survey of 1525 is not detailed enough to mention them.[14] For better details of patterns of inland residences of farming fishers and the shoreline storage places which they rented, and of the linked occupations of farming and fishing, we look across the wide Exe from the parish of Woodbury to Kenton on the opposite shore.

5.1.ii The Kenton cellar rents

Today the parish of Kenton wears less of a maritime air than would have been the case in the past, because the proud embankment of the South Devon Railway (1845-6), running along the shore of the River Exe, in places completely obscures views of the river. Moreover, the parish once had watery northern and southern boundaries along the shores of two relatively large creeks (the *Sod* and *South Brook*), drained in the early eighteenth century and early nineteenth century respectively.[15]

The manor had a turbulent history of ownership during the Middle Ages, belonging to a succession of tenants-in-chief of the Crown and, in between, to the Crown itself. This means that there is no single consolidated medieval archive although there are, scattered about in time, inquisitions *post mortem* and account rolls in the Public Record Office. The post-medieval documentation is excellent, with many rentals and surveys (the earliest of 1578) and court rolls, all arranged and conserved first by William Chapple, an eighteenth-century steward of antiquarian inclination, and more recently by the Devon Record Office.[16]

That Kenton's fishery was an important one is shown by the fact that when Bishop Bronescombe settled ecclesiastical income from the parish in 1270 he made sure that the tithes of the fishery did not go to the vicar.[17] The first mention of a fishery in manorial documents is in 1297 and from then on there are numerous references to it. Described as 'of Exmouth' (i.e. the Exe Estuary) or 'of the sea', the fishery probably took in much of the river (over which lords of Kenton claimed extensive rights) and also the sea 'as far as a man may see a humber barrel'. The sum paid to the lord for the fishery remained at 4s. between 1297 and 1578.[18] Kenton people often showed a sturdy independence (like other inhabitants of ancient demesnes of the Crown) as, for example, when they paid a large sum in 1204 to farm the whole manor for themselves.[19] They may therefore have been able to resist any increase in the payment which they made for their fishery In the fifteenth century a clever lord or administrator perceived that, besides the fishers in the deep estuary, others were exploiting closer waters, perhaps those of the two creeks which formed the northern and southern boundaries of the manor. The owners of nine boats used for 'dragging and taking oysters and mussels' were to pay 6d. each and 4s. was raised from boats netting salmon. Further out, on a stretch of sandbank and mud called *Foghely*, a payment was made in 1297 for permission to 'fix up nets', almost certainly a reference to the stakes of a fixed or haking net, as described in Chapter 3. Salt, to preserve the products of the fisheries, was imported by Kenton people in 1321.[20]

Medieval sources refer to other estuarine occupations on the manor of Kenton. One was ferrying people across the Exe, for Kenton had a ferry which was a rival to the one operating from *Pratteshide* on the opposite shore. As early as 1297 lords were receiving 26s. 8d. from the farm (lease) of the ferry and this payment too remained fixed. Lords repaired the ferry as, for example, when extensive repairs and a new anchor cost them over 9s. in 1423, perhaps an unlucky and stormy year, for this sum was around one-third of their profit from the farm. Later documents confirm these arrangements: the lord provided 'a lawful boat ... with rope, anchor and two oars', which he then passed over to the lessee who made as much profit as he could from the tolls (practices similar to those on other South Devon ferries).[21] If the charge for one journey was 1d., as it certainly was for the passage over one South Devon estuary in the Middle Ages,[22] the ferry would have broken even after

Fishing Farmers and Cellar Settlements

carrying about 300 people, so that the lease was very valuable to the operator; Kenton was on a well-used routeway, for to cross the Exe here saved the traveller a journey of over 15 miles up to the bridge at Exeter and back again. Here, then, were many opportunities for employment – for the lessee, his oarsmen and assistants and people who provided victuals for travellers. Just offshore from Kenton, certainly in the seventeenth century (as shown by the *Coasting Pilot* and other maps) and probably earlier, the main channel of the Exe swept westwards and came close to the shore of the manor. Here, in the seventeenth century, Celia Fiennes saw 'the great ships ride' waiting for the tides to take them upstream to the port of Topsham.[23] At this time some landings of cargoes took place on the shores of the manor: in 1598 it was claimed that lords of Kenton could take 4*d.* from ships at anchor in the channel and could charge for the landing of salt for the fishery.[24] The same practices are to be found in the Middle Ages: one of the very earliest records of the city of Exeter's port customs, enrolled on the mayor's court rolls for 1288, records that 9 tuns of wine had been unloaded 'against the statute' at *Colepole* (almost certainly a place on Kenton shores). Later, more successfully, the city profited from occasional licences issued for landings, especially for ships heavily laden with wine, at the same place, against their statute which insisted that Topsham was the only official unloading port.[25] Here were further shoreline occupations for Kenton people.

The gathering of 'water rushes' is mentioned in a financial account for 1423; perhaps they were used in roofing. The seventeenth-century records of Kenton's special 'water court', and other documents, refer to the gathering of sand, mud ('oze') and seaweed and to the nurture of oysters by 'tenants or poor inhabitants'.[26] Domesday Book records salt making, perhaps in the two creeks – eight salt workers rendering the large sum of 20*s.*[27] This occupation may have lingered on into the twelfth century but in the thirteenth century there are no references to it. It is highly unlikely that lords who were gaining 20*s.* from the industry in 1086 would have forsaken these payments later, so lack of thirteenth-century references to it must be taken at their face value, revealing the demise of salt making as happened elsewhere along the South Devon coast at this time. As at a few other places there was a modest revival in the vicinity of Kenton in the early eighteenth century.[28]

Who were the people engaged in these shoreline activities? We have no listings of those who fished (like the lists for Woodbury) so we are forced to proceed by inference through analysis of the pattern of settlement sites recorded in surveys. Very detailed surveys of 1578 and 1598 give the location (by place-name) of every built structure on the manor, down to the last cottage, barn and stable; the latter even gives the number of bays in each building.[29] There is another useful list of settlements in the form of a schedule of places at which rents were collected in 1423, almost certainly the result of a journey around the manor by the reeve or another official, because the places are listed in their true geographical order.[30] Excellent eighteenth-century maps help in the location of settlements.[31]

Both of the sixteenth-century surveys and the list of 1423 are emphatic in placing no habitations near the foreshore. Of the three documents, that of 1578 is the most detailed and has been used to make a reconstruction of the manor's pattern of settlement as it was at that time (Fig. 5.1); there is no evidence to suggest that the pattern was radically different in the Middle Ages. The settlement pattern of Kenton manor was similar to that of Woodbury on the opposite shore of the Exe, with isolated farms, many hamlets (e.g. Venbridge with three farms in 1578, Southbeare with two farms and a cottage) and one straggling village, Kenton itself. All of these settlements were true agricultural places with farmsteads, their own field systems, their own commons and, in some cases, a complement of agricultural labourers living in cottages of one bay. Many were in rolling red countryside well inland.[32] Kenton, Southbrook and Staplake were the three agricultural settlements nearest to the waters but they can hardly be described as shoreline places, all being just above the 25-foot contour.

We know that fishing and other shoreline activities were practised by the people of Kenton manor in the Middle Ages, yet the manor had then no coastal cottages or farmhouses, nothing which could be described

---

Figure 5.1 Kenton manor: cellars and settlements

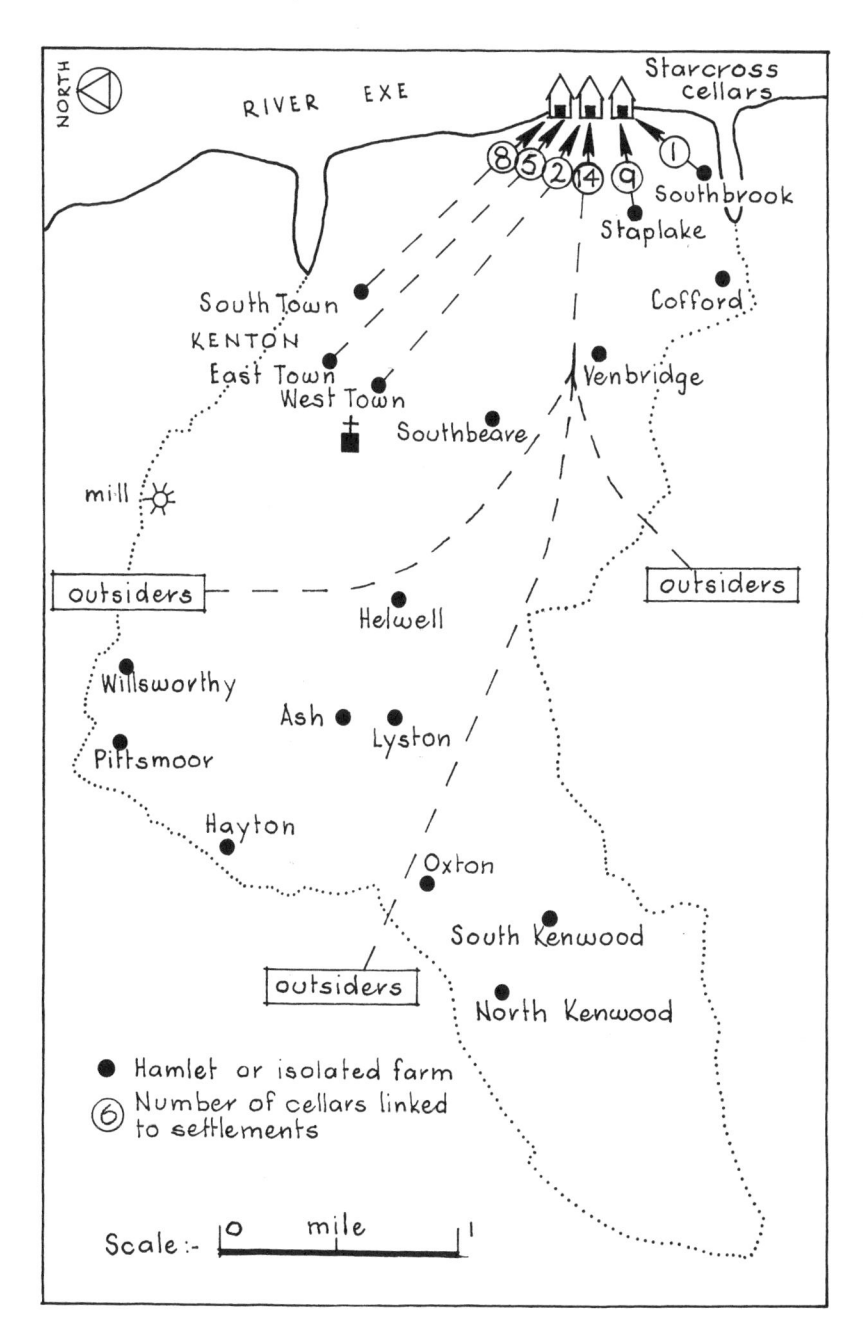

Fishing Farmers and Cellar Settlements

as an inhabited fishing village. The survey of 1578 provides the answer to this apparent contradiction, for it systematically lists just over fifty cellars (storage huts) at Starcross on the manor's eastern shore.[33] It was the usual neat Devonshire solution of inland residences and cellars on the strand from which shoreline occupations were followed – a late survival (for by this time many cellar settlements had become inhabited coastal fishing villages), but a fortunate one because it takes the cellar settlement into an era when detailed and explicit manorial surveys are available.

Fig. 5.1 is based on a linking of names of occupiers of cellars on the shore with names of occupiers of habitations inland, and shows which of the inland settlements were the homes of men and women who also rented a cellar at Starcross. In general, settlements nearest to Starcross (though a good mile away in some cases) provided most of the lessees of cellars. The reason may have to do less with nearness and more to do with the fact there was a tendency for the size of farm holdings in settlements near to the river to be relatively small, while those further inland were larger.

Table 5.2 explores the size of farm holdings belonging to people who were also involved with shoreline activities (by dint of their occupation of cellars). The results are very interesting and are similar to

Table 5.2 Kenton manor: size of farm holdings and occupation of cellars at Starcross, 1578

1½ – 10 acres	27%	of holdings have cellars attached
11 – 20 acres	27%	"
21 – 30 acres	20%	"
31 – 40 acres	8%	"
Over 40 acres	6%	"

Source: DRO, 1508M/Lon./manor/Kenton/6.

findings from Woodbury. Occupiers of holdings in the two lowest size bands comprise a good number of the cellar owners, while those in the two highest size bands were less likely to have been cellar owners. Two typical cellar owners were Richard Allerton who held a house in Kenton village and about 14 acres of land and Richard Melberry with a house in Staplake, 16 acres and two small parcels of unspecified size. Many holdings on the manor were of 32 acres or thereabouts (sometimes with small additions of leased demesne); in this group there were 29 occupiers without cellars but only three cellar owners. The cellar owner with the largest farm holding was Thomas Lux, who had engrossed two holdings, bringing his total acreage up to 59, but he was exceptional. He came from a family which provided one of that number of Kenton men who were ships' masters as well as farmers, a class frequently found in rural parishes close to great ports.[34] As in Woodbury, the really substantial farmers – such as John Thorn with 128 acres – were not involved in the activities of the foreshore and did not occupy cellars. Fishing and other estuarine activities were the province, as by-employments, of people who tended to be in the smallholder class.

There were some completely landless cottage labourers on the manor renting a cottage and no farm land, but these were not generally among the occupiers of cellars; of people with cellars the three smallest landholders were Maurice Danyell and William Randall with 1½ and 2 acres and Nicholas Hilling with a cottage only. This finding is a little surprising, because combination of labouring with a craft of some kind or another is a common feature of the English past; perhaps purchase of a boat and net, or shares in them, was beyond the means of those who earned only a labourer's wage.[35] A few occupiers of cellars did not have farm holdings or cottage holdings, yet had surnames also found among the landowning class. This group was a relatively small one, perhaps for the same reason as we have suggested for little involvement of landless cottagers on the foreshore, namely lack of capital. Some foreshore activities did, however, need relatively little capital and this applied especially to the raking of cockles and mussels at low tide which, in the eighteenth and nineteenth centuries, was especially an occupation among women. In this context it is interesting to note that, of the group of landless people who occupied cellars independently, two were women, Isobel and Maria Seleye.[36] Several Seleyes occupied farm holdings on the manor and, without analysis of parish registers, we cannot tell if these two were wives, widows or spinsters. We cannot say, but it would not be too rash to speculate that these two independent women of the late sixteenth century were distant predecessors of the legendary and much photographed female cockle rakers of a later age.

A final group of occupiers of cellars comprised people (almost all men) whose surnames cannot be traced elsewhere in the survey of 1578; in other words, they were not closely related to the settled population of the manor. These people are represented on Fig 5.1 as 'outsiders', perhaps from adjacent parishes without a foreshore, such as Mamhead and Kenn. This is only a supposition, but it is a reasonable one: there were probably outsider-fishers at Woodbury, studied in the previous section, while at Ringmore Strand (or Shaldon) on the Teign estuary, not far from Starcross, the taking of cellars by outsiders was disapproved of in the eighteenth century, presumably through fear of competition.[37]

5.1.iii The Stokenham custumals
On the Start Bay manor of Stokenham, as at Kenton, particularly detailed sources allow us to visit some of the homes of the fishing farmers. The manor's coastline consisted of some stretches of rocky cliffs, the small cove of Lannacombe and some fine long beaches which were excellent for the drawing in of seines.[38] During the fourteenth century when information concerning the fishery of the manor is at its best, lordship was first in the hands of Mathew fitz John, who died in 1309, then a succession of owners, then the de Montacutes. The last fourteenth-century de Montacute to hold the manor was John, who by succession became third earl of Salisbury, poet, crusader and Lollard who was murdered because of his religious beliefs. A significant event in the very chequered history of the Salisbury estate ('Salisbury lands') during the sixteenth century was the marriage of an heiress to the future second earl of Huntingdon which led to the preservation of a few early Stokenham documents in that family's archive and, eventually, in the Huntington Library in California.

Despite these illustrious connections, documentation for the manor of Stokenham is a little disappointing, for there are no court rolls before the sixteenth century and the oldest surviving account roll for 'Salisbury lands' is dated 1506-7.[39] To compensate there is a detailed survey and custumal (though without names of tenants) in the inquisition *post mortem* for John Fitz Mathew in 1309; a full rental and custumal which almost certainly dates from the accession of the de Montacute family in 1346, for long unrecognized as a Stokenham document because of the damaged head of the roll; another, later fourteenth-century rental and custumal of about 1360; and a Tudor rental of 1548.[40] It is from the first three of these documents that we have a detailed picture of the mullet fishery off the coast of Stokenham. The picture is so full that the relevant passages (already in part used earlier in this monograph) are worth quoting here in full.

> 1309. Some of the bondmen are under obligation to . . . station themselves, each day between Candlemas and Hock-day [2 February until the second Tuesday after Easter], by three rocks on the sea shore, nine by each rock, with their own boats and tackle, to catch mullet; and the lord has the option of taking one-third of the mullet which they net or one-third of the price if it is sold.
>
> About 1346. And she [Johanna the widow of Gervase: exemplar for some of the other tenants] shall sit upon the sea shore at *le Hole* from the feast of the Purification until Hockday [2 February until the second Tuesday after Easter] expecting the coming of the mullet and, with the men of Frittiscombe [a hamlet in the manor], she will catch the said fish and they shall have two-thirds and the lord one-third.
>
> About 1360. And he [Richard Still: exemplar for some of the other tenants], on alternate days from the feast of the Purification until Hockday, with others, will watch on the beach near *le Hole* waiting for the coming of the mullet. He will fish for them with his neighbours and they will have two-thirds of the catch and the lord one-third.

These passages contain many items of interest about many topics: teams of nine fishers (conceivably the crew of two boats used to manage a seine); requisition of part of the catch by the lord as his profit from his tenants' fishery; a 'look-out' system, perhaps from the top of a cliff (the 'rocks' of the 1309 source), probably the earliest reference nationally to this practice. Here we are more concerned with the personnel of the fishery, but before we discuss them a few introductory points should be made if the passages are to be correctly interpreted. First, the patient Johanna described in the second extract is by chance a woman; the tenure chosen, by the official who drew up the document, to exemplify other tenures in the same class and to have its services spelled out in full, happened to be occupied by a woman. Second, lords of Stokenham clearly used the manor in order to stock up their larder with mullet in the weeks leading up to Lent, but the extracts printed above do not mean that tenants restricted their fishing to that species and that season. That would have been highly unlikely given their considerable investment in boats and nets and, indeed, we know from other passages in the custumals that porpoise, salmon, plaice, bream, skate and conger were caught off the shores of Start Bay in the fourteenth century. Third, it is unlikely that successive lords of Stokenham instituted the system of watching and fishing described in the documents. They simply 'manorialized' ancient custom, perhaps manipulating it a little to their own advantage. They insisted, for reasons explored in an earlier chapter, on some kind of payment from their tenants' fishery; they made sure that this payment would be in mullet if they wished; and to make doubly sure that they got what they wanted, they spelled out the need for the tenants to continue ancient practices of watching and teamwork, perhaps elaborating them a little.

Documents from Stokenham make it quite clear that those who fished were true farmers, the lord's bondmen, *nativi* in the words of the survey of 1309.[41] That survey does not give the names of the tenants and it is not until we come to the custumal of 1346 that the people of Stokenham appear before us as individuals. At that time the manor's tenemental structure was highly regular and highly polarized. There were about 150 tenanted farm holdings, an impressive majority being standard 30-acre tenancies, while smallholders were very few. At the other end of the scale there were 89 completely landless cottages, more than one for every two farm holdings, a very high figure by Devonshire standards; they were very important to the economic structure of the manor, as we shall see. The custumal of 1360 is in some senses in a

Fishing Farmers and Cellar Settlements 125

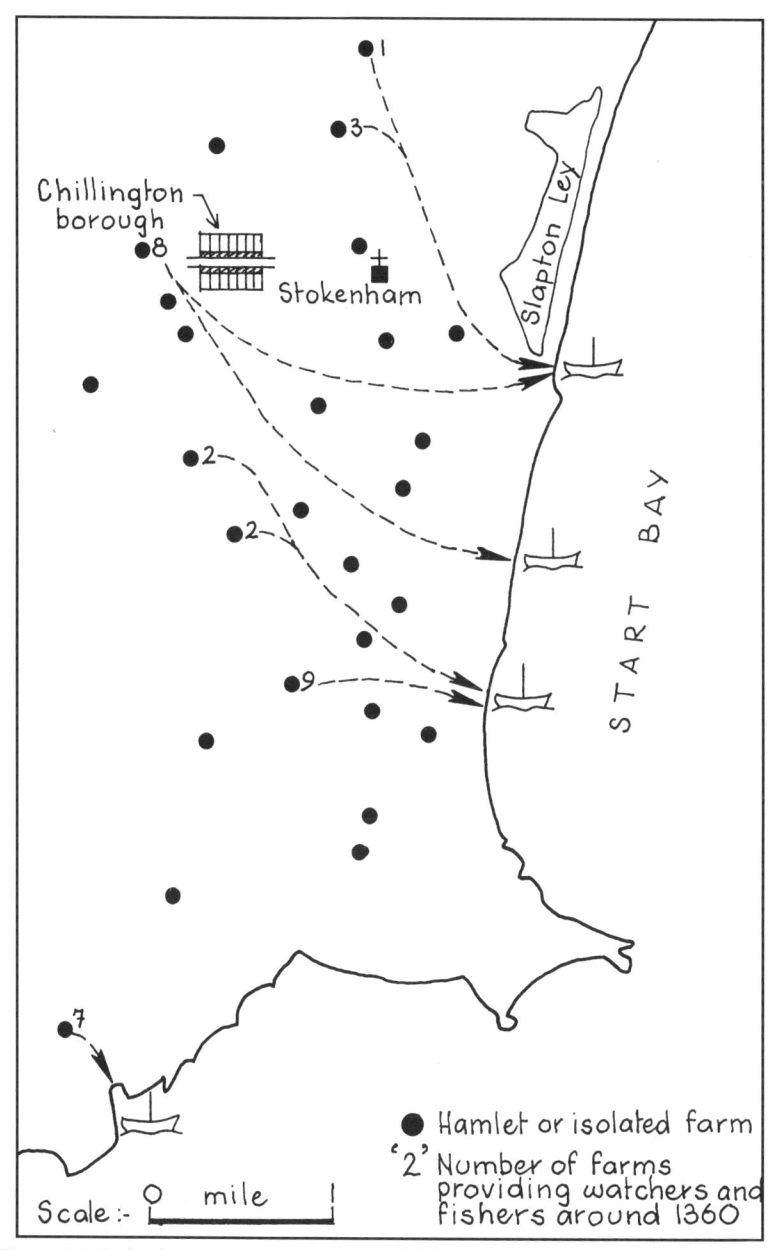

Figure 5.2 Stokenham manor: settlements and fishing according to the custumal of 1360

better state of preservation than that of 1346 (although it has some imperfections, surviving only as a later copy) and it allows us to identify all those who were obliged in that year to hand over one-third of their catch to the lord. By this time the average size of holdings had risen to 56 acres as a result of amalgamations after the Black Death; many of the cottages remained. Those who fished for the lord were, emphatically, not the cottagers; the profile of the fishers differed not at all from the profile of all farmers on the manor, for almost all of them occupied relatively large holdings of 30 acres and over. Their distribution is mapped in Fig. 5.2. which shows all of the hamlets and isolated farms scattered over the face of the manor, and mostly set well back behind the coast. It also shows (by use of numbers) the locations of the farms from whose occupiers the lord took mullet in 1360. The distribution at first sight seems rather unexpected because, with one exception, these farms were well inland.

The best explanation of the unexpected distribution shown on Fig. 5.2 is that the document upon which it is based catches obligations in only one specific year. Both in 1346 and in 1360 lords of Stokenham seem to have required the work of about 30 tenants in order to provide them with the desired quantity of mullet in the Lenten period. Rather than to burden the same tenures and families year after year it seems almost certain that they 'rotated' the obligation among all tenures, a practice found elsewhere in connection with other obligations owed to lords.[42] The custumal of 1360 therefore catches the rotation at a particular stage. This seems to be a reasonable explanation of the odd distribution of fishers in 1360, though to prove it would require a considerable amount of further research among Stokenham documents, which I hope somebody will carry out in the future. In any one year, about 30 tenant farmers fished partly for the lord; that many of the rest fished for themselves may be indicated by the fact that their work services on the demesne were reduced on February 2nd, just around the time of the arrival of the mullet.[43]

Also relatively unexpected, given the findings from Woodbury and Kenton – where fishing was to some degree in the hands of small farmers – is the large size of the farm holdings providing men and boats at Stokenham. The fact is that the manor had a highly rigid farm structure, with hardly any smallholders and a very large proportion of the farms at 30 acres (in 1346). This is quite typical of deep South Devon whereas further towards the east of the county smallholdings of between 5 and 10 acres were standard units in tenemental structures.[44] Reasons for these differences are very unclear at this stage. In the particular case of Stokenham it was certainly to the advantage of lords to have on hand the labour from large, well-equipped farms. Stokenham's demesnes, of which there were two, were large by Devon standards and remained in hand and cultivated by the lord and his agents until a relatively late date; situated in that part of the county most suitable for arable cultivation, the demesnes must have been highly profitable enterprises.[45] The custumals make clear that, until a relatively late date, much of the cultivation of the demesnes was done with the labour services of the tenants. These were not highly exacting (they did not have to be, because of the large number of tenants) but they were certainly heavy by Devon standards and required the tenants to use their own animals and equipment.[46] In short, the demesnes of Stokenham required a well-equipped, orderly labour force, so that it was in the interests of lords of the manor to maintain the standard 30-acre holdings (or, after the Black Death, multiples of them).

In discussions above of smallholders who fished at Woodbury and Kenton it was suggested that the second occupation arose partly out of need and partly from abundance of time. From the point of view of need, it seems unlikely that the large farmers of Stokenham would have allowed one of the longest and most fruitful of manorial coastlines in South Devon to go unfished, for here was a source not of untold wealth but certainly of welcome additional incomes. From the point of view of time, they solved the problem by constructing cottages (very well documented) near their farmhouses and, it could well be, the extra labour of those cottage families provided a solution to the triple demands which existed upon a farmer's time: on his own holding, on the demesne and at the fishery. We have already remarked upon the very large number of cottages which existed on the manor; also remarkable was the fact that they were mostly located not in a central village – an arrangement found elsewhere in Devon – but next to farmhouses in the scattered hamlets of the manor. Their occupants were very much under the thumb of the farmers and, after 1348, there was a tendency for the cottages to become tied to the farmhouses of their farmer-employers; such arrangements, as I have argued elsewhere in a recently published paper, were means by which farmers hoped to entice labour in an age when that commodity was becoming ever more costly.[47] This is all reasonable surmise; what we cannot guess about are the ways in which labour, on the farm, on the demesne and at the boats, was divided between farmer and his dependent cottage labourer. All that we can say is that the unusual presence of really abundant labour from cottagers (and their families, including females) injected extra labour into the working unit and therefore made time for the operation of the fishery.

The extracts from rentals printed above make it quite clear that watching for the arrival of the mullet was always done near *le Hole*, the local word for a cave which survives in the place-name Hallsands. From which beaches the boats set out we do not know but it is reasonable to suppose that the four beaches used for fishing on this stretch of coast in later times were the same as those used earlier on. When fish were seen to arrive offshore, extra hands had to be called from the inland hamlets (as explained in the extract above for 1346); there was no time to be lost so several fishing places were needed, each as close as possible to a group of inland hamlets.[48] These assumptions lie behind the positioning of the arrows and fishing stations on Fig. 5.2. The location of the hamlets and of those farms obliged to fish for and hand over mullet in 1360 are, on the other hand, firmly based upon what the custumal says.

At the fishing places there would have been cellars for the storage of nets and boats out of reach of the fierce storms which sweep this exposed coast. Passages from the custumals quoted above imply (if I have interpreted the rotation system correctly), that many Stokenham tenants had shares in boats used for fishing. The custumal of 1309 speaks of 'all tenants with boats' being obliged 'to convey by water from Totnes, Kingsbridge and Dartmouth all wine required by the lord for consumption on the manor'; these could have been the same small boats used for fishing, for the journeys stated are relatively short, though with hazardous and shoal-strewn headlands around which to steer.[49] We have already encountered cellars in case studies of Kenton and Woodbury. Medieval documents from Stokenham are silent on cellars though there are abundant references to them in the sixteenth century[50] and, in the nineteenth century, Beesands and Hallsands (by then inhabited fishing villages) still bore their old names of Beason Cellar and Hall Cellar, recalling their distant origins as fishing stations marked by collections of storage huts.

5.2 The cellar settlements

In the past the British landscape contained many sites and structures of a great variety of kinds which were used seasonally and were not permanent habitations lived in throughout the year. There were the cabins and lodges of the 'lookers' of Romney Marsh, the lone beehive-shaped herdsmen's shelters discovered by Peter Herring on Bodmin Moor, 'in positions offering impressive panoramic views over pasture', groups of corbelled stone huts, also of beehive form, in the seasonal pastures of the Dingle Peninsula and on Harris and Lewis (Hebrides), the 'summer houses' of Wealden dens, apparently lodgings for lords and officials as they exercised jurisdiction in a remote swine-pastures, the hut used by the guardians of the meadow at Dunster (an unusal reference), those 'little eminences called shepherds' tables . . . for shepherds to have a day of festivities at certain seasons of the year' which Throsby noticed in his tour through Leicestershire at the end of the eighteenth century.[51] At all of these places, as well as at sites with names derived from *scela*, *skali*, *hafod* and *havos* (in the northern half of England and in Scotland, in Wales and in Cornwall), secondary, seasonal use was connected to the rhythms of pastoral farming. Other activities could also generate seasonally used buildings: a fourteenth-century inquisition into the liberties and customs of the lead-miners of Alston Moor in Cumberland found that they operated from huts called *shelis*, presumably akin to the 'many little houses built for the stannary men to shroud them in near the works' which the ever-observant John Norden noted in sixteenth-century Cornwall. Nor must we forget that the present-day lodges of the masonic order are in direct descent from the medieval *logia* constructed at building sites or quarries by masons whose craft was also, to a degree, seasonal in nature.[52] And because fishing along the South Devon coastline was once, as described earlier in this chapter, a by-employment among people who were primarily farmers, we would expect that it, too, gave rise to secondary settlements used only at certain times of the year.

Such were the cellar settlements of the south Devon coastline. In a previous section we have already traced links between the homesteads of Kenton farmers inland and cellars on the coast at Starcross, using a rental of 1578. By the end of the sixteenth century Starcross was a late survival as a cellar settlement, for in many other places cellars had now been replaced by the permanently inhabited cottages of a fishing village. In the landscapes of relatively recent times the only legacies of cellar settlements are their successors, the fishing villages, and a few largely anachronistic place-names on maps. Recent 1-inch maps of the South Devon coast show only one place incorporating the element cellar: Coombe Cellars on the River Teign, now simply an inn, formerly the riverine cellars used by the people of inland Combeinteignhead. The 2½-inch map adds one more, Cellar Beach, tucked away just inside the mouth of the River Yealm.[53] From the first edition of the 1-inch Ordnance Survey map (Surveyed 1801-7, printed 1809) we can recover the names Slapton Cellars and Beeson Cellar on the coast of Start Bay and a place simply called Cellars on a tributary of the River Dart, in the parish of Littlehempston; Murray's *Handbook* of 1859, and its map, give Beason Cellar and Hall Cellar on Start Bay.[54] These Start Bay names, for present-day Beesands and Hallsands, are very interesting because they show that, although the places concerned were established fishing villages in the nineteenth century ('secluded little fishing hamlets' in Murray's words), and had been for some centuries, their distant origins as collections of cellars simply were still recalled in their alternative, presumably local, names.

By the time when the Ordnance Survey's officers first mapped the South Devon coastline and enquired locally about names, most fishing places were permanently inhabited and the cellar settlement was

Fishing Farmers and Cellar Settlements

a rare survival. In the Middle Ages the reverse applied: most fishing places were simply cellar settlements and permanent habitations on the shore were generally found only in the port towns (from which, naturally, some fishing took place). In many cases, as on Stokenham manor, the medieval documentation is not good enough to provide anything like a complete picture of a cellar settlement although we may infer its existence from the fact that those who fished were farmers with residences inland: when fishing was in progress structures on the shore would have been necessary for the safe storage of barrels, fish, salt, ropes and other paraphernalia and, in slack times, fishing farmers would have had the option either of carting these goods – and others such as nets, boats, anchors and so on – to their inland farms (an inconvenient option) or, more conveniently, of storing them away in shoreline cellars as safe as could be from the wild waves of autumn and winter. These cellar settlements, uninhabited, marginal, remote from manorial authority, are often screened from our view in medieval seigneurial documents, but not always. For example, a manorial account roll from St Marychurch in 1480 records rent received from a cottage near the site of the manor house and also its appurtenant *domus piscaria* which was almost certainly at Babbacombe; lords' rentals of 1513, 1517 and about 1522 mention cellars near Dawlish, on Ringmore manor (either at Ringmore Strand or at Shaldon) and at Warfleet near the mouth of the Dart.[55] It is notable that all of these medieval references are relatively late and it could well be that, at first, the construction by a tenant of a cellar, if noticed at all by a lord's officials, was permitted without charge, payment being subsumed within the general charge which the fisher paid for use of the lord's foreshore for beaching boats, drying nets and hauling in seines. Then, towards the end of the fifteenth century and the beginning of the sixteenth, when inhabited cottages began to replace cellars on the beach (as will be described in the following chapter), landlords slowly became more interested in income from structures built on the foreshore and began to expect separate payments both from cottages and from cellars where these survived.

Because the medieval documentation is rather poor, we have to use later evidence about late surviving structures in order to bring these cellar settlements to life. According to the *Oxford English Dictionary* a cellar is a 'store house . . . whether above or below ground', the cellars of the Devon coast being in the former category. Only three documents, as far as I know, give the dimensions of Devonshire cellars: on the manor of Nutwell, according to a survey of 1566, there were, 'lying next the sea-shore', cellars with dimensions of 18 by 12 feet, 20 by 16 and 25 by 16; a seventeenth-century survey of Lympstone, gives 32 by 16 feet as the dimensions of one cellar there; and a survey of Paignton manor describes a cellar of 20 by 16 feet near Roundham Head.[56] Devonshire cellars were therefore small compared with the substantial medieval farmhouses of mid-Devon and North Devon which could be up to 50 or 60 feet long, but they were large compared with a labourer's cottage which could be of only 12 by 9 feet (South Devon, 1416).[57] The length of cellars could well have been influenced by the size of craft stored away in them, boats of about 20 feet long designed for estuarine and inshore use only and relatively easily pulled on to a beach and into a cellar when out of use.[58] They probably had a ground floor only as did the old, traditional Devon-type cellars which survived to be sketched in the nineteenth century on the beach at *Barrepta* (in Carbis Bay) in the far west of Cornwall.[59] Many cellars were of substantial enough construction to be turned into dwellings later in their lives, for there are several references to a 'seller now converted to a dwellinghouse' from Cockington and to 'one cellar now a dwelling house' at Hope.[60] Possibly these 'barn conversions' involved the addition of a first-floor storey to give dry and roomy accommodation above, while the ground floor retained its traditional use; first-floor dwellings are traditional in fishing villages everywhere. Other cellars seem to have been less substantial, perhaps weather-boarded throughout, such as the 'boarded cellar' which still stood on Lympstone Strand in the eighteenth century, or the wooden structure depicted on a drawing of the beach at Beer in the early nineteenth century.[61] This seems to be the only explanation of several references to cellars at Starcross being 'taken down and carried away'.[62] The more substantial cellars would have been built of the common building material of the locality, cob from the New Red Sandstone along the eastern part of the coastline surveyed here, horizontally laid slatestone further west. Fenestration was minimal, as in the late-surviving cellars at *Barrepta*, for some of the items stored in these buildings needed to be kept cool. The roofing material of the cellars was probably thatch, no doubt obtained from the farms to which they belonged, and thatching continued to be common practice in fishing villages long after most cellars had been replaced by cottages.[63]

As we have guessed, boats were probably stored away in some cellars, out of reach of the winter waves, although only once has a specific reference to a boathouse been found: a fifteenth-century account roll for the manor of South Allington records rent from a cellar called a 'botehouse' at a place named *Ivacove*.[64] Other uses are revealed by the terms employed to describe these structures: cellar is overwhelmingly the most common term, but nethouse is used for some cellars at Lympstone and there were 'reek rooms' at Hope, used for smoking fish. 'Seahouse or cellar' has been found once and this is a word which has given rise to coastal place-names, though not in Devon.[65] Most cellars, no doubt, had multiple uses. Fish house or fishing house, occurring as early as 1480, probably usually refers to a cellar where fish was stored and from which fishing was practised, not to a habitation: thus 'one dwelling house formerly a fish house'.[66] The term palace, of obscure origins, is occasionally found in Devon sources but more often in those from Cornwall where, in later times at least, most structures connected with the storage and curing of fish were rather different from the Devonshire ones.[67]

No sizeable Devon cellar settlements survived into the age of large-scale maps, so we can only judge their appearance and morphology from their legacy in the landscape, the inhabited fishing villages which succeeded them on the same shoreline sites. This approach is permissible because conversion of the former into the latter often involved the physical conversion of cellars into structures used for habitation or into structures for both living and storage. Drawings in perspective, like the water-colours of Hooe by Cocks or those by Swete of Torcross and Clovelly, the bird's eye view of Hooe done by Edmund Spoure in 1694 and eighteenth-century estate maps such as those of Dawlish and Shaldon, all show that the fishing village (and, by implication, the cellar settlement which preceded it) was, typically, a close-knit disarrangement of buildings, densely packed together, with no hint of a planned, orderly shape.[68] This is as one would expect, given the origins of these places. Slowly, over a long period of time, one fishing farmer after another builds a storehouse on the beach; the buildings are set down close to one another at what is perceived to be the safest spot; an uninhabited cellar belonging to a farm inland does not, by definition, need a garden or orchard so these are not settlements with large enclosed crofts, as are found in a farming village. Fishing settlements 'have neither grounds belonging to them nor yet any room . . . to make any gardens or orchards but only houses', to quote a sixteenth-century Northumberland survey.[69] Cellar settlements were built on very restricted, contested sites. They needed to be beyond the reach of ordinary high tides and safe from the waves of the strongest remembered storm, and this pushed them landwards. But the fields of inland settlements approached close to the shore, pushing a cellar settlement towards the waters. Restricted sites made for close-packed structures as a cellar settlement grew in size and, eventually, was transformed into a fishing village. Today the visitor to fishing villages is instructed to delight in the charm and quaintness of the winding narrow lanes (for example, in Devon, at Shaldon and in the fishing end of Dawlish and in The Lanes at Brighton and similar patterns in fishing villages everywhere) which, in origin, are simply the interstices between cellars and cottages. On the Continent, where many fishers' settlements have the same morphology, it is often claimed in guide books (especially by Mediterranean shores) that these tangled patterns of lanes were constructed deliberately in order to confuse pirates, but such a view is almost certainly erroneous because the lanes did not come first as a skeletal plan along which huts and cottages were strung. They are simply legacies of the narrow spaces between close-packed structures. 'Huddled old houses and thatched cottages . . . an incredible number of recesses and sub-corners . . . cottages . . . [which] have no ground floors at all': these words of Stephen Reynolds sum up the morphology of settlements on cramped squatters' shoreline sites.[70]

The place-names of some fishing sites tell something of the nature of their buildings and of the occupation practised at them. As mentioned at the beginning of this section the word 'cellars' is or was found in a number of place-names and sometimes continued in use even after cellars had been replaced by inhabited cottages; how old it is we cannot tell because the place-names of these isolated and remote coastal sites are not common in the early written record. In the North Country, Anglian and Old Scandinavian languages have special words – *scela*, *skali* – denoting seasonally used settlements, words which were mostly employed in the context of upland pastoralism but also for seasonally used fishing places, as in the coastal names Seascale and North Shields, discussed in the final chapter.[71] West Saxon had no word with this special meaning although many a place with a name incorporating an element used mostly for unpretending places or buildings may have started off as a seasonal settlement: names, for example, in *stede*, *cot*, *aern* and *wic*. Fishwick on the River Teign is a lone case (in Devon) of *fisc* combined with *wic* in A. H. Smith's sense of a building or site 'for a particular occupation', or in the sense of 'specialised . . . unit' or 'temporary camp' proposed by Richard Coates.[72] We find *wic* again in Week, now in Dawlish parish, but once a detached part of Kenton parish and manor, and possibly a fishing place.[73] 'Fisher' occurs in only one South Devon coastal name, *Fisherton* (at the place now called Blackpool), and there is only one recording of it, by the incumbent in 1613, so it could possibly be a literary invention.[74] Names in *aern* ('building') combined with *salt* take us back to the time when the salt-making industry was of some importance along the South Devon coast, or to its decline.[75] The name Saltings (River Teign, manor of Bishopsteignton where there were salt-works recorded in Domesday Book) was *Salternehay* in 1361, the last element probably referring to some kind of enclosure around the saltern; Saltern Cove survives as a name in the parish of Paignton; Salterton (in East Budleigh parish) was always *Salterne*, or the like, until some time, probably in the seventeenth century, when the *ton* was added; *Coombe Salterns* was apparently an alternative name for Coombe Cellars.[76] One would expect there to have been some fishing activity at all of these places although the shed for salt-making, or for storage of salt, may have been the most prominent, or the most unusual, building at each; the shed which gave the unusual, simplex, name of

Arne (on the shore of Poole Harbour, Dorset) probably has its origin in this industry.

Other fishing sites take their names, as we might expect, from some prominent physical feature which was important in the lives of those who fished as a landmark, or from the beach at which so much activity began and ended. Oreston's name is recorded long before there was a permanent settlement here; the stone, a word used hereabouts for a large rock, may have been a feature at which people waited for the medieval ferry which plied across the Cattewater or by which ferrymen guided in their craft. Hallsands takes its name from a prominent cave ('hole' in South Devon) in the cliffs there. The importance of the beach for putting out to sea, for the drawing in of nets and drawing up of boats and for building cellars upon is the reason why 'strand' was so often used in coastal place-names in Devon and elsewhere. Dawlish Strand was the coastal offshoot of inland Dawlish; Ringmore Strand served Ringmore in the same way; Strand survives as a street name in the riverine part of Lympstone and Strand was apparently once the name of part of Starcross (also surviving today in a street name); the Strand is a familiar name still in Stonehouse, Torquay and Exmouth.[77]

Finally, a little further detail, about ecclesiastical provision, may be added through speculation raised by the names of the two former cellar settlements, later fishing villages, called Torcross and Starcross which share a second element 'cross'. The former is the easier. The editors of *Place-Names of Devon* give 1714 as the earliest recorded mention of the name, but we can now push this back to 1569 (*Torcrosse*) after inspection of court rolls which were still in private hands when that survey was published.[78] There is a very prominent cliff-top just to the south of the cellar settlement and later fishing village, clearly the tor of the first part of the name; the name quite unambiguously calls for the existence of a cross on this hill and there is some suggestion that a cross-shaft now situated in a lane leading to Widdicombe is the one which once stood above the village.[79] Starcross, the cellar settlement discussed at length in an earlier section of this chapter, is a more difficult name. The editors of *Place-Names of Devon* give *Star Crosse* (1689) as the earliest known mention but this can now be pushed back to a *Sterrcrosse* in about 1578; the editors of this volume confess that it is a difficult name but hazard the guess that the cross may have been shaped like a star.[80] Far more likely is 'cross by the stair', the latter word referring to a set of steps or stairs (O.E. *staeger*) which took people down a small bluff to the beach at low tide. We can compare one definition of 'stairs' in the *Oxford English Dictionary*, 'a landing-stage, especially on the Thames', and the many named landing places of the Thames such as Billingsgate Stairs.[81] At Starcross, then, we have another cross at a fishing place and cellar settlement, this one being at the top of a flight of steps.

These coastal crosses at Torcross and Starcross would have served several purposes. They would have made excellent landmarks, that at Starcross, for example, guiding the medieval Exe ferry as it approached the shore in an early morning or autumn mist. They were also in all probability crosses which could be used for devotional purposes; those whose livelihoods depended in part on God's command over the sea and over the capricious creatures of the sea were, in the words of the people of St Mawes, 'glad to pray in public for good speed when they go out to sea and likewise to give God thanks for their prosperity when they return'.[82] That a cross could serve in such a way is no idle speculation, for there was a wooden cross on the rocks near Lanteglos by Fowey, noticed by John Leland in the sixteenth century and surviving until recently through the actions of fishermen who renewed it if it was damaged by storms.[83] The curious crosses shown on a sixteenth-century map of the Dorset coast may have been of the same kind.[84]

Most cellar settlements were, almost by definition, distant from the inland churches of the parishes in which they lay. A cross near a beach which bustled with activity at certain times of the year may therefore be seen as a necessary, if minimal, item of devotional apparatus at a site of this kind. Might some cellar settlements have had chapels of ease for the same purposes, like the chapel on the shore near Great Yarmouth which, according to the register of Norwich Cathedral Priory, was used only 'during the time of the herring fishery' (*tempore piscationis allecium*)?[85] Along the South Devon coastline one chapel is a possible candidate for this role, that dedicated to St Nicholas near Ringmore on the Teign estuary. From inspection today, and according to a detailed estate map of the eighteenth century, its situation is highly eccentric to the agricultural settlement of Ringmore; it relates rather to Ringmore Strand, at which there is a possible reference to a cellar in a rental of 1517.[86] Evidence for its existence at an early date and for the dedication is very respectable by any standards. The windows are lancets and St Nicholas is possibly referred to in the twelfth century and certainly in 1445; he was a favourite saint of people with maritime connections from the Aegean westwards and, in the South-West, was patron of churches at several parishes inhabited partly by fishing families, such as St Buryan, Fowey, Saltash and Sidmouth (late evidence only for Sidmouth), as well as of the chapel-with-light overlooking Ilfracombe harbour, the chapel on Drake's Island (formerly the Island of St Nicholas) in Plymouth Sound and of the Benedictine priory on Tresco, Scilly Isles.[87] We can suggest that the chapel near Ringmore Strand was built partly for use by those who set out to fish from this spot; if the suggestion is valid it pushes the evidence for fishing here back to the twelfth and thirteenth centuries.

[1] For tithe accounts in general see P. Heath, *Medieval Clerical Accounts* (St Anthony's Hall Publications, 26, 1964). A recent paper which uses and describes a collection of tithe accounts is R. N. Swanson, 'Economic change and spiritual profits: receipts from the peculiar jurisdiction of the Peak District in the fourteenth century', in N. Rogers, ed., *England in the Fourteenth Century* (1993), pp. 171-95. A printed example is N. H. Bennett, 'Blunham rectory accounts', in J. S. Thompson, ed., *Hundreds, Manors, Parishes and the Church* (Beds. Hist. Rec. Soc., 69, 1990), pp. 124-69. The arrangement of the Blunham accounts differs from that of Woodbury's: it is by person not by commodity.
[2] N. Orme, 'The medieval clergy of Exeter Cathedral: I, the vicars and annuellars', *TDA* 113 (1981), pp. 79-102.
[3] ECA, VC 3357.
[4] VC 3366, 3358; G. R. Dunstan, ed., *The Register of Edmund Lacy* (5 vols, DCRS, new ser., 7, 10, 13, 16, 18, 1963-72), vol. 1, pp. 187-8.
[5] VC 3357, 8, 9, 60, 1, 2, 3, 4, 3354.
[6] Houndbeare was formerly a detached part of Woodbury parish and is now in the parish of Aylesbeare; I am not entirely certain about my attribution of Thomas to this place.
[7] H. S. A. Fox, 'Farming practice and techniques: Devon and Cornwall', in E. Miller, ed., *The Agrarian History of England and Wales*, vol. 3, *1348-1500* (1991), p. 318.

[8] PRO, E315/385.

[9] H. S. A. Fox, 'Servants, cottagers and tied cottages during the later middle ages: towards a regional dimension', *Rural History* 6 (1995), pp. 1-30.

[10] ECA, VC 957 which gives the numbers of owners and 'associates' for each boat. My calculations assume equal shares, which is unlikely, because the master would have taken more than the rest.

[11] Stokenham: see next section but one. East Budleigh: G. Oliver, *Ecclesiastical Antiquites in Devon*, vol. 1 (1840), p. 134 which refers to the fish tithe of those parishioners 'who have boats'.

[12] PRO, E315/385.

[13] U. W. Bridghouse, *Woodbury: a View from the Beacon* (1981), p. 59; there were probably two John Westcotes in Woodbury parish in the 1420s, so the accountant occasionally gave place of residence in order to distinguish them; for John Ley, see ECA, VC 3364.

[14] ECA, VC 3370; DRO, Z17/3/19.

[15] Good discussion of the shoreline before drainage is to be found in M. Parkinson, 'Salt marshes of the Exe Estuary', *TDA* 112 (1980), pp. 17-41.

[16] H. S. A. Fox, 'William Chapple', *New Dictionary of National Biography*, forthcoming.

[17] F. C. Hingeston-Randolph, ed., *The Registers of Walter Bronescombe and Peter Quivil* (1889), p. 193.

[18] See above, Chapter 3, n. 14 for this fishery.

[19] D. M. Stenton, ed., *Great Roll of the Pipe for the Sixth Year ... of King John* (Pipe Roll Soc., new ser., 18, 1940), p. 88.

[20] PRO, SC6 828/5; L. M. Midgley, ed., *Ministers' Accounts of the Earldom of Cornwall, 1296-7* (2 vols, Camden Soc., 3rd ser., 66, 68, 1942-5), vol. 2, p. 216; Kowaleski, *LCAPE*, p. 199. The *Foghely* of 1297 is *Fowley* on a map of 1743: DRO, 96add.M/E/11.

[21] Midgley, ed., *Ministers' Accounts*, p. 216; PRO, SC6 828/5; DRO, 1508M/Devon/surveys/Kenton/6.

[22] In 1424 or 1425 some officials acting on behalf of the Vicars Choral of Exeter Cathedral had business in Stokeinteignhead on the south bank of the Teign Estuary and they recorded their ferry expenses as 2*d*. (presumably 1*d*. each way): ECA, VC 3358. They presumably crossed from Teignmouth to where Shaldon is today. As on the Exe, there were two rival ferries here, one operating from Teignmouth and the other from the opposite shore: Midgley, ed., *Ministers' Accounts*, p. 216 and DRO, Carew of Haccombe MSS, MR/3b, Ringmore court of 23 Eliz. In the thirteenth century the toll (one-way) on the ferry which plied from Sutton across the Cattewater to Hooe (?) was ½*d*.: R. N. Worth, *History of Plymouth* (1890), p. 28.

[23] G. Collins, *Great Britain's Coasting Pilot* (1693); DRO, 96add.M/E/11, estuary map of 1743; *An Hydrographical Survey of the Coast of Devonshire from Exmouth Bar to Stoke Point* (a printed map of the 1770s); C. Morris, ed., *The Journeys of Celia Fiennes* (1949), p. 271.

[24] DRO, 1508M/Lon./estate/valuations/4. For more detail, see E. A. G. Clark, *The*

Ports of the Exe Estuary (1960), pp. 63-6.

[25] Kowaleski, *LCAPE*, p. 49; *ibid.*, p. 8 and n. Maryanne Kowaleski notes that the surname *Colepole* is found under Kenton in an early fourteenth-century lay subsidy. Another reference which shows that the place was on the western shore of the Exe (not the eastern as, mistakenly, indicated by some medieval documentary references: *LCAPE*, 8 and n.) is an account relating to the expenses of carrying produce from *Colepole* across the water to Nutwell, a place on the *eastern* shore: CRO, AR2/568.

[26] PRO, SC6 828/5 and 7; DRO, 1508M/Lon./manor/Kenton/2; M. G. Dickinson, ed., *A Living from the Sea: Devon's Fishing Industry and its Fishermen* (1987), p. 41.

[27] Domesday, 1/26.

[28] 'Among these sand-hills are some lagoons or lakes of salt water where the making of salt has lately been renewed with the prospect of answering very well': C. Vancouver, *General View of the Agriculture of the County of Devon* (1808), p. 44. See Parkinson, 'Salt marshes', pp. 33, 39-40 for the precise chronology of these new saltworks which were not strictly in Kenton manor, but a little way to the south.

[29] DRO, 1508MLon./manor/Kenton/6 and estate/valuations/4.

[30] PRO, SC6 828/5.

[31] DRO, 1508M/Devon/maps/Powderham/2 and maps/Kenton 1.

[32] See H. S. A. Fox, 'Outfield cultivation in Devon and Cornwall: a reinterpretation', in M. Havinden, ed., *Husbandry and Marketing in the South-West* (Exeter Papers in Economic History, 8, 1973), pp. 23-8, which is a detailed study of farming at Kenton.

[33] Most of the cellars are listed towards the end of the survey but a few are referred to in the body. The cellars in this document have also been analysed by Linda Pinkham in her dissertation, 'Starcross, Devon: "a small creek . . . noted only for a small fishery of oysters and cockles"' (unpublished M.A. dissertation, Department of English Local History, University of Leicester, 1985). In a few cases her figures differ from mine, but only marginally. In my analysis I have tried to take into account the names of people living in the minor manors of Kenton parish.

[34] J. Youings, 'Raleigh's country and the sea', *Procs British Academy* 75 (1989), pp. 287-9.

[35] A. Everitt, 'Farm labourers', in J. Thirsk, ed., *The Agrarian History of England and Wales*, vol. 4, *1500-1640* (1967), pp. 425-9.

[36] For female involvement in the nurture and capture of oysters, mussels and cockles, see J. H. Porter, 'The Teign oyster beds', reprinted in Dickinson, ed., *Living from the Sea*, pp. 43-4; R. Bush, *The Book of Exmouth* (1978), pp. 25, 33. One wonders if the bloodshed which took place in 1612 between two women on the shore of Kenton was connected with competition over shellfish: DRO, 1508M/Lon./manor/Kenton/2, court of April 1612. Jemima Fox dealt in oysters and cockles at Starcross in 1850: W. White, *History, Gazetteer and Directory of Devonshire* (1850), p. 410.

[37] DRO, Carew of Haccombe MSS, MR/48, undated list of those who put undertenants in their cellars on Ringmore manor. The document does not say where these cellars were: they were probably not on the restricted Ringmore Strand, because of their very number; more likely they were at Shaldon, which was in the manor of Ringmore.

[38] Fishing along Stokenham shores in the last century is acutely observed in M. Firestone, 'The traditional Start Bay crab fishery', *Folk Life* 20 (1981-2), pp. 56-75.

[39] PRO, SC2 168/32, courts of 34-5 Hen. VIII and 1-2 Edw. VI; DRO, Cary MSS, courts running from 20 Hen. VIII onwards, but not continuously; Huntington Library, San Marino, California, HAM box 74, account of 22-3 Hen. VII. Other accounts, from the reigns of Henry VII and VIII, are in the PRO.

[40] PRO, C134/16; PRO, SC11/765, which lacks a head and therefore a date but which certainly comes from before the Black Death, because all tenements are fully occupied and no engrossing has begun; Huntington Library, HAM box 64, rental of '1577' which, in fact, is the date of the copy, the lost original having been made around 1360 because, although the tenemental structure shows some scars as a result of the passing of the Black Death, a number of tenants from around 1346 still occupy their holdings; PRO, SC11/168, almost certainly defective in its listing of cottagers. Some Stokenham documents have been edited very usefully by Mr W. A. Roberts of Beeson. Most notable are: *Stokenham Occasional Paper* no. 1 (1980) containing an abstract of the rental of 1548; *Manorial Stokenham in the 14th Century* (*Occasional Paper* no. 4, 1982), containing an abstract of the rental of 1360; and *Elizabethan Court Rolls of Stokenham Manor 1560-1602* (1984).

[41] PRO, C134/16.

[42] For example, on some Suffolk manors, holdings became eligible to provide some of the officers of the vill in 17-year cycles: P. Warner, *Greens, Commons and Clayland Colonization* (Department of English Local History, Occasional Papers, 4th ser., 2, 1987), p. 49.

[43] Huntington Library, HAM box 64, rental of '1577'.

[44] A summary of the (increasing) size of holdings on the manor in 1346, 1360 and 1548 is given in H. S. A. Fox, 'Tenant farmers and tenant farming: Devon and Cornwall', in Miller, ed., *Agrarian History*, vol. 3, p. 724. I am now undertaking a thorough survey of differences in the size of holdings between one part of Devon and another, largely from thirteenth-century sources, and this, I expect, will bring out the distinctive nature of the smallholdings of East Devon.

[45] The two demesnes were near Stokenham itself and at Start: PRO, C134/16. Demesne was still in hand in 1400: *Cal. Inq. Misc.*, vol. 7, p. 71.

[46] Huntington Library, HAM box 64, rental of '1577'.

[47] Fox, 'Servants', pp. 12-17, which is a case-study of the Stokenham cottagers, and pp. 17-19.

[48] Firestone, 'Start Bay', names the fishing places.

[49] PRO, C134/16; also Huntington Library, HAM box 64, rental of '1577' where only Dartmouth is specified.

[50] For example, DRO, Cary MSS, Stokenham court rolls, court of Oct. 38 Eliz. and court of June 39 Eliz.

[51] M. Dobson, '"Marsh fever": the geography of malaria in England', *Jnl Hist. Geog.* 6 (1980), p. 369; P. Herring and J. Nowakowski, 'Beehive huts', in N. Johnson and P. Rose, *Bodmin Moor: an Introductory Survey*, vol. 1 (1994), p. 100; F. Aalen, 'Clochans

as transhumance dwellings in the Dingle Peninsula', *Jnl Roy. Soc. Ant. Ireland* 94 (1964), pp. 39-45; F. W. L. Thomas, 'Beehive houses in Harris and Lewis', *Procs Soc. Ant. Scotland* 3 (1857-60), pp. 127-49; K. P. Witney, *The Jutish Forest* (1976), p. 175; H. C. Maxwell Lyte, *A History of Dunster* (2 vols, 1909), vol.1, p. 314; Throsby's *Excursions in Leicestershire* (1790), cited in W. G. Hoskins, 'Croft Hill', in his *Provincial England* (1963), p. 168. For structures of all kinds, probably used seasonally, on Dartmoor, see B. Le Messurier, 'The post-prehistoric structures of central North Dartmoor', *TDA* 111 (1979), pp. 69-73. For the subject in general see the collection of studies in H. S. A. Fox, ed., *Seasonal Settlement* (1996).

[52] W. Nall, 'Alston', *Trans Cumb. & Westermorland Ant. & Arch. Soc.* 8 (1886), p. 14; Norden (late sixteenth century) cited in D. Austin, G. A. M. Gerrard and T. A. P. Greeves, 'Tin and agriculture in the middle ages and beyond: landscape archaeology in St Neot parish, Cornwall', *Cornish Archaeology* 28 (1989), p. 132 where there is also a discussion of an excavation of a tinners' shelter and a quotation from Beare, more or less contemporary with Norden, who noticed 'little lodges' which were 'made about with handsome benches' for the workforce at mealtimes; D. Knoop and G. P. Jones, *The Mediaeval Mason* (1949), pp. 56-62. The same work discusses seasonality in the building trades. For seasonality in medieval mining, see I. Blanchard, 'Labour productivity and work psychology in the English mining industry, 1400-1600', *Ec. Hist. Rev.*, 2nd ser., 31 (1978), pp. 2-3.

[53] There is also Pier Cellars in the parish of Maker-with-Rame, Cornwall, facing Plymouth Sound.

[54] *Murray's Handbook for Devon and Cornwall* (1859), p. 63 and end-map. For Slapton Cellars see R. Stanes, *A Fortunate Place: the History of Slapton in South Devon* (1983), pp. 54-6.

[55] DRO, Cary MSS, St Marychurch account of 19-20 Edw. IV; ECA, DC 3684, rental of Dawlish, 1513; DRO, Carew of Haccombe MSS, rental of Ringmore, 1517; DRO, Cary MSS, rental of Stoke Fleming, 1522.

[56] DRO, Z17/3/19, survey of Dinham lands; DRO, 346M/M/264; C. R. Straton, ed., *Survey of the Lands of William, First Earl of Pembroke* (2 vols, 1909), vol. 2, p. 399.

[57] Examples of the dimensions of farmhouses in mid-Devon and N. Devon are to be found in papers by N. Alcock and by Alcock and C. Hulland, *TDA*, 100 (1968), pp. 13-23 and 104 (1972), pp. 35-56. Labourer's cottage at Stoke Fleming: DRO, 902M/M/13, court near St Hilarius, 3 Hen. V.

[58] For the size of boats, above Section 3.4.

[59] Royal Institution of Cornwall, drawing of *Barrepta*, by E. W. Cooke, 1848.

[60] DRO, 48/13/4/2/4, survey of 1655; DRO, 1508M/Devon/estate/surveys/whole estate/2, survey of Galmpton.

[61] DRO, 53/6 box 38, deed of 1777; West Country Studies Library, Exeter, P & D 08722.

[62] DRO, 1508M/Lon./manor/Kenton/2, court of 1629. See also a similar case in the court of 1598. I am most grateful for these references to Linda Pinkham and her 'Starcross', p. 39.

[63] See the illustrations in T. Gray and M. Rowe, eds, *Travels in Georgian Devon* (4 vols, 1997-2000), vol. 1, p. 96 (Warfleet) and vol. 2, p. 156 (Coombe Cellars).

[64] PRO, SC6 Hen.VII/1099, account of S. Allington, 23-4 Hen. VII. Also BL, Add. roll 64341, undated account of S. Allington.

[65] Antony House MSS, PE/C4/1A, Lympstone survey of 1554; DRO, 1508M/Devon/estate/surveys/whole estate/2, Bolberry Beauchamp survey of around 1700; DRO, 48/13/4/2/4, Cockington survey of 1655. The three place-names – Seahouses or the like – are in Northumberland.

[66] DRO, Cary MSS, St Marychurch account of 19-20 Edw. IV; DRO, 48/13/4/2/4, Cockington survey of 1655.

[67] DRO, 48/13/4/2/4, 48/13/3/1/50, Cockington survey and lease of 1655 and 1623; DRO, 1962B/W/M/3/2, Kingswear court of 5 & 6 Philip & Mary. For Cornwall, see N. J. G. Pounds, 'Cornish fish cellars', *Antiquity* 18 (1944), pp. 36-41.

[68] Hooe by Cocks reproduced in I. V. Langdon, *The Plymstock Connection* (1995), p. 135. Gray and Rowe, eds, *Travels*, vol. 1, p. 194 and vol. 3, p. 101; CRO, FS3/93/3/130B; ECA, DC M/4; DRO, 563Z/P/1.

[69] M. W. Beresford, *New Towns of the Middle Ages* (1967), p. 474.

[70] S. Reynolds, *A Poor Man's House* (paperback edn, 1982), p. 9.

[71] Below, Chapter 7.

[72] A. H. Smith, *English Place-Name Elements* (2 vols, 1956), vol. 2, p. 259; R. Coates, 'New light from old wicks: the progeny of Latin *vicus*', *Nomina* 22 (1999), pp. 98, 106.

[73] Above, Section 3.1.

[74] DRO, glebe terriers, Blackawton perambulation of 1613. There is a Fisherton in N. Devon, parish of Bishop's Tawton, by the Taw. There are also three places in Devon called Fishleigh and Fishley, all relating to inland stream fisheries. The second element is *leah*, wood or clearing in a wood, which seemed strange to the editors of *PND*, vol. 1, p. 143, but cannot we envisage a wood or clearing adjacent to a stream which was renowned for fish or where there was a fishery?

[75] For the industry and its decline, see above, Section 3.5.

[76] *PND*, vol. 2, p. 489 (Saltings); vol. 2, p. 583 (Salterton); O. J. Reichel, 'The hundred of Exminster in early times', *TDA* 47 (1915), p. 227 (Coombe Cellars). *PND*, vol. 1, pp. 255 and 328, derive Saltram in Plymstock and possibly Goodshelter in East Portlemouth from words connected with salt-making. 'Saltern' on the first edition of the 1-inch map (parish of Dawlish) is probably not a place-name but refers to the thing itself. Woodbury Salterton, 2 miles *inland* from the shore of the Exe, is a mystery still. Might some salters have lived inland, close to the sources of fuel?

[77] For the ferry at Oreston, see *Cal. Pat Rolls, 1461-1467*, p. 536. For the names Dawlish Strand and Strand near Torcross, see *An Hydrographical Survey of the Coast of Devonshire from Exmouth Bar to Stoke Point* (a printed map of the 1770s) and W. L. D. Ravenhill, ed., *Benjamin Donne. A Map of the County of Devon 1765* (DCRS, new ser., 9, 1965).

[78] *PND*, vol. 1, p. 332; DRO, Cary MSS, Stokenham court of Sept. 11 Eliz.

[79] Local supposition.

[80] *PND*, vol. 2, p. 500; DRO, 1508M/Lon./manor/Kenton/6.

[81] *O. E. D.*, *s. v.* stair. Compare the 'stares' built to reach boats at low water in the port of Plymouth: R. N. Worth, *Calendar of the Plymouth Municipal Records* (1893), pp. 18-19.
[82] G. H. Doble, *Saint Mawes* (2nd edn, 1938), p. 24 (notes by Charles Henderson).
[83] Leland, *Itinerary*, vol. 1, p. 207; C. Henderson, *The Cornish Church Guide* (1925), p. 135.
[84] BL, Cott. Aug. I i 31, 33.
[85] H. W. Saunders, ed., *The First Register of Norwich Cathedral Priory* (Norfolk Record Soc., 11, 1939), pp. 30-3.
[86] DRO, 563Z/P/1; DRO, Carew of Haccombe MSS, rental of Ringmore, 1517.
[87] N. Orme, *English Church Dedications with a Survey of Cornwall and Devon* (1996), pp. 198, 241.

Chapter Six

TRANSITION: FROM CELLAR SETTLEMENT TO FISHING VILLAGE

6.1 Dating

A few cellar settlements, like Starcross, survived as such into the seventeenth century, or even later. Likewise, no small number of fishing farmers continued to ply their dual occupations until very late, such as Geoffrey Wheller of Chivelstone parish who died in 1598 leaving a small flock of sheep, 4 acres of sown crops and a quarter of a share in a seine, or Richard Benett of Cockington (d. 1569) who left oxen and sheep, corn, nets and 'an old boat'.[1] At many places, however, a transition took place, from cellar settlement to fishing village, beginning at some time towards the end of the fifteenth century or the early years of the sixteenth.

In order to date the emergence of fishing villages highly accurately, in an ideal world, continuous runs of court rolls and account rolls would be needed, and such runs we do not have for any manor on the stretch of shore studied here. But we should rejoice in what we have and try to use it to the full. For five fishing villages – Dittisham, the three Cockwoods and Hallsands – the evidence is relatively good and is discussed here. The earliest inhabited fishing village on our stretch of shore may well be waterside Dittisham on the River Dart, 3 miles above the river mouth and separated from the parent village and church of Dittisham by a little more than half a mile; rather unusually, the estuarine offshoot had the same name as the parent and today the two have more or less coalesced. No court rolls or surveys survive. The first manorial account is from 1404-5 and thereafter there is a series, discontinuous but not wildly so, into the reign of Henry VII, some being of part of the manor and others of a rather lowly kind, lacking in sophistication.[2]

The earliest account rolls tell us little about estuarine activity, even though it may have existed. Then in the late 1470s and 1480s, the accountant can be seen catching up with the rents of newly built cottages, some of them 'at ye wall' or 'at the sea wall' (*murus maris*), a simple riverine quay. This was clearly a new shoreline settlement, for one cottage 'next to the church', that is, in the inland part of Dittisham, is separately distinguished in an account. A new rental is made (it has not survived but is mentioned in 1480) and the accountant introduces a new heading, 'rent of the cottages', into his accounts. We read of the letting of a parcel of waste, possibly just above the high water mark, 'to build there', and of another piece of waste let next to an existing cottage, perhaps resulting in the beginnings of a terrace, an arrangement often found in fishing villages where space was at a premium. Fines indicate that brewing was taking place in this new settlement, a sure sign of its independence from inland Dittisham. Shoreline Dittisham became a village from which quite ambitious voyages set out to fish longshore on the south coast of England and which was also known for its locally nurtured shellfish, 'Dittisham oysters' being mentioned in an Exeter customs account from the late fifteenth century.[3]

After transcribing the account rolls of Dittisham in the Public Record Office, I visited the village which I had not seen since childhood and, like T. S. Eliot, 'seemed to arrive where we started | And know the place for the first time': still the terrace of cottages on the strand, still another cottage on a low river wall, still an inn, the successor perhaps to the place where the brewings of the late 1470s were made. We cannot precisely date the origins of waterside Dittisham, because of inadequacies in the record, but there was much building activity and interest in land here in the late 1470s and the 1480s and these probably date the beginnings of the fishing village.

Just a little later, and better recorded, are the origins of three fishing villages on the shore of Dawlish manor, Westwood, Middlewood and Cockwood. Very close together, yet separate settlements, the three Cockwoods all lay on the shore of a small creek, now drained but still called Cockwood Marsh.[4] The land on which the cottages and their gardens are situated is steeply sloping and was almost certainly once wooded, as steep slopes often were in this part of Devon; hence the place-names. Rather unusually for fishing villages, in length they extend inland rather than along the shore.

Documents from the manor of Dawlish do not satisfy the ideal criteria mentioned above, but they are relatively abundant: after 1410 there is hardly a decade which lacks either an account roll, court roll or rental. The accounts contain lists, quite long in some cases, of properties in hand or subject to reduced rent. Court rolls mention properties in hand and those whose occupiers changed hands. The medieval rentals of Dawlish, like those of many other Devon manors with dispersed settlement patterns, are arranged topographically, tenures being grouped under sub-headings which name the settlements.[5] Under these circumstances it is unlikely that an occupied settlement site would have gone unrecorded for long. The Cockwoods appear in no documents before 1483 when they suddenly burst upon us in the records; in particular, they are not mentioned in a very detailed rental of 1422.[6] Dawlish people certainly fished before the late fifteenth century, for there are sporadic references to fishing in the documents, but the craft was practised from inland settlements.[7]

The first reference to inhabited structures at one of the Cockwoods (which one is not specified) is in an account roll for 1483 when three 'new rents' for cottages are mentioned. The previous surviving account roll is for 1464 and mentions no cottages, so the beginnings of the establishment of these three villages can probably be dated to around 1480, because the account roll for 1483 shows that settlement was yet small and faltering a little.[8] We can see further new cottages being added in the early years of the sixteenth century, through account rolls, and in 1513 the three settlements are named in a detailed rental, then having (from west to east) ten, thirteen and seven cottages respectively.[9] All of the cottages were landless at this time (except one with a 'hemphay', that is, a small garden for hemp); the elongated closes associated with some of the cottages, still to be seen in the landscape today, are probably enclosures from the waste said to be 'new' in a late eighteenth-century document.[10] Rarely in the annals of medieval settlement history do we have such a good account of village origins.

Although the process of settlement of the Cockwoods seems to have been faltering a little in its very early stages, these cottages were soon relatively eagerly competed for, vacancies being very few.[11] The new settlements on the shore were associated with an increase in fishing activity, for the fish tithes of Dawlish parish rose from £7 3s. 9d. in 1465 to £22 11s. 1d. in 1511, the latter figure representing a total catch worth the very large sum of £225 (multiplying by ten).[12] From 1524 there is the first reference to a market at Dawlish, the account for that year recording 16s. as the lords' income from 'the new rent of *le stondynges* outside the *curia* of the lords' house with the profits at the time of the market there', the whole being let 10 years later 'to the wife of Thomas Wyse'.[13] There is no record of a market at Dawlish in the thirteenth and fourteenth centuries[14] and this new one springs up following an expansion of fishing activity. One may surmise, therefore, that it was (partly) a fish market and that the enterprising wife of Thomas Wyse was a rather grand kind of fishwife, perhaps paying over to the lords a fixed rent, taking tolls from sale of fish and pocketing the difference herself.

One further point should be added about the establishment of the Cockwoods as fishing villages. Much of the cottage building was, no doubt, done spontaneously by the new tenants. But the owners of the manor, the Dean and Chapter of Exeter, seem soon to have realized that good profits were to be made here and, if I am reading the documents correctly, it seems that some at least of the cottages were actually constructed by them. In several of the account rolls there are references to cottages *de novo per capitulum edificatur*.[15] This could possibly mean that the Chapter was simply repairing ('building anew') cottages in order to attract tenants, a common feature of estate management in the fifteenth century throughout England.[16] But a more likely interpretation is that these were new cottages actually built by the lord. There may possibly have been philanthropic motives (housing for the landless), but profit too may have been an important consideration. In the early sixteenth century the new rents from cottages at the Cockwoods brought in a total of £6 8s., the tithe of the fishery, as we have seen, was running at over £20 at this time and the new market made 16*s.* for the Chapter. If much of the trade at the market was indeed in fish, this means that about £27 came yearly to the Chapter from fish-related activities on this single manor, at a time when the average rent from a farm holding of standard size was about 8*s.* In addition there were more occasional windfalls from the entry fines for the cottages when they changed hands. To suppose that the Chapter stimulated some of this economic development by constructing a few cottages seems reasonable enough.

For one other place, Hallsands, a rough date may be put on the origins of the fishing village, although there are some difficulties with the documentation. The site, on the coast of Stokenham manor, is known as a watching place for fish as early as the fourteenth century (above chapter 5). Then, in 1505-6, an indulgence was granted to all those who would contribute to the building of a chapel of ease, almost certainly at this spot.[17] A simple story – and it may be the true one – would explain that the fishing farmers of the manor had been content with, perhaps, a simple cross at their fishing station when it had been no more than that, but that some of them petitioned for a chapel of ease when the transition took place and a permanently occupied village developed. There are some difficulties in this interpretation, presented by documentation relating both to the chapel and to the settlement itself, though these can be surmounted with some confidence.

Evidence of a more circumstantial kind adds a number of other sites to the list of places where fishing villages probably grew up in the late fifteenth century and the first half of the sixteenth. We can now say that the three Cockwoods on a creek of the Exe, Lympstone Strand on the opposite shore, Dawlish Strand just beyond the mouth of the Exe, Babbacombe in Babbacombe Bay, Cockington (where there is record of a newly built cottage in 1528)[18] in Tor Bay, Dittisham and Warfleet on the Dart, Hallsands and, perhaps, some of the other three fishing villages of Start Bay, Hope, Hooe and Oreston opposite Plymouth – all very probably date from this time. And, of course, there are many more for which any type of evidence for their origins around this time is non-existent.

6.2 Climatic change and coastal security

Fishing is notoriously prone to surges and setbacks resulting from the fickle behaviour of the waters and of the creatures inhabiting them. 'In this year, 1740, God was pleased to send his blessing of a great fishery amongst us after a failure of many years', wrote the vicar of Clovelly in his parish register. Then: 'In this year, 1742, the fish was small and poor and less in quantities. In this year, 1743, but an indifferent fishing. In this year, 1744, worse than in the preceding. In the year 1745 still worse.[19] In the year 1746 much worse.' Here the vicar gave up his recording in despair.

Thanks to the scientific work of Southward, Boalch and Maddock we know that, in the South-West, as elsewhere, the relative abundance of fish of different types has been affected in the recent past by climatic change which has an impact on the temperature of the sea.[20] The departure of fish from the sea off Clovelly in the middle of the eighteenth century was probably, therefore, caused by some change, perhaps minor and local, in water temperature. All recent commentators on the changing English climate pick out the period between about 1450 and about 1530 as a time of improvement, especially from the point of view of temperature, and it is intriguing to find that it was then that there took place a permanent development of fishing villages along the South Devon coast. Could there have been a connection between the two?

Martin Parry, basing his comments on a great variety of evidence, writes of 'a run of mild, wet winters and dry, warm summers' between these years. Christopher Dyer, using data on the prices of grains, calculates that in only four years between 1462 and 1520 were harvests disastrously bad, and three of those were consecutive (1481-2, 82-3, 83-4), which may reflect only one climatic disaster, that affecting the subsequent two years because of shortage of seed corn. No other 60-year period of the Middle Ages was fortunate in having so few years of dearth. Of course, we cannot say, from this type of information, precisely what type of weather resulted in such a run of good harvests: presumably we are dealing with a period in which summers were warm and also dry, causing grains to ripen well. Finally, Lamb, in a synopsis based on a

Transition: from Cellar Settlement to Fishing Village

great variety of evidence, describes a warmer climate at the end of the fifteenth century, marked especially by mild winters.[21]

It is interesting to speculate that an improving climate might have resulted in an abundance of fish (of what types it would be rash to guess) and that this, in turn, encouraged the development of fishing villages. But this argument cannot be sustained. First, when climate began to deteriorate after the 1530s, to produce the so-called second ice age which lasted into the seventeenth century and later, the fishing villages did not disappear (although that could have been because modern scientific evidence suggests that some species of fish proliferate in warming climates while others become more abundant when climate cools). Second, people will not begin to fish full-time for a livelihood unless there is a quick and increasing demand for their catches; this demand (discussed later in this chapter) must have been the fundamental stimulus, while a warmer climate and greater abundance of fish may simply have been a coincidental secondary cause, adding to the confidence of fishing communities as they were developing.

It is also worth pondering on the relationship between coastal security and the development of coastal settlement, because the political historian will quickly point to the coincidence between the establishment of the first permanently occupied fishing places on the coast and the conventional date for the ending of the Hundred Years War (1475). There is no doubt that the whole of the southern coast of England was unsafe for much of the duration of the war (1328-1475). If we confine ourselves to the South-West, there are references to 'incidents' at many places, record of these being most likely to have survived for the larger and wealthier communities – the port towns – rather than for obscure stretches of coastline in between them. Teignmouth, always the most exposed of the ports, was attacked in 1340.[22] Near Dartmouth in 1404 a Breton force landed and attempted to sack the port; the event is recorded in both English and French chronicles, though with different emphases dictated by patriotism; and also in a letter from the town's mayor to Henry IV.[23] Fowey was attacked in the reign of Henry VI (1422-61) according to John Leland who probably heard accounts of the raid from the immediate descendants of those who had experienced it.[24] On this occasion, and in other accounts of foreign raids on port towns, the role of women in defence is stressed; this is understandable because many of the menfolk may have been absent at sea. Plymouth, too, was attacked on several occasions.[25]

References to raids and attacks on lesser places and on the rural coastlands can also be found. An abbot of Torre, whose house was highly visible from enemy ships or pirates scouting in Tor Bay, claimed that he had incurred 'intolerable charges for the defence of those parts'. The people of East Budleigh, in what the crown clerk called a 'lachrymose complaint', petitioned Edward III in 1347 for reduction of taxation because foreigners had destroyed three ships and twelve boats (probably merchant ships and fishing boats); Parliament agreed to the request. The plight of the people of Revelstoke was even more desperate: when, in the fifteenth century, the parish went on a wake to the inland mother church of Yealmpton, the enemies of the realm were accustomed to row or sail in and burn and spoil the whole district.[26] In Cornwall, the vicinity of Polruan and Bodinnick was burnt and wasted in 1380, and the manor of Dorset, close by, was said to be 'devastated and desolate' in 1487.[27] Attacks on rural manors and their cellar settlements, for the purpose of securing supplies, were probably more numerous than the sources indicate, for the burning of a few poor houses and barns is not the stuff of which chronicles are made.

The unsafe nature of the South Devon coast in the fourteenth and fifteenth centuries is clear not only from the references given above but also by a perception of insecurity which lay behind the building of defences.[28] The corporate defences – castles, block-houses, chains – of the larger ports of Plymouth, Dartmouth and Fowey are well documented. Leland thought that the town of Teignmouth once had a wall, Stonehouse had defences quite separate from those of Plymouth, while new work on the walls of Exeter in 1377 may have been connected with a fear of foreign attack.[29] Defences were also built by individual lords who were constantly requested by the Crown to live in those of their manor houses which lay near the coast. Philip Courtenay's manor house at Powderham was, unusually, as close as could be to the shore and in the 1390s he fortified it; 'no toy castle this'[30] for in 1455 it withstood a serious siege as part of the bickering and battles between the families of Courtenay and Bonville. Powderham Castle looked out over the Exe to Nutwell House on the opposite shore, another manor which was probably fortified, while the bishop's palace at Paignton, vulnerable because it faced long sands which made for easy landing by the enemy, had defensive walls and also towers, one of which survives.[31] At Exminster, on the western shore of the Exe, Leland saw remains of a manor house 'embattled in the front' while the manor houses at Hooe, Ilton and Stonehouse are further examples of defended residences near the coast; Cockington manor house, very close to the exposed landing place of Livermead Sands, seems to have had defences of some kind.[32] At each of the port towns of Fowey and Kingswear there was at least one fortified private residence.[33]

All of this evidence reveals that the coast of South Devon was regarded as unsafe during the Hundred Years War which is sometimes said to have ended at the treaty of Picquigny (1475). 'Was this, indeed, as has been asserted, the real end of the Hundred Years War?' – so asks one influential work on the subject. 'It is permissible to doubt it', runs the answer, for towards the end of his life (1483) Edward IV was again in the course of military preparations against the old enemy and in the early sixteenth century, under Henry VIII, there was 'an uneasy system of truces kept in an atmosphere of mutual suspicion' and also open war and invasion of France.[34] Towards the end of Henry's reign the clouds hung more darkly still over the south coast of England as it seemed inevitable that there would be invasion from a new powerful combination of catholic countries intent on overthrowing England's presumptuous king and his ecclesiastical reforms. At this time people who lived near the coast must have been as anxious as were the compilers of the huge coastal chart of about 1540, with its annotations noting likely landing places and its depiction of fortifications 'made' and (mostly) 'not made'.[35] Some of the latter were eventually constructed as blockhouses or bulwarks of earth: for example at Dartmouth (by the town), at Brixham (possibly by the town), at Salcombe (possibly by the Crown), at Powderham (likewise) and at Blackpool, Exmouth and Slapton (all apparently built by the county).[36] These did not precede, but *followed*, the establishment of fishing villages. Moreover, threats from piracy – which were so severe in western Cornwall that the armed mariners were paid 'for keeping the fishermen safe from pirates' – did not diminish in the early sixteenth century.[37]

We can conclude, then, that fishing villages were established *despite* perceived and real dangers along the South Devon coast. Some force of a strong nature therefore lay behind their establishment. That force was probably the powerful, relentless, many-sided process of economic development which took place in South Devon at the end of the fifteenth century and the beginning of the sixteenth, which is discussed in detail in the following section.

6.3 Social and economic contexts

Fig. 6.1 provides a simple model which relates establishment of fishing villages to increase in population. In this section population will be discussed first and the various linkages in the diagram later on.* The diagram limits itself to developments at home, but ventures to distant fisheries and foreign demand (the export trade in fish) are dealt with at the end of the section.

The most simple and direct link is between increase in population and what the diagram rather crudely calls an 'overflow' of people from rural settlements, in coastal or inland parishes, towards the shore. To regard fishing villages as having been peopled by the surplus produced by a growing population is a novel theme, but it fits in very well with the observations of many historians on squatters' cottages in other situations during the sixteenth century. Growth of population soon produced new buildings in forest regions: for example, the 'great number of unnecessary cabins and cottages built . . . by strangers' in the Forest of Dean and in Kingswood in Gloucestershire or the 'continual erecting of new cottages' reported from Rockingham Forest. In some cases the building of these new cottages on the 'waste soil of the manor' gave rise to new settlements, just like the fishing villages of the South Devon coast. In sixteenth-century England emigrants from rural parishes were

---

*The figure is presented at p. 164 so as to be close to the main discussion of the links.

also attracted to towns where the poor urban inmate 'became for the town what the poor cottager on the waste was for the village'. Many of these immigrants to towns were attracted to outskirts and suburbs where 'mansions were fewer and poor tenements much more common', and here 'ribbon development was beginning in the later sixteenth century' as, for example, in the poor, extra-mural parish of St Sidwell in Exeter or along Foregate in Worcester.[38]

The fishing villages of the South Devon coast fit very well into the same pattern, but for this argument to stand a case must first be made for an increase in population beginning as early as the last two decades of the fifteenth century and first two of the sixteenth when the villages were becoming established. Historical demographers who study medieval England warn us that there is every reason to expect variations in population trends from place to place and from region to region.[39] In some parts of England the demographic recession of the fifteenth century came to an end rather late. Thus Ian Blanchard showed that in parts of the Midlands a turning point in demand for land took place in the 1520s, probably reflecting an increase in population. On the West Midlands estate of the Bishops of Worcester there was an upturn in the 1470s and 1480s in the level of the fines which tenants paid when they entered holdings (with some set-backs in the early sixteenth century). On the same estate, lists of serfs show that families were significantly larger in the first two decades of the sixteenth century (between three and four children per family) than they had been in the 1470s, when average family size shows a population of serfs which was barely replacing itself. Finally, a commencement of population growth whose timing was highly variable between different manors comes from the Essex studies of Larry Poos: on some manors population was falling or static around 1500, but, on two, upsurges were recorded in the last decade of the fifteenth century.[40] In short, while parish registers leave no doubt that population was rising rapidly in the 1540s, the onset of growth was highly variable.

For Devon, when we investigate this topic we must make do with indirect evidence – from the fishing villages themselves, from trends in the land market and from the sizes of towns. First, evidence from the fishing villages themselves has been discussed earlier in this chapter: on several manors new cottages were being built on the shore between the 1480s and 1510s. These could possibly reflect a *shift* in population, that is the relocation of families which had previously held farms inland; but such an explanation is highly unlikely because there is no evidence for growing vacancies in the stock of farm holdings at this time; indeed there was growing competition for farm holdings, which indicates a demand for land rather than a reluctance to occupy it. It is far more likely that the newly built cottages on the shore represent the 'overflow' from a growing population and gave chances for family formation among people for whom there were now no niches left in rural settlements.

Second, evidence relating to the land market indicates that in South Devon there was a relatively early recovery from the recession of the fifteenth century. For two manors we have relatively good series of court rolls spanning much of the century: Stoke Fleming, a coastal manor next to Dartmouth, and Sidbury, a little way inland from the coast just east of the Exe. Some figures are presented in Table 6.1 which shows the expected trough in demand for holdings in the 1430s, then a recovery towards the end of the century. In the 1430s, on both manors, many holdings became vacant and very few were taken up again rapidly, some lying empty for many years. This situation is characteristic of low demand for land, probably a result of a shortage of population. The turning point, when no holdings remained vacant at the end of the year, has recently been described by Margaret Yates as an indication of 'recovery from the recession of the mid-fifteenth century':[41] at Stoke Fleming it took place a little earlier (in the 1480s) than at Sidbury (1490s). After this turning point, there are many indications of demand for land, of competition for land and, by implication therefore, of a growing population. Thus at Sidbury in 1495, Thomas Spray made sure that his wife Matilda and their son were added to his existing copy – a type of arrangement which was rare in earlier decades – and paid an extra sum for this privilege. Entry fines for single holdings were always £2 or above in the 1490s whereas they had been 26*s.* or below in the 1420s; even cottages without land raised fines of £2 in the 1490s, a sure sign of a high demand for accommodation among the landless. At Stoke Fleming in 1498, a long line of tenants came before the manorial court in order

Table 6.1 Demand for land at Sidbury and Stoke Fleming as indicated by numbers of holdings remaining vacant at the end of the year, 1420s–1490s

Vacant holdings at the end of each year (means for each decade)

	Sidbury	Stoke Fleming
1420s	3	no data
1430s	5	5
1440s	2	2
1450s	3	no data
1460s	3	3
1470s	no data	2
1480s	3	1
1490s	0	0

Sources: ECA, DC 4798–4835; DRO, 902M/Stoke Fleming court rolls.

to insert the names of their wives and sons on to their copies, in some cases paying substantial sums for doing so: these tenants were making sure that they kept holdings within the family, a desire which reflected greater competition for land.[42] Analysis of entry fines from several other manors near the coast in East Devon reveals that payments made for entry into particular holdings were far higher in the 1490s and 1510s than they had been in the 1460s and 1470s.[43]

Third, a suggestion of the beginnings of population growth in Devon at a relatively early date comes from an oblique direction: from estimates of the sizes of towns, particularly Exeter. The best estimate of the medieval population of Exeter is for 1377 because in that year two relevant sources survive, a record of the first poll tax and a list of heads of households who contributed to a levy of murage (the expenses of repair of walls). Luckily the two sources concur in giving a total population figure for city and suburbs of around 3000.[44] For the early sixteenth century, several authorities have suggested a less safe figure of around 8000, based on the lay subsidy and military survey of the 1520s.[45] This last figure should not surprise us, for Exeter was England's fourth most wealthy provincial town at this time, having risen from a rank of only twenty-second in 1377. The oblique argument which is being proposed here is that an increase in population of the order of 5000 people must have taken many decades to complete, especially since cities must have had high death rates in the Middle Ages, as they did in early modern times. During the period between 1420 and 1450, Exeter's people 'did not entirely escape the woes that beset so many other English towns'.[46] Growth in population must have come later. An increase in the order of 5000 people cannot possibly have been crammed into the first two decades of the sixteenth century (the growth rate would have been phenomenal and unparalleled); Maryanne Kowaleski believes that much of this demographic expansion took place in the later decades of the fifteenth century.[47] Carus-Wilson was of the opinion that East Devon towns such as Tiverton and Bradninch sprang to life again, presumably with increasing populations, in the 1470s and 1480s.[48] Moreover, for some other towns, such as Tavistock, it is possible to argue a case similar to that presented above for Exeter. Tavistock housed about 320 people in the 1370s but by the 1520s had 650, at a very conservative estimate, and it is unlikely that this doubling in size occurred in the first 20 years of the sixteenth century – it must have begun earlier.[49]

This is not the place to discuss, in depth, the reasons for a local surge in population – after the set-backs lasting for much of the fifteenth century – which was precocious by any standards. One suggestion should, however, be briefly made. The southern parts of Devon seem to have been distinctive (though perhaps not unique) in the early commencement of population growth. The region was also distinctive in having *two* industries, tin working and cloth making, which were likely to prosper again as a result of the general revival of English foreign trade which took place in the 1470s; no other county, perhaps, had this dual advantage. The revival in trade is not in doubt. General synopses and studies of trade in particular commodities all agree in finding 'relief and expansion', 'marked recovery' and 'general recovery' in the 1470s and 1480s,[50] encouraged by restoration of relations with France, Burgundy and the Hanse and by the ending of civil war at home. Tin working expanded rapidly: there is only one figure for Devon's tin output in the 1480s but by 1494 it had reached over 300 thousand pounds weight for the first time (compared to figures around 100 or 140 thousand in the 1440s and 1450s), the 500 thousand mark was passed in 1515 and the 600 thousand mark in 1521.[51] This is a remarkable rate of growth. Cloths exported from the port of Exeter reached a height of over 10 thousand in 1501-2 whereas the level in 1460s had been around one thousand.[52]

The impact of these industrial developments was all the greater because they were highly concentrated in space; on the southern and western borders of Dartmoor (because of the tin industry); in that same area, in towns to the south of it and in countryside to the east of Exeter (by virtue of the cloth industry). We must also remember that the whole of this truly industrialized zone was fringed to the south by a coastline with two large towns (Exeter and Plymouth), many ports and diverse fishing stations, all prospering at the end of the fifteenth century. There can have been few other English regions which shared so many advantages for economic development at this time.

There were many positive links between different sectors of the economy. When tin production was increasing, tin workers had money to spend and this stimulated both agriculture (purchase of foodstuffs by non-farming tinners) and the urban economies of the stannary towns as well as towns distant from the stannaries, such as Exeter with its redistributive role. Likewise, when cloth production was increasing, agriculture prospered and towns grew in size; the latter because a proportion of the cloth workers were urban and because the towns were markets for wool, yarn and cloth as well as for foodstuffs needed by non-farming cloth workers. There may well have been positive links between tin working and cloth making, for it is remarkable that almost all of the towns officially connected with the stannaries – most especially Tavistock and Ashburton – and others close to tin working areas, for example South Zeal, were important for cloth making, and this also probably applied to their adjacent countrysides.[53] The connection needs much more investigation, but it may well be that families were involved in both trades, the division of labour being either seasonal or sexual; alternatively, cloth making may have been taken up when there were temporary set-backs in metal extraction, as happened on the medieval lead fields of Derbyshire.[54]

The connection between economic development and growth in population is made by the newly created opportunities for the formation of families. The getting of tin was in the hands of two types, farmer-tinners who combined both of those occupations, and labouring tin workers, a workforce among whom young, landless men (perhaps life-cycle tin workers) may have predominated and which was highly mobile, with men seeking employment in the stannaries for a year or two, then leaving them.[55] Likewise, cloth-workers belonged to different groups. Certain towns – such as Exeter, Cullompton, Tiverton, Bradninch, Ottery St Mary, Honiton, Crediton, Ashburton, South Zeal and Tavistock – contained concentrations of cloth workers.[56] In the countryside there were smallholders who also engaged in cloth making and cottagers who combined the craft with labouring. Both are in evidence in manorial sources[57] and also in the charming picture painted in the sixteenth century by John Hooker who saw 'at the hall door . . . of the house . . . the wife, their children and their servants at the turn spinning or at their cards carding'; no husbands are mentioned – clearly they were away from the house, labouring or running a smallholding.[58] The importance of cloth working in the countryside is clear from the presence there of many fulling mills and also from the will of John Lane of Cullompton (d. 1529), a merchant clothier, in which he bequeathed money not only to the town but to 100 parishes around about, as if to emphasize his debt to workers living in them.[59] Among most of these types, in both industries, extra income might follow from industrial expansion: in the stannaries production of tin *per capita* was often very low, so there was usually spare time to be taken up,[60] and increasing demand for cloth could be met by taking up slack within a smallholding or by the spreading of work within the family. Among the unmarried – young male workers in the stannaries and young female spinners – higher incomes, if saved, could lead to earlier acquisition of a cottage or urban property and, therefore, earlier family formation. Parents with some involvement in these industries might be able to save a little in order to help some of their children set up in marriage; in both cases the occupation of the recently formed family was, as likely as not, to have been in industry or labouring – or fishing – because (as discussed above)

Transition: from Cellar Settlement to Fishing Village

niches in the world of rural landholding were not increasing, indeed were becoming scarcer towards the end of the fifteenth century. The connection between earlier family formation and increase in fertility and growth in population is a well known theme in English demographic history.[61]

This simple model, which links two distinctive features in the economic development of South Devon during the last decades of the fifteenth century – early beginnings of population growth and expansion in two key industries – seems very plausible. It gives a key role to fertility in population change, thus avoiding the problem of mortality which appears, from a number of local studies in different parts of England, to have been at high levels at this time.[62] It is realistic because it involves a high proportion of the population of Devon south of Dartmoor and east of Exeter: we shall never be able to calculate the figure precisely, but it would not be surprising if between one in five and one in ten of the population was involved in tin working and cloth making at the end of the fifteenth century. Finally, the model accounts for the beginning of population growth by linking it to two industries whose products were largely traded abroad, thereby avoiding the problem of having to reconcile industrial growth with relatively low home demand in England at large. Demand in far-off places (for tin, as distant as Egypt and Syria) was presumably translated back to tin and cloth workers through trading chains and chains of credit: for example, in the tin industry, master tinners had close relations both with merchants and also with the workers in the stannaries to whom they advanced cash.[63]

Having examined some of the evidence for growth of population in South Devon during the late fifteenth and the early sixteenth centuries, we may return to Fig. 6.1 (p. 164) and look at the connections between that growth and the establishment of fishing villages. The most simple connection is what the diagram calls 'overflow', a rather crude term for the extra people of both sexes who are born in a place when its population begins to rise through increased fertility. Let us take a hypothetical and largely rural parish half way (say 6 miles) between the coast and the stannary districts of southern Dartmoor. When population began to rise as a result of greater involvement of family members in cloth working and tin working (or in both), the overflow of people could either continue living in the parish, combining farm labouring with another craft, or they could migrate to places where there were full-time non-agricultural occupations to follow, namely in towns or along the coast where fishing villages were developing. Acquisition of land within their home parish was not normally an option, because subdivision of holdings was not an established practice (a topic discussed in Chapter 7).

And, in fact, we have good evidence for migration towards the coast even before fishing villages were established: there was always the lure of the port towns with their exotic connections and of the unknown seas beyond, while to live in a rural coastal parish was to have access to all of the diverse resources of the shore mentioned in Chapter 3. In 1355, Thomas Knollyng, a villein of Ashburton, 10 miles from the coast, was manumitted (freed) by his lord so that he could practise his 'trade of mariner' with more success.[64] During the fourteenth and fifteenth centuries there is evidence in court rolls of villeins fleeing from Stoke Fleming to the adjacent port town of Dartmouth, from Waddeton to Churston Ferrers and Galmpton with coastal and estuarine shores respectively, from Ide to Dawlish, from Uplyme to Lyme Regis and from Hartland in North Devon to Northam, a parish which contained the minor port of Appledore.[65] Lists of the descendants of two serfs of *Schylhall* (near Menheniot in Cornwall) show that many of them ended up in towns by sea or river, at East Looe, Saltash (two), Plympton and Plymouth.[66] From about the time when fishing villages were being established we can trace migration to shoreline manors in the lay subsidy rolls for 1524 and 1525 for the hundreds of East Budleigh and Colyton, both east of the Exe. From Farringdon there was movement to Exmouth, from Gittisham to Woodbury and Lyme Regis, from Colyton to Axmouth and Sidmouth, from Northleigh to Branscombe, from Ottery St Mary to Woodbury. All of these movements were of males who had paid the subsidy in 1524; the source excludes most women and many young men who were subsumed within the household of a parent (and who were likely additional migrants).[67] We do not know how such moves were predetermined. In cellar settlements which survived late into the seventeenth century one finds that some cellars were rented by outsiders to the parish, a practice,

Transition: from Cellar Settlement to Fishing Village

which, if it existed in the Middle Ages, might have influenced the destinations of later permanent migration towards the shore.[68]

The examples in the last paragraph are largely of movements to the coast from places a few miles inland. In a coastal parish, already with a cellar settlement, 'overflow' population might lead to some offspring becoming full-time fishermen instead of practising fishing as a by-employment in the manner of their forefathers. Here, in a coastal parish, the neatest solution in a family with two sons would be for one to have retained the family holding when the father died or retired, while the other took over the old cellar belonging to the farm and converted it into a dwelling; the one was now engaged almost wholly in farming while the other became primarily a fisherman (with, perhaps, a little mutual help in both directions when the occasion required). The son who became the fisherman would have gained his experience working alongside his father at the nets, an association for which some evidence exists in the Woodbury tithe payments.[69] It is possible to discern what may have been relationships of the kind suggested here in the rental of 1513 for the three Cockwood fishing villages discussed in the first section of this chapter: the rental (of Dawlish manor), it may be remembered, catches them very soon after formation. Thus John Badford who held a fishing cottage at Middle Cockwood could well have been the brother of William Badford who farmed at Shutterton, inland; William Brasent who held another fishing cottage may have been the brother of William Brazent who farmed at Eastdon; and the rental reveals other relationships of this kind. However, a good number of the cottage holders in the rental had surnames not found elsewhere in the document, nor in earlier rentals of Dawlish manor, and it is probably correct to regard these as immigrants from other parishes, pushed out by pressure of population and drawn towards nascent fishing settlements by the lure of being able to make a livelihood from fishing. One of these bore the relatively unusual name of Winkleigh which comes from the inland parish of Winkleigh, 30 miles away to the north-west, in poor Culm measures countryside. It is interesting to suggest a relatively long-distance migration in his case, though it has to be said that there are some dangers in using surname evidence of this kind in the early sixteenth century.[70]

Another very simple connection shown in Fig. 6.1 is between growth of population and that growth in demand for fish without which villages occupied by full-time fishing families probably could not have developed. As the population of South and East Devon expanded in the late fifteenth century and early sixteenth, demand for fish must also have increased and must have continued to grow during the rest of the sixteenth century and first decades of the seventeenth when we know, from studies using parish registers, of continued expansion of population at a high rate. Demand for fish may, in fact, have increased at a higher rate than increase in people, because demand is affected by the social composition of a population as well as by numbers. If the proportion of the population classed as poor increased – as it did in the sixteenth century, which witnessed rapid inflation in prices, though not in real wages, as well as rapid growth of population – then the likelihood is that more fish was consumed *per capita* (Fig. 6.1) because fish was the cheapest form of protein. Thus the Privy Council, investigating the

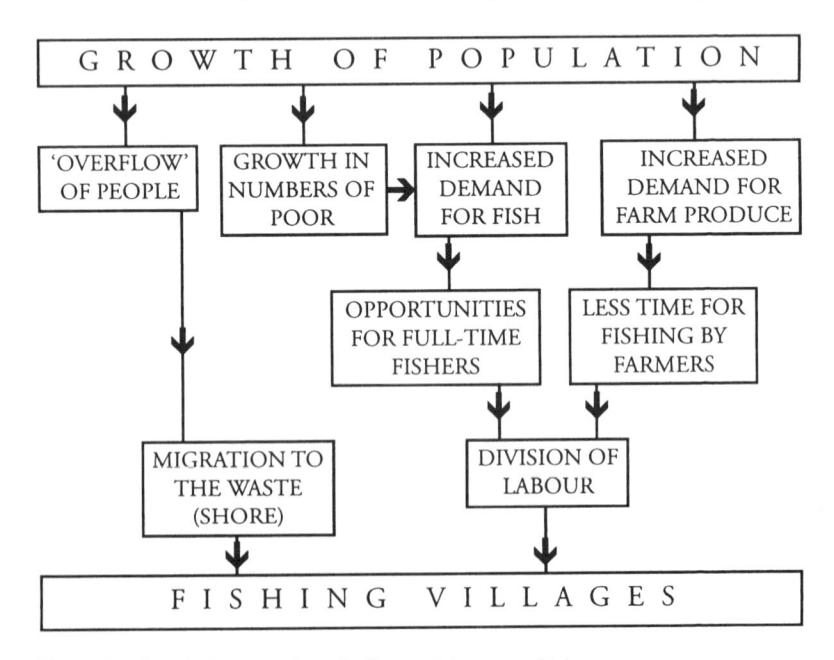

```
                     GROWTH OF POPULATION
                              │
        ┌─────────────┬───────┴───────┬─────────────┐
        ▼             ▼               ▼             ▼
   'OVERFLOW'    GROWTH IN       INCREASED      INCREASED
   OF PEOPLE    NUMBERS OF    →  DEMAND        DEMAND FOR
                   POOR          FOR FISH      FARM PRODUCE
        │                          │               │
        │                          ▼               ▼
        │                   OPPORTUNITIES    LESS TIME FOR
        │                   FOR FULL-TIME    FISHING BY
        │                      FISHERS        FARMERS
        │                          │               │
        ▼                          ▼               │
   MIGRATION TO              DIVISION OF ◄─────────┘
   THE WASTE                   LABOUR
   (SHORE)                       │
        │                        ▼
        └────────►  FISHING  VILLAGES  ◄──────────
```

Figure 6.1 Population growth and village origins: some links

export of pilchards from Plymouth in the 1580s, ordered that a proportion should be retained at home because this food sustained the poor; William Chapple, writing of Devon towards the end of the eighteenth century, knew that cheap fish 'much alleviate the distresses of the poor'; and several historians have argued that, earlier on, in the Middle Ages, fish was a very important cheap and readily available food for those with small incomes, the main reason, perhaps, for the controls on exports which were imposed from time to time by the Crown. To Sylvia Thrupp, 'fish was the most important food of the ... poor', next to bread, and this explains why the authorities of the City of London, and of other towns, tried to ensure that it was cheap and fresh and not a great source of profit to illegal dealers.[71] In short, growth of population – at first in South Devon, then in more distant parts of southern England within Exeter's extensive hinterland – and increase in the numbers of the poor, was bound to have an important impact on demand for fish. There was no problem in the transmission of knowledge from centres of demand to those who fished, because, as we have seen, sophisticated networks of fish carriers and fishmongers were already in place by the end of the fourteenth century.[72]

A new development shown on Fig. 6.1 is the 'division of labour' when fishing on rural manors as a by-employment among farmers gave way (in places only partially) to fishing by people who may now call themselves fishing families, and fewer farmers fished. The two occupations became divided from one another to a large degree; they were split as settlement was split too, farms, hamlets and villages remaining largely agricultural and the people of the new coastal cottage settlements being occupied primarily with fishing and other maritime occupations. Ian Blanchard found the same type of division of labour in the Mendip lead mining settlement of Chewton: 'under conditions of recurrent population pressure, . . . the farmer-miner [was] . . . replaced by either the cottar . . . or the professional miner'.[73] Division of labour may be approached from two directions. First, from the agrarian point of view, greater demand for foodstuffs, as population grew, would have brought about an intensification of farming. From the small amount of evidence which is available on this topic, we know that intensification on Tavistock Abbey's demesne at Hurdwick involved an increase in the application of sand to the soil in the 1490s and another one during the first two decades of the sixteenth century (giving rise to fuller employment among the sand gatherers of the coast and the bargemen of the estuaries). Intensification probably also took the form of an increase in the acreage of cropped land, rendered easy under Devon's convertible system of husbandry in which all that was needed was a reduction in the proportion of the acreage of a farm that was in ley grass. Intensification of farming also involved enclosure of strip-field systems in South Devon, during the late fifteenth century and the early sixteenth. There may also have been an increase in the number of dairy cattle, a speciality of South Devon, and an increase in the acreage of cider orchards. Certainly, by the time that John Leland saw South Devon in the 1540s, the region was 'the fruitfulest part' of the shire, while a century later it seemed to Tristram Risdon to be 'the garden of Devonshire'. All of these changes – more sanding, enclosure, more acres under crops, more cattle and orchards – were labour intensive, so that among those who had been fishing farmers, less time was now available for fishing. At first, and to some degree, they provided extra employment in the countryside for servants in husbandry of both sexes and for labourers, delaying a little the 'overflow' effect shown on Fig. 6.1 but, given the relentless expansion of population, only for a time.[74]

From the point of view of those who forsook the land to live in a newly established fishing village, the greater demand for fish which now existed meant that they could spend more time on fishing and related activities, visiting more grounds and working at all seasons. Now no time was lost in switching from farming to fishing and back again and all of a family's application could be devoted to the shoreline and the sea. Adam Smith, who assigned a central role to the division of labour in economic development, explained this last point rather brutally and with some exaggeration: he wrote of a workman 'who is obliged to change his work and his tools every half hour' and who, therefore, is 'incapable of any vigorous application'. Smith also saw that, in some cases, division of labour resulted in a worker more frequently carrying out the same task, so that 'a frequency of action insensibly fits men to a dexterity of accomplishing it', those who came to live solely from the sea, the rivers and the foreshore becoming ever more adept at exploiting their resources. He also thought that division of labour to the ultimate degree could be stultifying, but he excluded farming from that generalisation because an all-round farmer must by definition have 'a great variety of knowledge and experience'.[75] The same could be said for fishing and other shoreline occupations: a family which gained all of its livelihood from the shore and waters needed to be acutely aware of a vast number of facts which today we label as ecological, climatic and culinary; it needed to have intimate knowledge, in all seasons and weathers, of the sea, the sea bed, the foreshore and the strip of land above high water mark on which, as likely as not, it dwelt; it also needed to appreciate the properties of wood of many types, of hemp (nets, ropes) and of iron. Thus, when division of labour took place, were intensified the skills, inventiveness and resilience for which fishing families are well known.

We end this section with a brief discussion of developments beyond the coastline of Devon and beyond the realm. The full-time fishermen of fishing villages would have been able to visit more grounds than their farming predecessors who, by definition, could not generally be absent from their home manors for very long. These grounds might be along the coastline of Devon or, increasingly from the end of the fifteenth century, beyond the county and beyond the realm, developments which we are only now beginning to piece together thanks to the work of Maryanne Kowaleski and Todd Gray. Even before the Black Death some Devon boats were to be found fishing on the east coast of England, for the murage accounts of Great Yarmouth (documents recording monies collected for repair of the town's walls) reveal them there during the herring season. They were in small numbers, however, and came from the port towns, including the minor ones such as Brixham and Exmouth.[76] Generally, it is not until the 1450s and 1460s that we begin to hear again of longshore fishing voyages by Devon men around the English coast: off Lyme Regis (Dorset) in the 1450s, off Lydd (Kent) in the 1460s and off Great Yarmouth (Norfolk) in the 1450s.[77] By the 1450s, too, ships from Devon and Cornwall are to be found in the Icelandic fishing grounds and by the last decade of the fifteenth century off the Atlantic coasts of Ireland.[78] Again, most vessels on these long fishing voyages were from the port towns: from Exmouth to Yarmouth, for example, from Saltash to Iceland and from Plymouth.[79]

It was not until later that the smaller places, the fishing villages themselves, seem to have begun to participate in these voyages to distant shores. In the 1540s Paignton ships went as far as Mount's Bay in Cornwall, the Scillies, Winchelsea in Sussex and Ireland. A Kenton man, Philip Crope, fished off Great Yarmouth and Scarborough and also in Ireland in the later 1550s, details of his voyages surviving in a church court case concerning tithes to be paid on catches in distant waters. Men from Stokeinteignhead fished off Scarborough and off Winchelsea in the 1560s. Newfoundland attracted mariners from Tormoham, so it was claimed, from 1565 onwards, Stoke Gabriel men from 1568 and men from St Marychurch from 1570; these were not ports, involvement of the port towns in this fishery being earlier, from Plymouth in 1544 and from Kingswear probably in the late 1550s.[80] Two important points arise from this evidence. First, as we might expect, distant fisheries were not generally exploited by the people of rural parishes until fishing villages had grown up in them and until a division of labour had taken place, allowing fishing mariners to make these long, time-consuming voyages. Dittisham seems to be a conspicuous exception to this generalisation. Second, the home parishes of the people involved (the sources, being largely from cases concerning tithe, specify parish rather than residence) in the main had quays or creeks which provided shelter for ships between voyages. Paignton had a quay, possibly since the fifteenth century, Kenton had two sheltered creeks, the parish of Stokeinteignhead contained two fishing stations, at Shaldon and Ringmore Strand, with the possibilities of a quay at the latter, Stoke Gabriel had a quay of some kind by 1566 as well as a creek, the parishes of St Marychurch and Tormoham could use the quay at Torquay. The earliest venturers to distant fisheries did not come from more exposed fishing villages, such as those of Start Bay, at which it would have been difficult to protect ships of a size suitable for these voyages.

Earlier in this section we mentioned home demand for fish, not only in Devon but also in the extensive territory which formed the hinterland of the great redistributive centre of Exeter. Foreign demand must also be discussed, because it too was growing at the time when fishing villages were becoming established. Wendy Childs has shown that, by the 1490s, valuable exports of hake, especially, and of herring, rays and pilchards were being shipped abroad from the ports of the South-West and Maryanne Kowaleski has conclusively demonstrated that, by the same decade, a significant proportion of ships leaving those ports for overseas destinations were carrying consignments of cured fish. France and Iberia were the principal destinations and, in Devon, Dartmouth and Plymouth were the chief places from which these voyages originated.[81] The volume of the trade is difficult to measure because of a complicated system of exemptions, and it is difficult to chronicle trends over time in detail because of the patchy survival of customs accounts. We shall never know the proportion of these exports which was made up of catches of fishing farmers living in rural manors (catches then taken to the port towns for curing and export), and the proportion contributed by the full-time fishermen of the ports who worked on inshore, longshore and foreign fisheries. On these and related matters we can only deal in probabilities. It is highly probable, given the great number of rural fisheries, that these were already contributing to foreign exports in the era when fishing by farmers was the norm, for the value of exports from south-western ports almost trebled during the fifteenth century. There may have been a threshold beyond which the combined contribution of fishing farmers and of the mariners of the port towns could not satisfy foreign demand (on top of home demand), although it is unlikely that this in itself would have resulted in the development of fishing villages without the necessary demographic developments described earlier. However, knowledge of the existence of foreign demand must have served to boost the confidence of the first men and women who settled permanently on the shores of rural manors and created the first fishing villages. It is equally probably that the people of these villages, once established, helped in the further expansion in exports, through their fishing activities which were now carried out on a full-time basis.

170   *The Evolution of the Fishing Village*

[1] Gray, *E-SMS*, p. xvi; DRO, 48/13/2/3/3, Cockington probate inventories. See also Cockington leases from the eighteenth century which show that some farmers also still had cellars: 48/13/3/1/78.
[2] PRO, SC6 827/17-32; SC6 Hen. VII/93.
[3] PRO, SC6 827/24-31; reference from customs account kindly supplied by Maryanne Kowaleski.
[4] ECA, DC 3684 gives *Cokwood West*, *Middelwode* and *Estcokwode*.
[5] Accounts: ECA, DC 5030-5044 (up to 1538-9). Court rolls: 4784-91 (up to 1536-7). Rentals: 2937, 5053, 2936, 3684.
[6] ECA, DC 5037 (account); 5053 (rental).
[7] For example, in one of the earliest surviving account rolls, tithe of fish is mentioned: ECA, DC 5031, account of 7-8 Hen. V.
[8] ECA, DC 5037, 5036.
[9] ECA, DC 3684.
[10] DRO, 1508M/Lon./estate/legal correspondence.
[11] A full statistical study could be made of rents and entry fines during the early years of the existence of these villages, and also of the early occupants. I hope that somebody locally will do so.
[12] ECA, DC 5036, 5113.
[13] ECA, DC 5041, 5042.
[14] Kowaleski, 'Markets'.
[15] For example, in the account of 1511: ECA, DC 5040.
[16] See, for example, C. Dyer, 'English peasant building in the later Middle Ages', *Med. Arch.* 30 (1986), pp. 22-3; H. S. A. Fox, 'Occupation of the land: Devon and Cornwall', in E. Miller, ed., *The Agrarian History of England and Wales*, vol. 3, *1348-1500* (1991), pp. 171-2.
[17] N. Orme, 'Indulgences in the Diocese of Exeter 1100-1536', *TDA* 120 (1988), p. 31. The difficulties start here. The chapel is said, in the register of Bishop Oldham, used by Orme, to be dedicated to St Mary and to be situated at Start. Strictly Start means 'tail', 'tongue of land' (O. E. *steort*), so sticklers for accuracy might expect the chapel to have been on the headland itself; in fact Hallsands is just over 1 mile from the tip of Start Point, but it can still be regarded as on the 'tail'. There are no later references to a chapel on the point itself. There are, however, good references to a chapel at Hallsands: J. James, 'Medieval chapels in Devon' (unpublished M.Phil. thesis, University of Exeter, 1997), p. 140; PRO, SC11/168, Stokenham rental of 1548. The rental of 1548 introduces a further problem: it mentions only one cottage at Hallsands. It is, however, a suspect rental, especially so in its recording of small cottage properties: it mentions hardly any at all, whereas in about 1360 there had been 61 (Huntington Library, HAM box 64). It is hardly likely that such a large number had all disappeared, so it would seem that the rental, drawn up for the Crown by distant officials, is defective. In the introduction to his excellent *Elizabethan Court Rolls of Stokenham Manor, 1560-1602* (1984), p. xvi, Mr. W. A. Roberts dates the beginnings of Hallsands much later, in the early seventeenth century. However, his arguments do not take into account the fact

that there can be a lag between the establishment of a settlement and first references to it in some kinds of documentary sources (the length of the lag depending on the types of sources which are being used and the strength of vigilance by lords and officials). It must also be noted that my argument associating the new chapel with an *inhabited* village, rather than a cellar settlement, contradicts my views on Ringmore chapel, above Section 5.2.

[18] DRO, 48/13/4/1/8, account of 20-1 Hen. VIII.

[19] M. Dickinson, ed., *A Living from the Sea: Devon's Fishing Industry and its Fisherman* (1987), p. 57.

[20] A. Southward, G. Boalch and L. Maddock, 'Climatic change and the herring and pilchard fisheries of Devon and Cornwall', in D. J. Starkey, ed., *Devon's Coastline and Coastal Waters* (1988), pp. 33-57.

[21] M. Parry, *Climatic Change, Agriculture and Settlement* (1978), p. 66; C. Dyer, *Standards of Living in the Later Middle Ages* (1989), pp. 262-3; H. H. Lamb, *Climate, Present, Past and Future*, vol. 2, *Climatic History and the Future* (1977), pp. 440, 461.

[22] E. M. Thompson, ed., *Adae Murimuth Continuatio Chronicarum* (Rolls Series, 1889), p. 109 n. 6.

[23] L. Bellaguet, *Chronique du religieux de Saint Denys* (1839-52), vol. 2, p. 181; F. C. Hingeston, *Royal and Historical Letters of Henry the Fourth* (1860), pp. 270-3.

[24] Leland, *Itinerary*, vol. 1, p. 204. See also F. E. Halliday, ed., *Richard Carew of Antony: the Survey of Cornwall* (1953), p. 209.

[25] C. Gill, *Plymouth, a New History: Ice Age to the Elizabethans* (2nd edn, 1979), pp. 76-91; M. M. Oppenheim, *The Maritime History of Devon* (1968), pp. 13-19.

[26] *Cal. Pat. Rolls, 1348-50*, p. 206; *Cal. Pat. Rolls, 1345-8*, pp. 467-8; G. R. Dunstan, ed., *The Register of Edmund Lacy Bishop of Exeter, 1420-1455* (5 vols, DCRS, new ser., 7, 10, 13, 16, 18, 1963-72), vol. 4, pp. 314-8.

[27] *Cal. Inq. Misc.*, vol. 4, p. 77; *Cal. Inq. Post Mortem Hen. VII*, vol. 1, p. 94.

[28] The best recent summaries are R. A. Erskine, 'The military coast defences of Devon, 1500-1956' (with earlier references), *NMHD*, vol. 1, pp. 119-21 and R. Higham, 'Public and private defence in the medieval South West', in *idem*, ed., *Security and Defence in South-West England before 1800* (1987), pp. 42-6. These two works give the principal references to defences at the port towns of Plymouth, Dartmouth and Fowey. Plymouth is now very well covered by A. Pye and F. Woodward, *The Historic Defences of Plymouth* (1996).

[29] Leland, *Itinerary*, vol. 1, p. 225; Pye and Woodward, *Historic Defences*, p. 151; I. Burrow, 'The town defences of Exeter', *TDA* 109 (1977), p. 35.

[30] Higham, 'Public and private defence', pp. 41-2.

[31] T. Risdon, *The Chorographical Description or Survey of the County of Devon* (1811), p. 56; C. R. Straton, ed., *Survey of the Lands of William, First Earl of Pembroke* (2 vols, 1909), vol. 2, opposite p. 388, drawing showing the walls and gatehouse at Paignton but not the tower which still survives.

[32] Leland, *Itinerary*, vol. 1, p. 232; CRO, FS3/93/3/130B, facsimile of a drawing of Hooe by Spoure, showing crenellated walls and a gatehouse; Risdon, *Chorographical*

Description, p. 176; BL, Aug. I i, map of about 1540; DRO, 48/13/4/1/2, Cockington account of 18-19 Hen. VI. This last document mentions what was probably the gatehouse to the manor, suggesting a walled outer enclosure.

[33] Place at Fowey and Gommerock at Kingswear. For Place, see Leland, *Itinerary*, vol. 1, p. 204. For the licence to crenellate said to be for Gommerock, see M. A. Watts, *Archaeological and Historical Survey at Gomerock, Kingswear, Devon* (Exeter Archaeology, 1997), p.5. This is an excellent report, but the matching of the documentary to the physical evidence is not easy and the tower could possibly have been on the opposite shore.

[34] E. Perroy, *The Hundred Years War* (1959), pp. 347-8.

[35] BL, Cott. Aug. I i 35.

[36] Dartmouth: Leland, *Itinerary*, vol. 1, p. 221 and H. R. Watkin, *Dartmouth*, vol. 1, *Pre-Reformation* (1935), p. 268. Brixham: *Letters and Papers, Hen. VIII*, vol. 3, pt 2, p. 997. Salcombe and Powderham: H. M. Colvin and others, *History of the King's Works*, vol. 4, *1485-1660*, pt 2 (1982), pp. 595, 594 and n.; Erskine, 'The military coast defences', pp. 120-1. Blackpool and Slapton: R. Stanes, *A Fortunate Place: the History of Slapton in South Devon* (1983), pp. 50-2. Exmouth: Erskine, 'The military coast defences', pp. 120-1; *Letters and Papers, Hen. VIII*, vol. 20, pt 2, p. 106; R. Bush, *The Book of Exmouth* (1978), p. 23. The references in Stanes and Bush come from the churchwardens' accounts (some of which I have checked) of parishes which did not contain the sites at which these defences were constructed; the accounts specify contributions towards the costs of the defences.

[37] C. J. R. Fletcher, *Short History of St Michael's Mount Cornwall* (1951), p. 61 for payments to mariners. Pirates: T. Gray, 'Turkish piracy and early Stuart Devon', *TDA* 121 (1989), pp. 159-71; idem, 'Turks, Moors and the Cornish fishermen: piracy in the early seventeenth century', *Jnl Roy. Inst. Cornwall*, new ser., 10 (1990), pp. 457-75; S. Bhanji, 'The involvement of Exeter and the Exe Estuary in priacy', *TDA* 130 (1998), pp. 23-49.

[38] J. Thirsk, 'The farming regions of England', in *eadem*, ed., *The Agrarian History of England and Wales*, vol. 4, *1500-1640* (1967), pp. 71, 96; P. Slack, *Poverty and Policy in Tudor and Stuart England* (1988), p. 68; A. L. Beier, *Masterless Men: the Vagrancy Problem in England 1560-1640* (1985), p. 47.

[39] R. M. Smith, 'Human resources', in G. Astill and A. Grant, eds, *The Countryside of Medieval England* (1988), p. 194.

[40] I. Blanchard, 'Population change, enclosure and the early Tudor economy', *Ec. Hist. Rev.*, 2nd ser., 23 (1970), pp. 439-41; C. Dyer, *Lords and Peasants in a Changing Society: the Estates of the Bishopric of Worcester, 680-1540* (1980), pp. 230-2, 288; L. R. Poos, *A Rural Society after the Black Death: Essex 1350-1525* (1991), pp. 96-103.

[41] M. Yates, 'Change and continuities in rural society from the later middle ages to the sixteenth century: the contribution of west Berkshire', *Ec. Hist. Rev.*, 2nd ser., 52 (1999), p. 635.

[42] Sources for this paragraph are given in the note to the table. The figures in the table are for all tenancies except leased demesne.

[43] B. E. Morris, 'The south-western estates of Syon Monastery in the later middle ages'

Transition: from Cellar Settlement to Fishing Village 173

(unpublished M. A. thesis, University of Kent, 1977), pp. 125-6.

[44] Kowaleski, *LMRTE*, pp. 371-5.

[45] W. T. MacCaffrey, *Exeter, 1540-1640: the Growth of an English County Town* (printing of 1978), p. 11; W. G. Hoskins, *Two Thousand Years in Exeter* (1960), p. 51.

[46] Kowaleski, *LMRTE*, p. 90.

[47] *Ibid.*, p. 88.

[48] E. M. Carus-Wilson, *The Expansion of Exeter at the Close of the Middle Ages* (1963), p. 18.

[49] An urban rental of the late thirteenth century (DRO, W1258M/D/84/2) gives 120 burgage plots; multiplied by 4.5 (number of people per plot) this gives a population of 540 at that time. I assume a decline of only about 40% to take into account falling population in the plagues of 1348, 1361 and 1369 in order not to be seen to be fuelling my argument; many historians would give a more severe estimate. The resulting figure is about 320 people in the 1370s. The figure for the 1520s is from T. L. Stoate, ed., *Devon Lay Subsidy Rolls 1524-7* (1979), pp. 152-3. This source gives about 130 taxpayers in 1525. I have multiplied these by a factor of 5 but, again, many historians would have used a higher figure for a growing and thriving town.

[50] J. L. Bolton, *The Medieval English Economy 1150-1500* (1980), p. 293; E. M. Carus-Wilson, 'The overseas trade of Bristol in fifteenth century', reprinted in her *Medieval Merchant Venturers: Collected Studies* (1967 edn), p. 48; H. L. Gray, 'English foreign trade from 1446 to 1482', in E. Power and M. M. Postan, eds, *Studies in English Trade in the Fifteenth Century* (1933), p. 33.

[51] J. Hatcher, *English Tin Production and Trade before 1550* (1973), pp. 158-9.

[52] E. M. Carus-Wilson and O. Coleman, *England's Export Trade 1275-1547* (1963), p. 145.

[53] Evidence of cloth working in South Zeal and in its parent manor of South Tawton: PRO, C132/31; E179 95/12 (draper, tucker, and wool-beater as surnames); E101 388/11 (aulnager at South Zeal); C139/94 and 123 (fulling mills mentioned in inquisitions *post mortem*); *Cal. Inq. Misc.*, vol. 6, p. 126 (fulling mill); Stoate, ed., *Devon Lay Subsidy*, pp. 63-4 (weavers, tuckers and tanners). On rural manors where tin working took place there was often a fulling mill also, an outstanding example being the small and remote Dartmoor manor of Jordan in Widecombe in the Moor: DRO, 48/13/2/4/1, court of 26 Oct., 27 Eliz., and following courts.

[54] I. Blanchard, 'Industrial employment and the rural land market 1380-1520', in R. M. Smith, ed., *Land, Kinship and Life-Cycle* (1984), pp. 229-35.

[55] Hatcher, *English Tin Production*, pp. 63-4.

[56] All of the towns named (except Tiverton) were places visited by the aulnager (royal quality control official) in the late fourteenth century: Kowaleski, *LMRTE*, p. 24; H. S. A. Fox, 'Medieval rural industry', in R. Kain and W. Ravenhill, eds, *Historical Atlas of South-West England* (1999), p. 328. For Tiverton, see Carus-Wilson, *Expansion of Exeter*, pp. 18-19.

[57] Examples are Sibil Pounde, 'spinster' and cottager of Sidbury, who in 1499 stole wool dyed a 'bloody colour' from a neighbour; Stephen Ham, another cottager from Sidbury,

whose chattels included wool, 'a pair of cards' and a 'turn'; and William Mochknap, a small farmer of Clayhidon, whose chattels in the autumn of 1381 included grain, sheep and wool, perhaps stored away for winter work: ECA, DC 4835, Sidbury court near St Denis, 15 Hen. VII; CRO, AR MSS, Clayhidon court near Michaelmas, 5 Ric. II. In East Devon and south of Dartmoor, the presence of numerous cottages and cottagers at a place is usually a sure sign of the presence of cloth-workers. Examples are 21 cottages at Uffculme in the 1420s, alongside no less than three fulling mills; numerous landless cottagers at Sidbury; and the growing number of cottagers at South Brent (with its teazle mill and fulling mills) in the sixteenth century: PRO, C138/52, 139/51, extents of Uffculme; H. S. A. Fox, 'Servants, cottagers and tied cottages during the later middle ages: towards a regional dimension', *Rural History* 6 (1995), pp. 10-12 (case study of Sidbury cottagers); DRO, 123M/E/31, 37.

[58] W. J. Blake, 'Hooker's Synopsis Chorographical of Devon', *TDA* 47 (1915), p. 346.

[59] For the distribution of fulling mills see Fox, 'Medieval rural industry', pp. 326-7; for Lane, see E. M. Carus-Wilson, 'The significance of the secular sculptures in the Lane Chapel, Cullompton', *Med. Arch.* 1 (1957), pp. 113-17.

[60] Hatcher, *English Tin Production*, pp. 85-6.

[61] E. A. Wrigley and R. S. Schofield, *The Population History of England 1541-1871: a Reconstruction* (1981), pp. 454-84.

[62] J. Hatcher, 'Mortality in the fifteenth century: some new evidence', *Ec. Hist. Rev.*, 2nd ser., 39 (1986), p. 28; Poos, *Rural Society*, p. 120; B. Harvey, *Living and Dying in England 1100-1540: the Monastic Experience* (1993), p. 144.

[63] Hatcher, *English Tin Production*, p. 133 (exports), p. 51 (chains of credit in the tin industry). Blake, 'Hooker's Synopsis', p. 346 for chains of credit in the cloth industry: 'first the merchant or clothier buys of the weaver his cloth and pays money, the weaver buys his yarn of the spinster and pays his money. And the spinster buys her wool and pays her money.'

[64] F. C. Hingeston-Randolph, ed., *The Register of John de Grandisson, 1327-1369* (3 vols, 1894-9), p. 1159.

[65] DRO, 902M/Stoke Fleming court rolls; DRO, CR 23, Waddeton court near Corpus Christi, 22 Ric. II and CR 29, Waddeton court near Trinity, 16 Hen. VI; ECA, DC 2857; Longleat House MSS, Uplyme court rolls; CRO, AR MSS, Hartland account of 6-7 Hen. IV.

[66] BL, Add. ch. 64453.

[67] Stoate, ed., *Devon Lay Subsidy*, pp. 1-27. These pages cover the Hundreds of East Budleigh and Colyton in which the tax collectors for 1525 recorded movements made by tax payers since 1524; the same was not done for other hundreds.

[68] Above, Section 5.1 (Woodbury and Kenton) for outsiders.

[69] Above, Section 5.1 (Woodbury).

[70] ECA, DC 3684.

[71] A. L. Rowse, 'A dispute concerning the Plymouth pilchard fishery', *Economic Journal* (*History Supplement*) (for 1932); W. Chapple, *A Review of Part of Risdon's Survey of Devon* (1785), p. 33; A. S. Littler, 'Fish in English economy and society down to the

Reformation' (unpublished Ph.D. thesis, Swansea, 1979), *passim*; S. L. Thrupp, *The Merchant Class of Medieval London* (1989 edn), pp. 95-6.

[72] Above, Sections 4.2 and 4.3.

[73] I. Blanchard, 'Labour productivity and work psychology in the English mining industry, 1400-1600', *Ec. Hist. Rev.*, 2nd ser., 31 (1978), p. 9.

[74] H. P. R. Finberg, *Tavistock Abbey* (1951), p. 91; H. S. A. Fox, 'The chronology of enclosure and economic development in medieval Devon', *Ec. Hist. Rev.* 2nd ser., 28 (1975), p. 187; *idem*, 'Farming practice and techniques: Devon and Cornwall', in E. Miller, ed., *The Agrarian History of England and Wales*, vol. 3, *1348-1500* (1991), pp. 315-7; Leland, *Itinerary*, vol. 1, p. 244; Risdon, *Chorographical Description*, p. 5.

[75] Adam Smith's *Wealth of Nations* (1776) cited in D. A. Reisman, *Adam Smith's Sociological Economics* (1976), pp. 149-50, 154.

[76] A. S. Littler, 'Fish in English economy and society down to the Reformation' (unpublished Ph.D. thesis, Swansea, 1979), Appendix 3. The author notes ships of 'Hope' and 'Hooe' at Great Yarmouth, as well as those of Brixham and Exmouth. From all that is known about the development of the Devon places with these names it would appear that the ships at Great Yarmouth were from places with similar names in other counties.

[77] M. Kowaleski, 'The expansion of the south-western-fisheries in late medieval England', *Ec. Hist. Rev.,* 2nd ser., 53 (2000), p. 441.

[78] *Ibid*, pp. 442-3.

[79] *Ibid.*, p. 441 (Exmouth); E. M. Carus-Wilson, 'The Iceland venture', reprinted in her *Medieval Merchant Venturers: Collected Studies* (1967 edn), pp. 119, 128 (Saltash). For Plymouth, Kowaleski, 'The expansion', pp. 435-7, and especially the table on p. 437 which shows the dominance (in Devon) of that port both in exports of salt, to be used for preserving fish on long fishing voyages, and in exports of fish, some of which would have been caught on such voyages.

[80] T. Gray, 'Devon's fisheries and early-Stuart northern New England', *NMHD*, vol. 1, pp. 140-2.

[81] W. R. Childs, 'Devon's overseas trade in the late middle ages', *NMHD*, vol. 1, p. 80; Kowaleski, 'The expansion', pp. 435-7.

Chapter Seven

CONCLUSION:
FISHERIES AND SETTLEMENT HISTORY

This conclusion is not a summary of the findings of previous chapters: conclusions, when such are possible, are included in almost all of the sections of this monograph and the list of contents has been made especially detailed so that readers can easily seek out the pages in which they are most interested. Rather, this final chapter offers some further observations on two types of coastal settlement around which much of this work has pivoted – cellar settlements and fishing villages. All of the themes dealt with here are explored with a light touch, and I leave it to others to add further detail.

Because fishing in the past has often, in England at large, been a by-employment among farmers, and because farms tend not to be sited directly on the shore, it would be surprising if something akin to the cellars and cellar settlements of Devon were not found elsewhere. In making a rapid and selective examination of the printed evidence, one comes across several examples of shoreline structures which offer instructive parallels. On Birnbeck Island near Weston-Super-Mare the sprat and herring fishermen dried their nets and maintained a hut, 'low, thatched and kept in repair by a fund raised among themselves'. On the beach at Hythe were 'lodges', presumably used for the storage of nets.[1] A little further to the south along the Kentish coast, on the shingle of Dungeness, the fishermen of inland Lydd maintained 'cabins' which are well documented back to 1356 and survived into the twentieth century. The late eighteenth-century description of Hasted sets the scene: here fishermen had 'cabins, and a common dining room, erected on the shore . . . where they remained the whole time of the fishing season'. Further details have been given in a recent article by Mark Gardiner.

The earliest reference to the 'cabons' of Dungeness is in a financial account of 1356 and they are further mentioned in a rental of 1402. Fifteenth-century references imply that fishermen sometimes slept in these structures overnight and that the roofing material was thatch. By the late fifteenth century some cabins were being let out to stranger fishermen, including some from Devon, and in 1571 a company or fellowship of Lydd fishermen was set up.[2] So here at Dungeness was a well documented seasonal settlement of fishermen who had their own common facilities and common rules for the better governance of their activities. 'Lodges' were apparently a feature of other places on the coast of Kent.[3] The writer of the register of Norwich Cathedral Priory, looking back to the reign of Henry I (early twelfth century), describes five sheds (*domuncule*) on the beach near Great Yarmouth, 'for the reception of fishermen' during the herring season, while at Mousehole and Penzance in Cornwall, a survey of 1327 mentions lodges 'of foreign fishermen'.[4]

One can add to these examples. W. G. Hoskins, speculating on the place-name Winterton on the Norfolk coast, wrote imaginatively as follows: the 'winter quarters . . . [were] for the purpose of catching the larger codling which move inshore as the colder weather sets in. This source of food, in a primitive economy, was too valuable to ignore . . . Huts provided the winter quarters in the first place, probably more like a camp than a regular settlement.' The transition (in this case from a seasonal fishing site to an agricultural village, perhaps with fishing still practised as a by-employment) took place relatively early, for Winterton had the normal accoutrements of a farming settlement according to Domesday Book. Another suggestive place-names on the east coast of England is Somercoates in Lincolnshire, now some way inland. Again, one may speculate: could these 'cots' have originally been huts used in summer by fishermen and salt-makers? Salt-making on this coast leaves large accumulations of debris, mounds called 'maures', and on those mounds, safe from the sea, salt-makers erected huts for storage and cottages as summer dwellings: 'those [maures] that have cottages now upon them are at the present used for salt', runs an explanation of a late sixteenth-century map of Marsh Chapel, south of

Conclusion: Fisheries and Settlement History

Grimsby (Lincolnshire). Eventually maures could be reclaimed, which would explain why Somercoates is now so relatively far from the sea.[5]

The search for seasonally used fishing settlements has been most fruitful in the North, where place-names are especially informative, for only there (and in Cornwall and Wales) do we have names which specifically denote seasonal settlement. Names in Old English *scela*, 'a temporary hut, especially a shepherd's hut on the summer pastures', and in Old Scandinavian *skali*, a 'temporary hut or shed', are especially revealing. It is clear from these interpretations, taken from A. H. Smith's *English Place-Name Elements,* and also from similar ones in the *Oxford English Dictionary,* that shiels were, in the vast majority of cases, seasonal dwellings – usually in uplands – connected with the movement of animals of all types (not simply sheep as in Smith) to summer pastures, sometimes over relatively short distances.[6] In a minority of cases the terms could, however, be used to describe dwellings or shelters associated with other activities: thus a fourteenth-century inquisition into the customs and liberties of the lead-miners of Alston Moor in Cumberland found that those men operated from seasonally used *shelis*, while Angus Winchester has recently described the 'peat scales' of Eskdale, where turves were dried before collection.[7] It would be surprising if the term were not used in northern Britain for seasonally used fishing sites. And three diagnostic references show that this was indeed so. First, an early thirteenth-century deed relating to a property of Paisley Abbey refers to 'the shielings of the fishermen' *(scalinge piscatoribus).* Second, a description of the River Tweed, communicated in 1830 to the Society of Antiquaries of Newcastle-upon-Tyne, states that it was normal for a fishery to have a building called 'a "shiel" or "shield", in which the fishermen at certain seasons kept their nets . . . and use as a dwelling'.[8]

A third, most graphic, reference comes from the medieval town of North Shields (Northumberland), built on land belonging to Tynemouth Priory.[9] By the end of the thirteenth century the place had become a minor port, importing coal and fish, exporting hides and wool and containing around one hundred dwellings. Upstream the anger of the people of the Crown's grand borough and port of Newcastle-upon-Tyne was roused. They could boast a royal charter which dated back to the twelfth century and they were recognised by the Crown as one of the official ports of the realm when, for example, a levy on trade was taken in 1204; now the little upstart downstream was attempting to divert their trade to its own good. In about 1267 the resentment burst out into violence when the mayor of Newcastle and a party of armed men descended upon North Shields, assaulted the monks, burnt mills and houses, confiscated coal and did damage estimated at £300. The dispute rumbled on and in 1290 the Priory was brought to Parliament to answer the King and the burgesses of Newcastle.

It is in the course of the long proceedings of this case that we hear from the mouths of local people, speaking through their attorneys, what their forebears had told them about the origins of North Shields. Tynemouth was originally an agricultural settlement inland; it had villeins holding bovates (a measure of agricultural land) and owing servile works, it had labourers in husbandry and village fields. Then, probably in the early thirteenth century, 'three huts (*sciales*) only' were made on the bank of the Tyne, by fishers: so it was said by protagonists in Parliament who could not themselves have witnessed this event, although they could have heard it as a 'foundation story' from their fathers and grandfathers. For both parties the story had its point, because the Prior of Tynemouth could claim that the first event in the foundation of Shields was spontaneous and not at his house's instigation, while Newcastle could complain that the place had become, by the end of the thirteenth century, monstrous and a commercial threat, compared to its state in its earlier humble beginnings. There would have been no objection to a few huts on the shore but subsequent additions to the settlement were hurtful to Newcastle: first, in about 1225, a prior of Tynemouth had built cottages for fishermen who, in return for the privilege of using his shore for their boats, were to provide fish for the monks; then the Priory built further houses and mills (often associated with ports) and bakeries which provided visiting ships with bread. But it is the beginning of the story, not its end, which concerns us here: either because they well knew what the name Shields meant in a coastal context, or because they had heard tell of the beginnings of the settlement, those who spoke before Parliament in

Conclusion: Fisheries and Settlement History

1290 described those beginnings as a small cluster of fishermen's storage huts on the river bank.

The three crucial references given here indicate beyond doubt that place-names in shiel or the like can relate to fishing huts akin to the cellars of the South Devon coast. Because of this there is some need to reinterpret coastal place-names containing this element, even where there is no independent evidence of their having started out as fishing places. Such place-names have been noted before, by J. McDonnell, who thought that they denoted seasonally used pastoral settlements for keepers of animals feeding off the grass of sand-dunes.[10] This could have been so in some cases, but it is worth looking at the sites in a little more detail. Sandscale, north of Barrow-in-Furness, and North Scale, west of it, are so markedly perched upon the shore that a mainly piscatorial rather than agricultural function seems probable. The same could be said for Seascale in Cumberland and possibly for the field-name *Winscales* (near Sellafield) just to the north of it, while, from the same county, another Scandinavian term with connotations of intermittent use (*both* 'a booth, a temporary shelter') has given us the coastal name *Scaddebothes*, the first element probably referring to a type of fish.[11] Further research, by those closer at hand, needs to be carried out on these intriguing sites.

The establishment of fishing villages along the South Devon coast is the *dénouement* of this monograph and I want to end by discussing three themes concerning that type of settlement. The first is about chronology. In supposing that fishing villages in some parts of Britain began as storage huts, like those of the South Devon coast, I certainly do not wish to imply that the transition from one to the other took place everywhere at the same time as it did in Devon – namely at the very end of the fifteenth century and in the sixteenth. Differences from coast to coast in ease of access to markets, in the behaviour of shoals of fish and in coastal topography must mean that there were different chronologies in different places. However, one point must be stressed: some fishing villages are, emphatically, earlier than the eighteenth century. It is necessary to make this point because, in the literature of fishing, it has often been claimed that few such villages pre-date relatively recent times. Thus Paul Thompson, in his influential and acclaimed *Living the*

Fishing, states that (with certain exceptions) 'there are not many small independent fishing communities proper, of the village type, which can be traced back before the eighteenth century', the reason being that 'it was not easy to find – or supply – a regular fish market' before then. The same view is to be found in T. C. Lethbridge's expert *Boats and Boatmen*: 'specialized fishing appears to be a phenomenon of recent growth . . . because the roads ashore were so bad that you could not dispose of the catch before it was rotten'. Mark Bailey, also, has wondered whether the 'specialist fishing village of the 20th century is more a product of the industrial revolution than a feature of the Middle Ages'.[12] All this may well have been true of parts of the Scottish coast and the islands off it where much of Thompson's innovative research was done and where there were severe marketing problems because of great remoteness and lack of urban markets close at hand. Here – although fishing crofters remained very common into the eighteenth and nineteenth centuries and although there may have been a few specialist fishing villages at an early date as evidenced by small-scale maps from the seventeenth and early eighteenth centuries – many settlements of full-time fishers are relatively late creations. Some were set up by landowners in programmes of estate improvement (following clearances in some cases): examples are East Buckie, Banffshire (1723), Gardenstown, a little way along the coast, established by Alexander Garden of Troup (1720) and Leverburgh, Outer Hebrides, founded by the first Lord Leverhulme. Others were the results of work by the British Fisheries Society, founded in 1749 (Ullapool, 1788, and Tobermory, Mull).[13]

But the view that fishing villages are very late developments certainly does not apply to all English coasts. Many Devon fishing villages date, as we have seen, from around 1500 and others to later in the sixteenth century; Staithes and Robin Hood's Bay (Yorkshire, North Riding) were probably in existence as fishing villages in the fifteenth century or the early sixteenth; at North Shields, Tynemouth Priory established a community of fishing families in the thirteenth century; Mousehole in Cornwall, where 40 heads of household were recorded in the early fourteenth century, was probably more of a fishing village than a port.[14] Reginald Lennard perceptively noticed that, at the time of

Conclusion: Fisheries and Settlement History

Domesday, Eaton on the Dee was a place rendering 1000 salmon each year, where six fishermen formed the majority of the inhabitants and this may be regarded as a fishing settlement of a kind. In Wiltshire at the aptly named Fisherton Delamere, another inland fishery, 26 bordars and cottars worked alongside 16 villeins in 1086, and if the former group were the fishers, this place too may be seen as specialized to some degree.[15] Other local historians will be able to think of further examples and to explain why fishing settlements developed at an early date in particular places.

Thompson and others also exaggerated the constraints of marketing. In fact, fresh salt-water fish was carried further than is commonly believed – to deepest inland Coventry from the coast (east coast or Severn? one wonders) in the Middle Ages and to London from the coasts of Kent and Sussex in the sixteenth century, frequented routes being divided into a series of stages each operated by its own trains of packhorses. The 'Scarborough fish' consumed at Westminster Abbey in the fifteenth century were almost certainly 'fresh', not preserved. Moreover, a good proportion of the volume of fish to be consumed was cured and the distance over which it was transported added only to price, not putridity. Hence the relatively long distances over which fish traders operated in the Middle Ages – from Grimsby to York and London, for example, from Exeter to Wiltshire.[16]

In order to explore a second theme, we move from fishing villages to coastlines which are notable for their lack of settlements of this kind. In his Leicester Ph.D. thesis on the Lincolnshire coast Simon Pawley rightly points out that true fishing villages, perched on the coast, whose people were virtually landless and engaged in full-time fishing and other maritime occupations, are generally absent from the county. Full-time fishermen were to be found, as is normal, in the ports, active and decayed, but a great deal of the county's commercial fishing was carried out from 'multi-occupational coastal villages', set a little way inland, housing people of the type which I have called fishing farmers in this monograph.[17] His thesis contains a great deal of evidence to back up his point and others have found the same thing. For example, Rod Ambler and his team have examined in detail the probate inventories of the parish of Clee, at the mouth of the Humber, from 1536 to 1742, concluding that 'all the men connected with fishing . . . [with two exceptions] were also involved to some degree in farming'. Then again, an eighteenth-century report described the people of the Isle of Thanet as 'amphibious animals, equally skilled in holding helm or plough, according to the season of the year'.[18] What is at issue is not the existence, on some coastlines, of 'multi-occupational coastal villages', but the reasons lying behind the persistence of this type of organization of fishing at some places and the emergence of true fishing villages at others. One reason may have to do with the physical instability of the Lincolnshire coastline: on some stretches, deliberate reclamation, salt-making and silting have extended the shore seawards by up to a mile and more, leaving old ports stranded inland, while other sections of the coast have been eroded away, leaving several churches and chapels, and a good deal of agricultural land, under the sea. As Pawley states, 'the frontier between land and sea was so variable' that settlements exclusively devoted to the latter would in some cases have found it hard to survive.[19]

Pawley's main argument, however, is that 'for a man to cut himself off, by placing all his energies and all his capital in fishing and maritime trade, was . . . unthinkable in a multi-occupational coastal village, because it would have implied rejection of the shared common culture', the dominant rural culture based on working the land and on the products of the land.[20] In other words, there was no splitting of settlement and function because the agricultural ties were the dominant ones. This could well have been the case in Lincolnshire, but it does not apply to all places along the South Devon coast. A tentative explanation of the difference involves farm size. In the Fenland of South Lincolnshire, examined in detail by Joan Thirsk, well over half (61%) of all farms were of under 5 acres according to surveys made early in the seventeenth century and a farm of over 30 acres was rare indeed (7%); smallholders lived from the profits of grazing, especially cattle, and from the products of the fen itself (wildfowl, fish, osier and sedge), with a little arable. Smallholdings were also very abundant in the Lincolnshire Marshland, though slightly less so than in Fenland, and large farms were likewise scarce.[21]

A complete contrast is provided by surveys of some coastal manors in South Devon. Thus surveys of South Huish and Galmpton, made in about 1715, give an average size of holding (cottages excluded) of 35 acres and reveal only two smallholdings of 16 acres or less. A picture of a landholding structure heavily skewed towards large farms may be reconstructed from an early sixteenth-century survey of Stokenham, taken just at the time when fishing villages had recently come into being on the coast here. The average size of farm holdings was 54 acres; only very few (7%) were under 16 acres and hardly any under 5 acres.[22] In the Fenlands, holdings fragmented partly through partible inheritance, partly because of the richness of soils and the presence of diverse other resources. In South Devon, there is hardly any sign of fragmentation and none of partible inheritance. Engrossing was common so that at Stokenham, for example, since the standard size of tenure was 30 acres, many farms of 60 acres (and even 90 and above) were to be found. Even when pressure of population was very great, in the sixteenth century, the stock of large farms remained intact, as can be shown where a succession of surveys survives.[23] In the Fenlands, the tradition was for new families to be accommodated on the land, in cottages or subdivided holdings, and a strong ethos of land-holding, described by Pawley, grew up. The ethos on many manors in South Devon was for holdings to be retained intact on the death of an occupier; this bound some family members securely to the land, but it repelled those who could find no niches there and, with population rising rapidly (Chapter 6), the only solution, apart from emigration, for some of these people was to build or occupy a cottage on the shore.

It is possible, in fact, to accommodate both this argument and Simon Pawley's to developments along the South Devon coast during the late fifteenth century and the early sixteenth. Where large farms predominated, as on the manors mentioned in the previous paragraph, agricultural ties prevailed among family members who were due for the succession to holdings; other members became redundant when population was expanding and, by force of circumstance, might become fisherfolk. On some other manors, especially in East Devon, there was a stock of small farms, probably of ancient origin and not the results of partible inheritence, so that at Woodbury in 1525, at Kenton in 1578 and at Cockington in 1655, smallholdings of 16 acres and under comprised 28%, 35% and 67% respectively of all holdings.[24] On such manors there was scope for a variety of responses: some people, mainly smallholders, retained their dual occupations of farming and fishing, like Pawley's Lincolnshire farmers, well into the seventeenth and eighteenth centuries while others, finding themselves without an agricultural inheritance, became coastal cottagers.

A final theme to be developed here is that the circumstances of the origins of a place can colour its character for many subsequent centuries. Circumstances of origin still have a profound influence on the morphology of the fishing village. 'Huddled old houses and thatched cottages... an incredible number of recesses and sub-corners... cottages... [which] have no ground floors at all' (Stephen Reynolds); 'full of quaint and interesting corners, rambling old streets and buildings picturesquely piled together' (Stanhope Forbes); streets 'intricate and capricious' (Richard Warner).[25] The apparent disarrangement of fishing villages along the South Devon coast is a result of their origins: first, collections of cellars on the shore, growing slowly, the buildings being added one by one; then evolution, also usually slow and un-planned in most cases, into inhabited places.[26] High density of buildings has been explained (Chapter 5) by the cramped sites on which these settlements stood and by the fact that cellars, later to be replaced by cottages, had no gardens, almost by definition, and were placed close together – although later in the evolution of these places, small plots might be enclosed, if there was space, to grow hemp for making nets (the 'hemphays' of the documents)[27] and for vegetables. The winding, narrow streets today are simply the interstices between these structures and enclosures.

Marginality and vulnerability are two characteristics of fishing villages which also reflect their origins. These villages were naturally marginal to the manors and parishes in which they were situated, pushed on to shingle banks or sand spits, as at Torcross and Shaldon. Their people were to a degree marginal to rural society, having found no rural employment niches in their home parishes, and hence, perhaps, their traditional sturdy independence and non-conformity. Marginality led to vulnerability. Shoals might desert a stretch of coast for several years on end, or cease to arrive altogether; a site on the sea shore invited battering to destruction from the waves, as happened to several settlements in the vicinity of Start Bay (above, Chapter 2). Fishing villages were vulnerable, also, because of the closely-packed cottages: a cottage 'burnt and not rebuilt' is recorded in a seventeenth-century rental of Oreston and over 50 cottages were destroyed by a fire at Lympstone in the early nineteenth century.[28] The people of fishing villages were vulnerable, too, to mortality from infectious diseases, not only because houses were huddled but also because, like port towns, they frequently received strangers from outside. Finally, they were vulnerable to dearths of grains, for their people were completely reliant on the market for bread: on the manor of Plymstock, in the serious 'national' dearth of 1625-6, large numbers of property holders died, not those from inland parts but among the landless cottagers of Oreston on the manor's shore.[29]

The response to a certain vulnerability was a certain inventiveness and adaptability. It is said that the making of lace of the Honiton type (so called because it was sold in that market town) may have begun as a result of some set-back in local fishing villages, perhaps some temporary desertion of shoals from inshore waters; certainly, the craft was very well developed among the coastal settlements of East Devon.[30] And when we read, in Westcote's seventeenth-century chorography, that the mining and fishing community of Combe Martin (North Devon) was the supplier of almost the whole county with shoemakers' thread, we cannot but wonder if that craft, too, arose during a slump in the fortunes of fishing, makers of nets readily adapting to become makers of thread.[31] Along the South Devon coast, fulling mills for beating cloth in the finishing process are recorded in a number of manors whose people were also involved in fishing; the coincidence of the two crafts is intriguing but lack of time has prevented research into the connections between them.

The nature of the community of fishing villages also connects with their origins. As these villages developed, no doubt a certain degree of social differentiation emerged. We have examples of men who operated from a number of fishing places, who were clearly magnates among their fellow inhabitants, making profits from them all. There was also the woman of Dawlish who cornered the local village fish-market by renting it from the lord, clearly a position of some influence. Towards the end of the fifteenth century we find a tendency for some lords to farm (lease out) the profits of a fishery to a single individual who then, so long as he paid the fixed rent for it, was in a position to exploit and profit from the more ordinary fishers; in the late fifteenth century a distinction was made on the manor of Dawlish between the 'masters' of boats and their 'associates'.[32] But, set against these examples, is the monolithic, uniform nature of the social structure of some fishing villages, well brought out by a rental of Strete Gate (Blackawton parish) in the middle of the eighteenth century. Almost all of the fourteen heads of household held a cottage dwelling alone. A few held two cottages (for sub-letting or perhaps for kin) and one had a garden, but these could hardly be called village grandees. Exactly the same kind of picture is given by a rental of Starcross, around 1700. Almost all heads of household paid a uniform rent of 1s. and all dwellings except one were called 'cottages'; gardens belonging to five out of over thirty properties were all that there was to differentiate a few of the inhabitants.[33] Fishing villages grew up on cramped and restricted sites so that there was not enough space for the development of the coastal equivalents of squire, yeoman, smallholder and cottager inland. On the coast most people, emphatically, were cottagers.

This trait, no doubt, gave a certain solidarity to the community of the fishing village. In addition, the necessity for teamwork and communal participation in many activities bound some families together, as when people co-operated to form the crews of boats or to manage large seine nets. At Stokenham in the fourteenth century, well before the days of the fishing village, people were already forming teams of nine, a team of six people is mentioned in a document from Woodbury in 1434, while on the manor of Dawlish in the late fifteenth century we hear of boats which generally had teams of this same size. Some activities were carried on by individuals on behalf of the community. From Ringmore (Teign) there is a fascinating glimpse of how the ferry over

Conclusion: Fisheries and Settlement History

the river was run: tenants took it in turn 'to help to put the passage boat [ferry] afloat as they are bound to do by custom'.[34] On the manor of Stokenham in the late fourteenth century, certain tenants were chosen to be 'watchers' for fish, 30 in all out of about 160 tenants; these would stand on some high spot on the look-out for the changing colour of the sea as shoals approached and would then warn the whole community of the coming of the fish.[35] We know a great deal about these 'huers', who were vitally important to the whole community, in Cornwall; an act of 1603 (permitting them to go to high places without fear of being sued for trespass) implies that they were just as common in Devon, but they do not frequently appear in documentary sources – understandably perhaps.[36] However, five 'sounders' are recorded under Blackawton in the maritime survey of 1619 and they may have been watchers on high places acting on behalf of the fishermen. At Hallsands, 'hill-men' as the watchers were called there, survived into the twentieth century.[37]

On occasion the community of the fishing village can be seen in action. When the Bishop of Exeter, in 1506, granted an indulgence for all who would help in the construction of a chapel at what was (probably) the new fishing village of Hallsands, presumably he was acting on a request from the majority of the community. Certainly, when the people of the minor port and fishing town of Exmouth desired a chapel of ease in about 1415, it was the 'the inhabitants of the vill' who drew up the petition.[38] We have seen how devotional crosses might be set up at fishing stations and these, if modern parallels can be trusted, were maintained by the community.[39] From Cornwall, one example has been found of a capstan (for winding in boats and nets) which appears to have been rented from the lord by the community, although there are also references to privately owned capstans whose owners presumably charged individuals for their use.[40] In 1434 the fishers of Newton Ferrers made an arrangement with the bailiff, under which they no longer paid individually for permission to fish, but gave a collective fine, so they must have come to some arrangement among themselves in order to divide the sum into shares. Some fishing communities may have owned a common seine, akin to the common plough of agricultural villages.[41] We find, too, that the people of fishing villages enacted by-laws in order better to regulate their fisheries: on Ringmore manor (Teign) in 1632, an individual who dredged for oysters out of season did so 'contrary to an ancient order' (i.e. by-law) and at Exmouth in 1566 there was a by-law giving the dates at which the gathering of mussels and oysters should begin and ordering that no one should take the 'greatest oysters and leave the little behind'.[42]

A strong sense of territoriality and a sometimes hostile reaction to outsiders were reflections of the community of the fishing village and almost certainly relate to concepts of conservation. They were exercised over the foreshore: a Topsham man was accused of taking sand on Kenton foreshore in 1606 while outsiders from Starcross were fined for taking cockles on Exmouth's land in the early eighteenth century. Territoriality also extended to the waters so that at Kenton, Dawlish men were accused of taking oysters in 1638, and in 1566 it was complained that boatmen from Slapton, with their companies, had 'come a tucking to Sidmouth'.[43] Whether or not these antagonisms ever resulted in communal acts of violence is not known – the precedent was there in the conflicts which took place between port towns, presumably over trade rivalries, but perhaps over fishing also. The men of Lyme Regis and the men of Dartmouth 'fought at sea' in the 1260s and in 1322 the people of Lyme were still behaving badly, aiding and abetting men from Weymouth and Portland who had attacked a Plymouth ship, then ransacked and scuttled her.[44] Ill-feeling could be defused by 'friendly' competition, such as the lively regatta on the Fal Estuary which John Leland witnessed in the early sixteenth century and described in verse. The Torcross regatta may have had its origins in rivalry between the fishing villages of Start Bay.[45] Moreover, under conditions of threat, cooperation between fishing communities might take place, as when the fishers of Salcombe Regis and Sidmouth joined together to draw up a petition concerning payment of tithe (probably in the seventeenth century), or in 1536 when all the fishing communities along the coasts of Norfolk and Suffolk petitioned about the oppressive nature of the tolls which they had to pay when selling fish at Hull.[46]

It is not our purpose here to give the impression that all life was harmonious and cosy in the fishing village: acts of theft, trespass and

Conclusion: Fisheries and Settlement History 191

battery all occur in court rolls relating to these communities. But a lack of much social differentiation, vulnerability to so many possible natural and man-made hazards, a strong sense of territoriality, the communal nature of many of the tasks which fishing involved – all of these tended to bind the people of a fishing village together. To a degree, communal activities, in watching and in making up the crews of boats, were already present when fishing was still a by-employment among farmers. This was so, we know from documentary sources, in the fifteenth and fourteenth centuries – and no doubt was also the case in all the misty years leading backwards to Domesday Book and beyond....

[1] *VCH Somerset*, vol. 2, p. 105; A. J. F. Dulley, 'Four Kent towns at the end of the middle ages', *Archaeologia Cantiana* 81 (1966), p. 105.
[2] Hasted's *History and Topographical Survey of the County of Kent*, cited in A. E. Everitt, *Continuity and Colonization: the Evolution of Kentish Settlement* (1986), p. 64; M. Gardiner, 'A seasonal fishermen's settlement at Dungeness, Kent', *Medieval Settlement Research Group Annual Report* 11 (1996), pp. 18-20; A. Hussey and M. M. Hardy, eds, *Records of Lydd* (1911), pp. 185-8.
[3] C. W. Chalkin, *Seventeenth-Century Kent* (1965), p. 150; E. Melling, ed., *Kentish Sources, III, Aspects of Agriculture and Industry* (1961), p. 135.
[4] H. W. Saunders, ed., *The First Register of Norwich Cathedral Priory* (Norfolk Rec. Soc., 11, 1939), pp. 30-3; PRO, C135/3.
[5] W. G. Hoskins, *Fieldwork in Local History* (1967), pp. 82-3; M. W. Beresford and J. K. S. St Joseph, *Medieval England: an Aerial Survey* (1958), p. 241.
[6] A. H. Smith, *English Place-Name Elements* (2 vols, 1956), vol. 2, *s. v. scela, skali*; O.E.D., *s. v. shiel, shieling*.
[7] W. Nall, 'Alston', *Trans Cumberland & Westmorland Antiquarian & Archaeological Society* 8 (1886), p. 14; A. J. L. Winchester, *Harvest of the Hills* (2000), pp. 130-1.
[8] O.E.D., *s. v. shieling*, citing the register of Paisley Abbey; R. Weddell, 'The salmon fishings in the River Tweed', *Archaeologia Aeliana* 4 (1855), p. 303. Both works give other references to shielings associated with fisheries, e.g. 'big scheillis... for resaweing of the fish' (1502); 'the shiel or house where the fishermen lodge' (1845); 'fisheries... called the Pool, South Yarrow, Hugh Shiel, Wen and Walton' (seventeenth century); 'the several fisheries... with all way-leaves, passages, netgreens, shealds, stells, standing places' (1653).
[9] This and the next two paragraphs draw upon H. H. E. Craster, *A History of Northumberland*, vol. 8, *The Parish of Tynemouth* (1907), pp. 248-52, 284-8 and *Rotuli Parliamentorum*, vol. 1, p. 26.
[10] J. McDonnell, 'The role of transhumance in northern England', *Northern History* 24

(1988), p. 4 and n.

[11] Information on *Winscales* kindly supplied by Angus Winchester. *Scaddebothes*: Smith, *Elements*, vol. 1, p. 43; A. J. Winchester, *Landscape and Society in Medieval Cumbria* (1987), p. 110 and p. 115, n. 64, where he prefers a type of fish to the wild plum.

[12] P. Thompson, T. Wailey and T. Lummis, *Living the Fishing* (1983), p. 13; T. C. Lethbridge, *Boats and Boatmen* (1952), p. 47; M. Bailey, 'Coastal fishing off south east Suffolk in the century after the Black Death', *Procs Suffolk Inst of Archaeology and History* 37 (1990), p. 113.

[13] D. Turnock, *Patterns of Highland Development* (1970), pp. 38-45; R. N. Millman, *The Making of the Scottish Landscape* (1975), pp. 156-8, 165-7; A. C. O'Dell and K. Walton, *The Highlands and Islands of Scotland* (1962), pp. 122, 157.

[14] A. Storm, 'Family and maritime community: Robin Hood's Bay c. 1653 - c. 1867' (unpublished Ph.D. thesis, University of Leicester, 1991), pp. 17-18; above, pp. 179-81 for North Shields and Chapter 2, n. 36 for Mousehole.

[15] R. Lennard, *Rural England 1086-1135* (1959), p. 251; *VCH Wiltshire*, vol. 2, p. 154; above, Section 3.1 for bordars as possible fishermen or fishing farmers. I am grateful to John Chandler for the Wiltshire reference.

[16] G. Hutchinson, *Medieval Ships and Shipping* (1994), p. 130; F. J. Fisher, 'The development of the London food market, 1540-1640', reprinted in P. J. Corfield and N. B. Harte, eds, *London and the English Economy, 1500-1700* (1990), p. 78 n.; A. J. F. Dulley, 'The early history of the Rye fishing industry', *Sussex Archaeological Collections* 107 (1969), pp. 51-4; B. Harvey, *Living and Dying in England 1100-1540: the Monastic Experience* (1993), pp. 47, 227 for Scarborough fish; S. H. Rigby, *Medieval Grimsby: Growth and Decline* (1993), pp. 66-7; above, Section 4.3 for Wiltshire.

[17] S. Pawley, 'Lincolnshire coastal villages and the sea c. 1300-c.1600: economy and society' (unpublished Ph.D. thesis, University of Leicester, 1984), pp. 154-97.

[18] R. W. Ambler and B. and L. Watkinson, eds, *Farmers and Fishermen: the Probate Inventories of the Ancient Parish of Clee, South Humberside 1536-1742* (Studies in Regional and Local History, School of Adult and Continuing Education, University of Hull, 4, 1987), p. 23; description of Thanet cited in Thompson, Wailey and Lummis, *Living*, p. 13.

[19] Pawley, 'Lincolnshire coastal villages', pp. 67-96.

[20] *Ibid.*, p. 272.

[21] J. Thirsk, *English Peasant Farming: the Agrarian History of Lincolnshire from Tudor to Recent Times* (1957), pp. 41, 74.

[22] DRO, 1508M/Devon/estate/surveys/whole estate/1; PRO, SC11/168.

[23] PRO, SC11/168; DRO, 123M/E/31 and 37, surveys of Churchstow and South Brent.

[24] PRO, E315/385; DRO, 1508M/Lon./manor/Kenton/6; DRO, 48/13/4/2/4.

[25] S. Reynolds, *A Poor Man's House* (1982 edn, with an introduction by Roy Hattersley, of a work first published in 1908), p. 9; S. A. Forbes, 'Cornwall from a painter's point of view', *Royal Cornwall Polytechnic Soc. Report* 68 (1900), p. 56; R. Warner, *A Tour Through Cornwall* (1809), p. 139.

Conclusion: Fisheries and Settlement History 193

[26] The Cockwoods, discussed in Section 6.1, may be exceptions.

[27] ECA, DC 3684 ('hemphey' at Middle Cockwood, 1513); PRO, E315/385 (½ acre of hempland at Ilfracombe, 1525); DRO, 346M/M/264 ('hemphaye' at Lympstone, seventeenth century).

[28] DRO, W1258M/add./7/1; E. Scott, 'Lympstone: a village story', *TDA* 88 (1956), p. 110.

[29] DRO, W1258M/D/74/7-8, Plymstock courts of April 1626 and April 1627. For very severe mortality in 1625-6, see E. A. Wrigley and R. S. Schofield, *The Population History of England 1541-1871: a Reconstruction* (1981), p. 333.

[30] G. F. R. Spenceley, 'The origins of the English pillow lace industry', *Agricultural History Review* 21 (1973), pp. 87-8, 90, although the theory I put forward in the text is not his. See also H. J. Yallop, *The History of the Honiton Lace Industry* (1992), p. 51.

[31] T. Westcote, *A View of Devonshire in MDCXXX* (1845), p. 253.

[32] Above, Section 6.1 for the fishwife of Dawlish; PRO, SC11/174 for the farm of the fishery at Yealmpton in 1548; PRO, SC6 Hen.VIII/495 for a farm at Holberton; Suffolk Record Office, 449/1/15.53/2.1 for the farm of the fishery at Slapton in 1483-4; ECA, DC 957.

[33] DRO, CR 20048, Blackawton survey of the middle of the eighteenth century; DRO, 1508M/Devon/surveys/Kenton/5.

[34] PRO, C134/6 and above, Section 5.1.iii; ECA, VC 3365; ECA, DC 957; DRO, Carew of Haccombe MSS, Ringmore court of 23 Eliz.

[35] Huntington Library, San Marino, California, HAM box 64, rental of '1577', and above, Section 5.1.iii.

[36] F. E. Halliday, ed., *Richard Carew of Antony: the Survey of Cornwall* (1953), p. 117; C. Noall, *Cornish Seines and Seiners: a History of the Pilchard Fishing Industry* (1972), especially Chapter 2; K. Harris, *Hevva!: an Account of the Cornish Fishing Industry in the Days of Sail* (1983), p. 37 ('hevva!' was the cry which went out when the shoals were spied). For the act of 1603, see *Statutes of the Realm*, vol. 4, pt 2, pp. 1048-9.

[37] Gray, *E-SMS*, p. 17; M. Firestone, 'The traditional Start Bay crab fishery', *Folk Life* 20 (1981-2), p. 59. See also *VCH Dorset*, vol. 2, p. 355.

[38] *Cal. Papal Letters*, vol. 6, pp. 487-8.

[39] C. Henderson in *The Cornish Church Guide* (1925), p. 135 and above, Section 5.2.

[40] PRO, SC6 823/38, account of Trethevas in Landewednack, 32-3 Hen. VI. CRO, AR 2/1346, seventeenth-century survey, mentions a privately rented capstan house in Gunwalloe parish, Cornwall.

[41] PRO, C116/37, Newton court near the Conversion of St Paul, 12 Hen. VI; DRO, Exeter City Archives book 57 for the 'town seine' of Dawlish.

[42] DRO, Carew of Haccombe MSS, Ringmore court of 1632; R. Bush, *The Book of Exmouth* (1978), p. 24.

[43] DRO, 1508M/Lon./manor/Kenton/2, court of May 1606; Bush, *Exmouth*, p. 25. DRO, 1508M/Lon./manor/Kenton/2, court of Apl 1638; DRO, Exeter City Achives book 57.

[44] *VCH Dorset*, vol. 2, pp. 180, 183; *Cal. Patent Rolls, Hen. III, 1258-1266*, p. 421.

Compare the affrays between Cinque Ports ships and those of Fowey: *VCH Sussex*, vol. 2, p. 136.

[45] T. Hearne, ed., *The Itinerary of John Leland* (3rd edn, 9 vols, 1768-70), vol. 9, p. xxi and J. Chandler, 'John Leland in the West Country', in M. Brayshay, ed., *Topographical Writers in South-West England* (1996), p. 47 for a translation; R. Stanes, *A Fortunate Place: the History of Slapton in South Devon* (1983), p. 56 for the regatta at Torcross. The regatta which Leland describes was a competition between ships, presumably representing their home-ports.

[46] T. Gray, 'Devon's fisheries and early-Stuart northern New England', *NMHD*, vol. 1, p. 141; *Statutes of the Realm*, vol. 3, pp. 532-3.

INDEX OF PLACE-NAMES (INCLUDING RELIGIOUS HOUSES) IN DEVON

Names in italics are names or forms of names not generally found on printed Ordnance Survey maps of the nineteenth and twentieth centuries.

Allington, South (Chivelstone), 133
Anstey's Cove (St Marychurch), 24
Appledore, 89
Ashburton, 159, 160, 162
Ashprington, 26, 47, 51, 90
Ashwater, 80 n. 64
Aunemouth (Thurlestone), 68
Aveton Gifford, 31
Avon, River, 9, 31, 68
Axe, River, 83 n. 105
Axmouth, 47, 51, 162
Aylesbeare, 138 n. 6
Babbacombe (St Marychurch), 26, 44 n. 83, 49, 131, 149
Barbican, 44 n. 83
Babbacombe Bay, 48, 149
Bantham (Thurlestone), 9, 31
Batson (Salcombe), 43 n. 76
Beer, 76 n. 3, 132
Beesands (Stokenham), 31, 129, 130
  Beason Cellar, 129, 130
Berry Pomeroy, 62
Bigbury, 31, 83 n. 105
Bishopsteignton, 26, 74, 82 n. 99
Blackawton, 8, 189
Blackpool (Blackawton and Stoke Fleming), 31, 135, 153
  see also *Fisherton*
Blegberry (Hartland), 12
Bolberry (Malborough), 43 n. 76
Bozomzeal (Dittisham), 26
Bradninch, 88, 98, 158, 160

Branscombe, 162
Braunton, 47
Brent, South, 174 n. 57, 192 n. 23
Brightson, 48
Brixham, 23, 26, 27-8, 32, 39 n. 26, 43 n. 69, 68, 97, 153, 167
Broadhembury, 68
Buck's Mills (Woolfardisworthy), 16, 82 n. 89
Budleigh, East, 114, 152
Budleigh, East, Hundred, 48, 162
Budleigh Salterton, 73, 135
  Salterne, 135
Burgh Island (Bigbury), 31
Cattewater (Plymouth), 30, 61, 136, 139 n. 22
Cellar Beach (Newton and Noss), 30, 130
Cellars (Littlehempston), 130
Challaborough (Bigbury), 31
Charleton, 31
Charlwood (Ashcombe), 75
Chesills, les (Lympstone), 27, 39 n. 18
Chillington (Stokenham), 91-3, 104 n. 29, 125
Chivelstone, 37, 145
Churchstow, 66, 192 n. 23
Churston Ferrers, 26, 162
Clayhidon, 174 n. 57
Clovelly, 16, 133, 149
Cockington, 8, 28-9, 58-9, 91, 132, 145, 149, 153, 170 n. 1, 186

Cockwood (Dawlish), 19, 23-4, 145, 146-9, 163
Estcokwode, 170 n. 4
Cockwood Marsh (Dawlish), 146
Cofton (Dawlish), 83 n. 105
Colepole (Kenton), 117, 140 n. 25
Coleridge Hundred, 38 n. 11
Columbjohn (Broadclyst), 87
Colyford (Colyton), 88, 95
Colyton, 48, 162
Colyton Hundred, 162
Combeinteignhead (Haccombe with Combe), 12, 130
Combe Martin, 187
Coombe Cellars (Haccombe with Combe), 12, 26, 130, 135, 143 n. 63
Coombe Salterns, 135
Cornworthy, 26, 47, 51, 54
Countess Wear (Topsham), 58
Crediton, 160
Cullompton, 88, 160
Dartington, 47, 54
Dartmoor, 9, 25, 65, 96, 142 n. 51, 159, 160, 173 n. 53
Dartmouth, 9-11, 15, 16, 24, 25, 26, 31, 32, 38 n. 11, 41 n. 49, 41 n. 52, 58, 63, 92-3, 94-5, 97, 128, 151, 152, 153, 156, 162, 169, 171 n. 28, 190
Dart, River, 11, 25, 26, 32, 36, 47, 54, 62, 77 n. 9, 145-6, 149
Dawlish, 3, 24, 49, 61, 63, 92, 113, 131, 133, 134, 136, 146-9, 162, 163, 188, 190
Dawlish Strand (Dawlish), 18, 26, 136, 149
Dawlish Warren (Dawlish), 18, 83 n. 105
Devon, East, 18, 48, 60, 72, 96, 98, 156-7, 158, 159, 161, 162, 164, 174 n. 57, 185, 187
Devon, North, 3, 16, 47, 62, 69, 71-2, 73, 81 n. 71, 82 n. 89, 89, 96, 103, 132

Dittisham, 16, 26, 38 n. 18, 145-6, 149, 168
Dock (Plymouth), 32
Dotton (Colaton Raleigh), 48
Drake's Island (Plymouth Sound), 138
  St Nicholas Island, 138
East ..., see under second element
Eastdon (Dawlish), 163
Ebford (Woodbury), 114
Erme, River, 30, 59-60
Ermington, 52, 62, 67, 68
Exe Bridge, 117
Exe, River, 3, 17, 18-24, 28, 36-7, 47, 49, 57-9, 61, 64, 74-5, 77 n. 14, 82 n. 89, 83 n.105, 91, 95, 96, 100, 107-22, 137, 139 n. 22, 153
Exeter, 2, 7, 18, 43 n. 67, 58, 76, 87, 88, 91-2, 95, 96-9, 101, 113, 117, 152, 157, 159, 160, 161, 165, 169, 183
Exminster, 19, 47, 57-8, 79 n. 34, 92, 153
Exmouth, 3, 7, 19, 21-3, 32, 47, 89, 136, 153, 162, 167-8, 189, 190
  see also *Pratteshide*
Exmouth (= Exe Estuary), 20, 21, 77 n. 14, 116
Exton (Woodbury), 114
Farringdon, 162
Fisherne Path (Sidbury), 95
Fisherton (Bishop's Tawton), 143 n. 74
Fisherton (? now Blackpool, in Blackawton and Stoke Fleming), 135
Fishleigh (Aveton Gifford), 143 n. 74
Fishleigh (Hatherleigh), 143 n. 74
Fishley (Tawstock), 143 n. 74
Fishmongers' Lane (Dartmouth), 11
Fishway, le (Stoke Fleming), 95
Fishwick (Kingsteignton), 135
Fowley (Kenton), 139 n. 20
  Foghely, 116, 139 n. 20
Frittiscombe (Stokenham), 123
Frogmore Creek (Kingsbridge Estuary), 62
Galmpton (Churston Ferrers), 26, 162

Index of Devon Place-Names

Galmpton (S. Huish), 185
Gara Bridge (Diptford), 105 n. 30
Gittisham, 162
Gommerock (Kingswear), 172 n. 33
Goodshelter (E. Portlemouth), 31, 143 n. 76
Great Mew Stone (Wembury), 72
Mewestone, 72
Haccombe with Combe, 48, 49, 51
Hackney (Berry Pomeroy), 26, 62
Hakyn, le, 62
Hackney (Kingsteignton), 62
Hakyng, 62
Haldon Hills, 72, 82 n. 100, 104 n. 25
Hallsands (Stokenham), 12, 31, 33, 61, 63, 128-9, 130, 136, 145, 149, 170 n. 17, 189
Hall Cellar, 129, 130
Hole, le, 123, 128
Hartland, 16, 17, 73, 81 n. 81, 162
Hartland Point (Hartland), 103
Heathfield (Woodbury), 114
Hill (Withycombe Raleigh), 22
Hogsbrook (Woodbury), 114
Holbeton, 30, 193 n. 32
Holcombe (Dawlish), 74
Hole's Hole (Bere Ferrers), 30
Holsworthy, 87-8, 103 n. 12
Honiton, 88, 160, 187
Hooe (Plymstock), 30, 133, 139 n. 22, 149, 153
Hope (Malborough), 31, 33, 132, 133, 149
Hope-key, 33
Hope (St Marychurch), 26
Houndbeare (Aylesbeare, formerly Woodbury), 109-10, 138 n. 6
Huish, North, 67
Huish, South, 31, 185
Hurdwick (Tavistock Hamlets), 67, 69, 71, 166
Ide, 162
Ilfracombe, 72, 138, 193 n. 27
Ilton (Malborough), 153
Ivacove (Chivelstone), 31, 133

Jordan (Widecombe in the Moor), 173 n. 53
Kenn, 122
Kennford (Kenn), 88, 91-2, 104 n. 28
Kenton, 2, 3, 13, 36-7, 45 n. 90, 48, 49, 51, 52, 55, 61, 63, 74, 82 n. 89, 82 n. 99, 92, 107, 112, 115-22, 126, 129, 130, 135, 140 n. 36, 168, 186, 190
Kenwood (Kenton), 75
Kingsbridge, 31, 92, 128
Kingsbridge Estuary, 32, 34-5, 50, 62, 86
Kingskerswell, 86, 100, 101
Kingsteignton, 26, 62
Kingston, 67
Kingswear, 23, 25-7, 32, 34, 42 n. 67, 68, 153, 168
Laira (Plymouth), 30
Langdon (Wembury), 72
Lannacombe (Stokenham), 122
Lawn, The (Dawlish), 25
Leigh (Milton Abbot), 69
Lincombe (Ilfracombe), 82 n. 89
Littleham, 21, 22, 23, 42 n. 58, 47-48, 71
Lulham, 41 n. 49
Littlehempston, 130
Livermead (Cockington), 26, 28-9, 40 n. 26
Livermead Sands (Cockington), 28, 57, 58, 91, 153
Lundy Island, 72, 73
Lympstone, 19, 39 n. 18, 132, 133, 136, 187, 193 n. 27
Lympstone Strand, 19, 23-4, 132, 149
Malborough, 44 n. 87
Mamhead, 122
Man Sands (Brixham), 68
Maristow, 30, 33, 44 n. 80, 67, 68
Martinstow, 44 n. 80, 80 n. 65, 81 n. 73
Middle Wood (Dawlish), 19, 23-4, 145, 146-9, 163, 193 n. 27
Middelwode, 170 n. 4

Modbury, 87-8, 96
Mohun's Ottery, 100, 101
Molton, South, 87
Monkleigh, 69, 80 n. 63
Moreleigh, 105 n. 30
Morwell (Tavistock Hamlets), 44 n. 80
Morwellham (Tavistock Hamlets), 15, 30, 33, 69
Newhouse (Mamhead), 75
Newton Ferrers, 30, 32, 56-7, 61, 62, 63, 65, 68, 101, 106 n. 48, 187
North …, see under second element
Northam, 162
Northleigh, 162
Noss Mayo (Revelstoke), 30, 44 n. 88, 101, 106 n. 48
Nutwell (Woodbury), 19, 24, 48, 65, 100, 101, 114-15, 132, 140 n. 25, 153
Okehampton, 98
Oreston (Plymstock), 30, 106 n. 48, 136, 143 n. 77, 149, 187
Otter, River, 74
Otterton, 51, 74, 90, 104 n. 20
Otterton Priory, 53, 74
Ottery St Mary, 51, 88, 98, 160, 162
Paignton, 15, 26, 39 n. 26, 71, 89, 97, 132, 153, 168
Pilehayes (Woodbury), 114
Plymouth, 7, 11, 23, 30, 37 n. 2, 43 n. 75, 61, 63, 89, 93-4, 97, 100, 101, 106 n. 53, 143 n. 81, 149, 152, 159, 162, 165, 168, 169, 171 n. 28, 190
Plymouth Sound, 138, 142 n. 53
Plym, River, 30, 68
Plympton, 52, 67, 97, 162
Plympton Hundred, 66
Plympton Priory, 68, 94
Plymstock, 100, 187
Pool, North (S. Pool), 31, 62, 63
Pool, South, 31, 49-50, 60, 79 n. 48, 86
Portlemouth (= Kingsbridge Estuary), 43. n. 76
Portlemouth, East, 31, 35

Portlemouth, West (Malborough), 43 n. 76
Postlake (Woodbury), 114
Powderham, 19, 24, 152-3
Pratteshide, 21-3, 41 n. 49, 116
Prawle (Chivelstone and E. Portlemouth), 31
Revelstoke, 45 n. 88, 152
Ringmore (near Bigbury), 31
Ringmore (St Nicholas), 26, 55, 82 n. 89, 131, 136, 137-8, 140 n. 37, 171 n. 17, 188, 190
Ringmore Strand (St Nicholas), 122, 131, 136, 138, 140 n. 37, 168
Roundham Head (Paignton), 132
St James Priory (Exeter), 20, 51
St Marychurch, 131, 168
St Sidwell (Exeter), 155
Salcombe (Kingsbridge Estuary), 23, 31, 32, 43 n. 76, 82 n. 92, 153
Salcombe Regis, 82 n. 92, 97, 190
Saltern Cove (Paignton), 135
Saltings (Bishopsteignton), 135
Salternehay, 135
Saltram (Plympton), 30, 143 n. 76
Sampford Peverell, 88, 100, 101
Sandweie (Broadhembury), 80 n. 70
Seaton, 83 n. 105
Seaton Bay, 95
Sewer (Malborough), 44 n. 87
Shaldon (St Nicholas), 26, 122, 131, 133, 134, 139 n. 22, 140 n. 37, 168, 186
Shutterton (Dawlish), 163
Sidbury, 48, 95, 156-7, 173 n. 57, 174 n. 57
Sidmouth, 6, 39 n. 18, 53, 61-2, 63, 71, 74, 90, 92, 95, 100, 101, 104 n. 20, 138, 162, 190
Sidmouth Bay, 2
Sid, River, 74
Slapton, 97, 153, 190, 193 n. 32
Slapton Cellars (Slapton), 31, 130
Slapton Ley, 34
Smithenestrete (Dartmouth), 10

Index of Devon Place-Names

Sod, the (Kenton), 115
South ..., for most names, see under second element
Southbeare (Kenton), 118-19
South Brook (Kenton), 115
South Sands (Salcombe), 31
South Town (Dartmouth), 38 n. 9
Southwood (Dawlish), 75
Staplake (Kenton), 118-19, 121
Starcross (Kenton), 3, 6 n. 4, 13, 19, 22, 23-4, 36, 119-22, 130, 132, 136-7, 145, 188, 190
  Star Crosse, 136
  Sterrecrosse, 136
  see also *Strand*
Starehole Cove (Malborough), 31, 34-5
Start (farm; Stokenham), 141 n. 45
Start Bay, 29, 33-4, 48, 49-50, 64, 96, 99, 122-9, 130, 149, 168, 187, 190
Start Point (Stokenham), 33, 170 n. 17
Stoke Damarel, 105 n. 36, 106 n. 48
Stoke Fleming, 38 n. 9, 77 n. 9, 95, 142 n. 57, 156-7, 162
Stoke Gabriel, 26, 168
Stokeinteignhead, 49, 139 n. 22, 168
Stokenham, 2, 3, 48, 49, 50-1, 53, 55, 56, 59-60, 63, 72, 88-9, 92-3, 96, 99, 101, 107, 114, 122-9, 131, 149, 170 n. 17, 185, 188, 189
Stoke St Nectan (Hartland), 16
Stonehouse, 30, 44 n. 77, 94, 106 n. 48, 136, 152, 153
Strand (part of Starcross), 136
Strand, The (Exmouth), 136
Strand, The (Lympstone), 136
Strand, The (Stonehouse), 136
Strand, The (Torquay), 136
Strete Gate (Blackawton), 31, 34, 188
  Startgate, 34
  Streate Sands, 44 n. 85
  Streate Under Cliff, 34
  Undercliff (and slight variants), 34, 44 n. 84
Sutton (Plymouth), 11, 55, 56, 68, 89, 93-4, 139 n. 22

Tamar, River, 3, 15, 30, 33, 56, 66, 68
Tavistock, 158, 159, 173 n. 49
Tavistock Abbey, 33, 60, 67, 69, 71, 94, 100, 101, 166
Tavistock Hundred, 66
Tavy, River, 30, 33
Taw, River, 81 n. 71
Tawton, South, 173 n. 53
Teignmouth, 11, 25, 26, 95, 139 n. 22, 151, 152
Teign, River, 12, 25, 26, 48, 49, 62, 74-5, 82 n. 89, 122, 130, 137-8, 139 n. 22
Thurlestone, 31
Tiverton, 60, 88, 158, 160
Topsham, 11, 15, 16, 18-21, 22, 27, 36, 51, 57-9, 72, 87, 117, 190
Tor Bay, 15, 24, 26, 27, 33, 36, 39 n. 25, 39 n. 25, n. 26, 51, 57, 61, 101, 149, 152
Torcross (Stokenham), 31, 133, 136-7, 186, 190
  Torcrosse, 136
Tormoham, 168
Torquay, 14, 15, 26, 39 n. 26, 136, 168
Torre, 14, 15
Torre Abbey, 51, 57, 61, 152
Torridge, River, 69
Totnes, 26, 63, 128
Totnes Priory, 51, 54, 90
Turnchapel (Plymstock), 30
Uffculme, 174 n. 57
Uplyme, 101, 162
Upton (Brixham), 68
Venbridge (Kenton), 118-19
Waddeton (Stoke Gabriel), 26, 162
Warfleet (Dartmouth), 15, 26, 31, 39 n. 23, 131, 143 n. 63, 149
  Welflut, 39 n. 23
Week (Dawlish, formerly Kenton), 48, 135
Wembury, 71
Werrington, 80 n. 64, 100
West ..., see under second element
Westwood (Dawlish), 19, 23-4, 145,

146-9, 163
Cockwood West, 170 n. 14
Whiteway (Kingsteignton), 74
Widdicombe (Stokenham), 136
Widecombe in the Moor, 42 n. 58
Winkleigh, 98, 163
Withycombe Raleigh, 22, 42 n. 58
Woodbury, 2, 19, 24, 77 n. 14, 107-15, 118, 121, 122, 126, 129, 162, 163, 186, 188

Woodbury Salterton (Woodbury), 114, 143 n. 76
Woodhouse (Ashcombe), 75
Woodhuish (Brixham), 68
Yealm (= Newton Ferrers), 43 n. 75
Yealmpton, 30, 52, 55, 60, 62, 65, 67, 97, 152, 193 n. 32
Yealm, River, 30, 44 n. 88, 72, 130
Zeal, South (S. Tawton), 159, 160, 173 n. 53

INDEX OF PLACE-NAMES (INCLUDING RELIGIOUS HOUSES) IN OTHER WEST-COUNTRY COUNTIES

CORNWALL

Barrepta (now Carbis Bay), 132, 133
Bodardle (Lanlivery), 86
Bodinnick (Lanteglos), 100, 152
Bodmin Moor, 129
Calstock, 30, 33
Cargoll (Newlyn East), 81 n. 77
Cornwall generally, 3, 62, 66, 80 n. 68, 83, 97, 101, 102, 129, 133, 142 n. 52, 189
Cornwall, north coast, 70, 100, 101
Cornwall, western, 154
Dorset (Lanteglos), 152
Fal, River, 100, 190
Fowey, 98, 100, 138, 151, 171 n. 28
Gerrans Bay, 68
Gunwalloe, 193 n. 40
Gurlyn (St Erth), 86, 106 n. 49
Halton (St Dominick), 15, 16, 17, 30, 33, 68-9
Helston, 66
Land's End, 7
Landulph, 30, 33
Lanteglos, 137
Launceston, 103 n. 13

Lelant, 15
Looe, 98
Looe, East, 162
Lynher, River, 30
Marazion, 15, 16
  Marghasyowe, 16
  Market Jew, 91
Marhamchurch, 100
Mount's Bay, 168
Mousehole (Paul), 15, 17, 40 n. 26, n. 27, n. 36, 45 n. 88, 55, 98, 182
Newlyn (Paul), 15
Newquay, 14
Padstow, 15
Penzance, 55, 98, 100, 101
Pier Cellars (Maker-with-Rame), 142 n. 53
Place (Fowey), 172 n. 33
Polruan (Lanteglos), 152
Probus, 100
Pulsack (Phillack), 80 n. 69
Roscarrock (St Endellion), 12
St Buryan, 138
St Columb Major, 103 n. 13
St Goran, 61
St Ives, 15, 40 n. 28

Index of Other West-Country Place-Names

St Mawes (St Just in Roseland), 15, 137
St Michael's Mount, 86, 90, 100, 104 n. 22
Saltash, 30, 56, 61, 89-90, 138, 162, 168
Schylhall (Menheniot), 162
Scilly Isles, 138, 168
Towednack, 77 n. 9
Trematon (St Stephen by Saltash), 68
Tresco Priory (Scilly Isles), 138
Trethevas (Landewednack), 193 n. 40
Whalesborough (Marhamchurch), 103 n. 12
Zennor, 80 n. 58

DORSET

Arne, 136
Chesil Beach, 63
Cobb, the, 16
Dorset generally, 38 n. 12, 47, 98, 102, 137
Lyme Regis, 16, 89, 100, 162, 167, 190
Poole Harbour, 136
Portland, 190
Shaftesbury, 98
Sherborne, 98
Weymouth, 190

SOMERSET

Birnbeck Island (Weston super Mare), 177
Chard, 98
Chewton, 165
Crewkerne, 98
Dunster, 54, 78 n. 20, 99, 101, 129
Glastonbury Abbey, 47, 60, 89, 101
Kilton, 82 n. 89
Kilve, 82 n. 89
Langport, 98
Lilstock, 82 n. 89
Mendips, 165
Minehead, 82 n. 89, 99
Old Cleeve, 82 n. 89
Porlock, 101
Quantoxhead, East, 82 n. 89
Severn, River, 62
Somerset generally, 3, 98, 102
Somerset Levels, 54, 99
Somerset, north coast, 62, 73
Stogumber, 101
Taunton, 98, 99
Watchet, 99
Weston super Mare, 177
Wincanton, 98
Yeovil, 98

INDEX OF OTHER PLACE-NAMES

Aegean Sea, 138
Alston Moor (Cumb.), 129, 179
Anjou, 76
Bay of Biscay, 75-6
Bayonne, 76
Billingsgate Stairs (Lon), 137
Blunham (Beds.), 138 n. 1
Bordeaux, 27, 76
Brighton (Sussex), 134
Burgundy, 158
California, 122

Cinque Ports (Kent & Sussex), 194 n. 44
Clee (Lincs.), 184
Coventry (Warcks.), 183
Dean, Forest (Glouc.), 154
Dee, River, 183
Dingle Peninsula (Co. Kerry), 129
Derbyshire, 159
Dungeness (Kent), 177-8
Dunwich (Suff.), 55
East Buckie (Banffs.), 182

East Anglia, 54
East coast (England), 59
East Fen (Lincs.), 65
Eaton (Chesh.), 183
Egypt, 161
Erlestoke (Wilts.), 99-101, 106 n. 53
Eskdale (Cumb.), 179
Essex, 155
Europe, southern, 9, 75
Fenland (Lincs.), 184-5
Fisherton Delamare (Wilts.), 183
Foregate (Worcester), 155
Foulness Island (Essex), 62
France, 158, 169
Gardenstown (Banffs.), 182
Gascony, 9, 20, 25, 76, 83 n. 104, 94
Genoa, 72
Grimsby (Lincs.), 77 n. 4, 183
Harris (Hebrides), 129
Hastings (Sussex), 63, 90
Hooe (unidentified), 175 n. 76
Hope (unidentified), 175 n. 76
Hull, 190
Humber, River, 184
Hythe (Kent), 177
Iberia, 169
Iceland, 167-8
Ireland, 67, 168
Kent, 177-8, 183
Kingswood (Glouc.), 154
Lanes, The (Brighton), 134
Leicestershire, 129
Leverburgh (Outer Hebrides), 182
Lewis Island (Hebrides), 129
Lincolnshire, 2, 60, 74, 75, 77 n. 8, 82 n. 97, 183
London, 39 n. 20, 96, 82 n. 90, 109, 165, 183
Lydd (Kent), 167, 177-8
Lymington (Hants.), 73
Malmesbury (Wilts.), 99
Marsh Chapel (Lincs.), 178
Marshland (Lincs.), 184
Mediterranean countries, 39 n. 20, 134
Midlands, of England, 155

Minchinhampton (Glouc.), 60
Montebourg Abbey (France), 47, 51
Mont St Michel, 90
Newcastle-upon-Tyne (Northumb.), 179-80
Newfoundland, 4, 9, 18, 21, 25, 168
Norfolk, 74, 75, 77 n. 8, 82 n. 97, 190
Norfolk Broads, 75
North Country (Britain), 129, 135, 179
North-East England, 82 n. 90
North Scale (near Barrow, Lancs.), 181
Northumberland, 134
Norwich Cathedral Priory, 137, 178
Oléron, 76
Paisley Abbey, 179
Poitou, 76
Robin Hood's Bay (Yorks., NR), 182
Rockingham Forest (Nthants.), 154
Romney Marsh (Kent), 129
Rye (Sussex), 2, 55
Salisbury (Wilts.), 99
Sandscale (near Barrow, Lancs.), 181
Scarborough (Yorks., NR), 2, 168, 183
Scaddebothes (near Maryport, Cumb.), 181
Scotland, 12, 21, 129, 182
Sea House (Ancroft, Nthumb.), 143 n. 65
Seahouses (N. Sunderland, Nthumb.), 143 n. 65
Sea Houses (Long Houghton, Nthumb.), 143 n. 65
Seascale (Cumb.), 135, 181
Severn, River, 53, 183
Shields, North (Northumb.), 54, 179-81, 182
Somercoates (Lincs.), 178-9
Southampton (Hants.), 99
South coast (England), 151, 153
Staithes (Yorks., NR), 182
Suffolk, 2, 141 n. 42, 190
Sussex, 73, 183
Syon Abbey, 2, 100, 101
Syria, 161
Thames, River, 27, 54, 137

Index of Other Place-Names

Thanet, Isle of (Kent), 184
Tweed, River, 179
Tidenham (Glouc.), 53-4
Tobermory (Mull), 182
Tyne, River, 180
Tynemouth (Northumb.), 180
Tynemouth Priory, 54, 179-80, 182
Ullapool (Ross and Cromarty), 182
Wales, 129, 179
Warblington (Hants.), 106 n. 53
Warminster (Wilts.), 99
Weald (Kent & Sussex), 129

West Fen (Lincs.), 65
Westminster Abbey, 182
Wiltshire, 99, 183
Winchelsea (Sussex), 55, 168
Winscales (near Sellafield, Cumb.), 181
Winterton (Norf.), 178
Worcester, 155
Wye, River, 54
Yarmouth, Great (Norf.), 137, 167-8, 175 n. 76, 178
York, 183
Yorkshire, 2, 54

INDEX OF SUBJECTS

boats (including barges), 8, 11, 27, 32, 55, 58, 62-3, 66, 68-9, 71, 90, 94, 99, 114, 116, 123, 126, 128, 131, 133, 145, 152, 166, 188, 189
  see also lerrets, punts
bordars, see farming
buildings
  boathouses, 133
  cabins, 177-8
  cellars, see settlements
  chapels, see ecclesiastical
  fish(ing) houses, 13, 29, 115, 131, 133
  lodges, 129, 130, 142 n. 52, 177-8
  net houses, 133
  palace, 133
  saltchambers, salthouses, 83 n. 105
  salterns, 135
  seahouses, 133
  sheds, 178
  summer houses, 129
  see also coastal defence, cottagers and cottages
by-laws, see fishing villages
capstans, 63, 189, 193 n. 40
cellars and cellar settlements, see settlements
chapels, see ecclesiastical

cliff top, uses of, 64
climate, 150-1
cloth-workers, see industries
coastal attacks, 12, 25, 32, 151-2
coastal defence, 12, 152-4, 171 n. 28, 172 n. 36
cockle rakers, 3, 121-2
cockle sellers, 140 n. 36
cottagers and cottages, 6, 13, 17, 22, 24, 28, 29, 35, 43 n. 71, 65, 121, 124, 127-8, 132, 141 n. 40, 146-8, 154, 160, 163, 165, 170 n. 17, 174 n. 57, 178, 180, 186, 188
cranes, 10, 14, 20
crusade, crusader, 25, 122
dockyards, 32
ecclesiastical subjects
  chapels, 16, 22-3, 34 (?), 42 n. 58, 43 n. 76, 137-8, 149, 170 n. 17, 189
  crosses, 136-7, 149, 189
  ingulgences, 16, 149
  parish boundaries, 8, 48-51, 77 n. 9
  pastoral care, 108
  tithes, 1, 2, 20, 27, 43 n. 69, 43 n. 76, 56, 57, 107-13, 115, 138 n. 1, 170 n. 7
  wakes, 152

farming, 3, 35, 66-7, 70-1, 108-10, 113, 127, 159, 165-6
bordars, 48, 76 n. 3, 183
farm holdings, 109-13, 120-1, 124-8, 141 n. 44, 163, 184-6
farm labourers and servants, 110-11, 128
fishing farmers, see fishing
land market, 147-8, 156-7
smallholders, smallholdings, 22, 110-13, 120-1, 127, 184-6
see also cottagers, fishing farmers, sand
ferries, 22, 27, 36, 116-17, 136, 139 n. 22, 188-9
fish, carriage of (not trade), 86, 99-101
fish, consumption of
 aristocratic, 72-3, 86-7, 100-1
 by poor, 85, 87, 164-5
 urban, 85, 96
fish, preservation of (includes use of salt), 3, 9, 58, 76, 83 n. 104, n. 105, 89, 106 n. 48, 116, 117, 131, 175 n. 79, 183
fish, price of, 102-3
fish, species, types of (includes shellfish and Phocaenidae)
 bass, 60
 bream, 89 124
 cockles, 3, 60, 121, 140 n. 36, 190
 cod, 60, 89, 178
 conger, 11, 60, 86-7, 89, 94, 101, 124
 eels, 54
 hake, 59, 60, 62, 86, 169
 herring, 20, 54, 60, 86-7, 94, 101, 169, 178
 ling, 60, 86, 89, 101
 lobsters, 60
 mackerel, 60
 mullet, 53, 58, 59, 60, 89, 123-4, 126, 128
 mussels, 36, 55, 60, 116, 121, 140 n. 36, 190
 oysters, 50, 55, 60, 63, 116, 140 n. 36, 190
 oysters 'of Dittisham', 146
 pilchards, 60, 164-5, 169
 plaice, 60, 61, 89, 124
 porpoises, 2, 60, 89, 100, 124
 prawns, 60
 rare fish, 53
 ray, 169
 royal fish, 100
 salmon, 41 n. 41, 50, 54, 55, 58, 60, 63, 86-7, 89, 116, 124, 183
 'Scarborough fish', 183
 skate, 60, 89, 124
 sprats, 20
 sticklebacks, 60
 trout, 58
 whiting, 20, 60, 61
 whiting, dried (buckhorn), 80, 101
fishbones, in excavations, 88
fish markets, 3, 53, 54, 88, 89-95, 98, 100-1, 103 n. 12, n. 13, 104 n. 20, 105 n. 36, 113, 148, 149, 188, 190
fish trade
 coastal, 27, 96, 97, 98, 105 n. 42
 fish sellers, 87-8, 92, 96-9
 overland, 68, 88, 92, 93, 95-9, 104 n. 25, 183
 overseas, 11, 93, 169
 see also fish, carriage of (not trade), fish markets, jowters
fisheries
 coastal and estuarine, *passim*, but especially 47-57
 farmed, 52, 116, 188, 193 n. 32
 inland, 2
 longshore, 4, 167-8, 175 n. 79, 178
 overseas, 4, 9, 11, 18, 21, 167-8, 175 n. 79
 port towns, fisheries of, 1, 4, 10-11, 25, 28, 55, 131, 175 n. 79, 183
 right to, 65-6
 seigneurial, 57-9
 technology of, 4, 59-63
 see also boats, capstans, haking, huers, nets

Index of Subjects

fishing farmers, 12, 29, 35, 102, 107-29, 145, 163, 165, 166, 167, 169, 177, 182, 183-6
fish(ing) houses, see buildings
fishing villages, 5, 12-14, 16, 23-4, 35, 40 n. 36, 45 n. 88, 107, 130, 145-50, 151, 154-5, 162, 163, 164, 168, 169, 181-3, 186-91
  by-laws of, 8, 189-90
  co-operation in, 5, 61, 63, 113-4, 188-9
  other occupations in, 13-14, 66
foreshore, 2, 64-6, 80 n. 57
haking, 62, 79 n. 48
hemp gardens, hemphays, 3, 147, 193 n. 27
huers or hill-men, 123-4, 128, 189
Hundred Years War, 151-3
industries
  cloth-workers, cloth making, 18, 88, 96, 158-61, 173 n. 53, n. 57, 187
  lace-makers, 187
  lead-miners, mining, 129, 159, 165, 179
  lime burning, 16, 33
  quarrying, 130
  salt making, salt-workers, 50, 51, 73-6, 76 n. 3, 77 n. 8, 82 n. 92, 117-18, 135-6, 140 n. 28, 143 n. 76, 178-9
  see also buildings
  thread-makers, 187
  tinners, tin working, 16, 25, 42 n. 64, 129, 142 n. 52, 158-61
jowters, 88, 96
lace-makers, see industries
lead-miners, mining, see industries
lerrets, 63
lime burning, see industries
lookers, 129
maps, coastal, 7, 24, 29, 37 n. 1, 64
markets and fairs, see trade
mills, 22, 41 n. 52, 52, 180
nets, 3, 11, 43 n. 72, 55-6, 57, 58, 60-2, 64, 88, 114, 116, 122, 123, 128, 131, 145, 167, 189
  see also buildings, sayndrayth
nonnys, 56
oyster and cockle dealers, 140 n. 36
pig-men, 75
pirates, 12, 23, 154
population, growth of, 154-8, 160-1
population, migration of, 162-3
population, mortality, 161, 187
porpoise, see fish
porths (Cornish), 3
port towns, see settlements
punts, 63
quarrying, see industries
quays, 8, 10, 14-17, 18, 20, 27, 33, 37, 39 n. 20, n. 21, n. 26, 69, 81 n. 73, 146, 168
regattas, 190, 194 n. 45
resort trade, 35
rural settlement, see settlement
rushes, 36, 117
saltchambers, see buildings
salt-making, salt-workers, see industries
saltways, 68
sand
  carriage of, 44 n. 80, 66-71, 81 n. 71, 166
  gathering of, 50, 65, 69-70, 117, 166
  sanders, 70, 81 n. 76
  sandways, 67-8, 80 n. 68, n. 70, 82 n. 89
  uses of, 66-7, 70-1, 166
sandleave, 63
sayndrayth, 50
seabirds, 65, 72-3, 87
seaweed, 67, 73, 81 n. 89
settlements
  cellar settlements and cellars, 12, 13, 24, 29, 34, 35, 36, 37, 63, 115, 120-2, 129-38, 145, 163, 177
  fishing villages, see fishing
  port towns, 1, 4, 8-11, 16-17, 18-35, 36-7, 38 n. 5, 44 n. 77, 55, 93-5, 131, 151, 167-8, 169, 178-80, 183, 190

see also fisheries
rural settlements, 5, 12, 36, 114, 118, 165
shielings, 12, 129, 135, 179-81, 191 n. 8
see also porths
shellfish, see fish
shepherds' tables, 129
shielings, see settlements
shipwrights, ship-building, 9, 10, 20, 22, 38 n. 9, 69
silver, 44 n. 80
smallholders, see farming
smiths, 10, 22, 105 n. 31
Spanish Armada, 72
stairs, 137, 144 n. 81
technology, see fisheries
thread-makers, see industries

tinners, tin-working, see industries
tithes, see ecclesiastical
trade
coastal, 15, 18, 20, 27
markets and fairs, 9, 10, 21, 23, 44 n. 76, 54, 78 n. 20, 88, 91-3, 98
overseas, 9, 18, 20, 25, 27, 36-7, 45 n. 90, 75-6, 95, 148, 158
see also fish markets, fish trade
turves, peat, 52, 65, 82 n. 100, 86, 179
urban developments, 85-6, 88, 91-3, 155, 157-9, 173 n. 49
vagrants, 108-9
weirs, 18, 58, 79 n. 34
woodland, 75, 146-7
wrack-roads, 67
wreck, 71-2

LIST OF OCCASIONAL PAPERS, DEPARTMENT OF ENGLISH LOCAL HISTORY, UNIVERSITY OF LEICESTER

First Series
1. H. P. R. Finberg, *The Local Historian and his Theme* (1952)
2. H. P. R. Finberg, *The Early Charters of Devon and Cornwall* (1953)
3. Joan Thirsk, *Fenland Farming in the Sixteenth Century* with an introduction by R. H. Tawney (1953)
4. M. Claire Cross, *The Free Grammar School of Leicester* (1953)
5. G. H. Martin, *The Early Court Rolls of the Borough of Ipswich* (1954)
6. H. E. Hallam, *The New Lands of Elloe: a Study of Early Reclamation in Lincolnshire* (1954)
7. C. F. Slade, *The Leicestershire Survey c. A.D. 1130* with a preface by Sir Frank Stenton (1956)
8. H. P. R. Finberg, *Roman and Saxon Withington: a Study in Continuity* (1955)
9. A. M. Everitt, *The County Committee of Kent in the Civil War* (1955)
10 and 11. Cyril Hart, *The Early Charters of Essex* (1957)
12. Basil E. Cracknell, *Canvey Island: the History of a Marshland Community* (1959)
13. W. G. Hoskins, *The Westward Expansion of Wessex* with a supplement to No. 2 in this series by H. P. R. Finberg (1960)
14. Thomas Garden Barnes, *The Clerk of the Peace in Caroline Somerset* (1961)
15. R. B. Smith, *Blackburnshire: a Study in Early Lancashire History* (1961)
16. L. A. Burgess, *The Origins of Southampton* (1964)
17. K. J. Allison, M. W. Beresford, J. G. Hurst et al., *The Deserted Villages of Oxfordshire* (1966)
18. K. J. Allison, M. W. Beresford, J. G. Hurst et al., *The Deserted Villages of Northamptonshire* (1966)
19. John S. Moore, *Laughton: a Study in the Evolution of the Wealden Landscape* (1965)
20. Margaret Spufford, *A Cambridgeshire Community: Chippenham from Settlement to Enclosure* (1965)

Second Series
1. Alan Everitt, *Change in the Provinces: the Seventeenth Century* (1969)
2. R. A. McKinley, *Norfolk Surnames in the Sixteenth Century* (1969)

3. Cyril Hart, *The Hidation of Northamptonshire* (1970)
4. Alan Everitt, *The Pattern of Rural Dissent: the Nineteenth Century* (1972)
5. David Hey, *The Rural Metalworkers of the Sheffield Region* (1972)
6. Cyril Hart, *The Hidation of Cambridgeshire* (1974)

Third Series
1. J. S. Morrill, *The Cheshire Grand Jury 1625-1659* (1976)
2. Katherine S. Naughton, *The Gentry of Bedfordshire in the Thirteenth and Fourteenth Centuries* (1976)
3. Prudence Ann Moylan, *The Form and Reform of County Government: Kent 1889-1914* (1978)
4. Charles Phythian-Adams, *Continuity, Fields and Fission: the Making of a Midland Parish* (1978)
5. B. J. Davey *Ashwell, 1830-1914: the Decline of a Village Community* (1980)
6. Beryl Schumer, *The Evolution of Wychwood to 1400: Pioneers, Frontiers and Forests* (1984)

Fourth Series
1. Charles Phythian-Adams, *Re-thinking English Local History* (1987)
2. Peter Warner, *Greens, Commons and Clayland Colonization: the Origins and Development of Green-side Settlement in East Suffolk* (1987)
3. K. D. M. Snell, *Church and Chapel in the North Midlands: Religious Observance in the Nineteenth Century* (1991)
4. Christopher Dyer, *Hanbury: Settlement and Society in a Woodland Landscape* (1991)

Associated Volume
Charles Phythian-Adams, ed., *Societies, Cultures and Kinship, 1580-1850: Cultural Provinces and English Local History*, with contributions by Mary Carter, Evelyn Lord and Anne Mitson (1993)

Note. Virtually all of the Occasional Papers listed above are out of print. Third series no. 6, by Beryl Schumer, has been republished by The Wychwood Press (Jon Carpenter Publishing), Charlbury, Oxfordshire.